Mary Douglas

In the active voice

Routledge & Kegan Paul
London, Boston and Henley

This collection first published in 1982
by Routledge & Kegan Paul Ltd
39 Store Street, London WC1E 7DD,
9 Park Street, Boston,
Mass. 02108, USA and
Broadway House, Newtown Road,
Henley-on-Thames, Oxon RG9 1EN
Set in 10/12pt Linotron Erhardt by
Rowland Phototypesetting, Bury St Edmunds, Suffolk
and printed in Great Britain by
St Edmundsbury Press, Bury St Edmunds, Suffolk

Library of Congress Cataloguing in Publication Data

Douglas, Mary Tew.
In the active voice.
Includes index.
Contents: Passive voice theories in religious sociology –
Goods as a system of communication – Money:
The contempt of ritual; Raffia cloth distribution in
the Lele economy; Primitive rationing – [etc.]
1. Economics, Primitive – Addresses, essays, lectures.
2. Food habits – Addresses, essays, lectures.
3. Ethnology – Addresses, essays, lectures. I. Title.
GN448.D68   306'.3   81-18263

ISBN 0-7100-9065-X   AACR2

In the active voice

Also by Mary Douglas
Purity and Danger: an Analysis of Concepts of Pollution and Taboo
Implicit Meanings: Essays in Anthropology
Essays in the Sociology of Perception

Contents

Preface

Some of these essays are very old. Respect for the publisher and for readers suggests they should be discarded or severely revised. After suppressing quite a few from the first list and shortening or combining some others, I have to explain why the resulting list is offered as it is. I cannot say that students' clamour has called for republication of the early papers. It is rather that for me they adumbrated intentions to work in certain directions, some of which I followed. It is salutary to recognize now how short and sketchy they were. But it is sometimes useful to be able to produce them now, as evidence of long-term goodwill. When the late, regretted Margaret Mead reproached me, together with all English anthropologists, for never quoting American anthropology, I was happy to be able to send her the little piece on rationing in which her work figured.

At a later stage in an academic career, published articles often originate as gestures of esteem and comradeship. Someone is organizing a conference or exhibition, some event is to be memorialized or a beloved teacher honoured. Then, however unworthy the result may be of the occasion that called it forth, it seems wrong either to remove it from the collection or clip it shorter still – as if the original celebration no longer mattered.

Even so, some of the essays need a lot of expansion or explaining. Sometimes the development of the basic idea has required at least one whole book. Then what appear here are the first intimations that more should be done. For example, several essays on economics or money, such as the reflections upon whether the role of raffia cloth in the Lele economy should be compared to money or to ration coupons, led eventually to writing, with Baron Isherwood, *The World of Goods* (1979). The passage of time gives curious twists in proving one's most confident predictions wrong. Little did I think that the Islamic revival and the victory of monetarist theory would make anachronistic my 1966 wish that a new enlightened view of ritual should match the enlightened Keynesian view of money as a medium of social relations.

A group of very sketchy essays on food represent work that is still in hand. In 1977 Ravindra Khare invited me to join him in developing the Commission on the Anthropology of Food established by the International Union of the Anthropological and Ethnological Sciences. Among its objectives are to encourage anthropologists to focus more upon world food problems and to make the distinctively anthropological work on food accessible to all concerned with food planning policy. These short essays on food appear trivial, even frivolous. But a more imaginative understanding of the social uses of food would not allow soup-kitchen almsgiving to seem so meritorious as it does.

Soon after I arrived at the Russell Sage Foundation a call from Judith Goode announced that a team of anthropologists in Philadelphia were already studying food habits by the so-called Nicod method. Subsequently, the Russell Sage Foundation sponsored research on domestic food cycles and patterns, which is now being analysed and written up. Michael Nicod's research on English food patterns was funded by the Department of Health and Social Security, a mere £3,000 which saw him through his master's degree. For describing this work in a too jocular form in *New Society* we received the British equivalent of the Golden Fleece Award for useless research. A Parliamentary question challenged the Minister of Health to justify squandering money on studying food habits when real hunger needed to be fed. There is a certain come-uppance in reprinting years later essays which insist that giving food to the poor is no substitute for addressing the problems of poverty direct. Inequalities in food distribution closely follow inequalities in the distribution of incomes and wealth. In the Introduction to Jessica Kuper's Cookbook I indicate that a very individualist competitive society rejects large numbers of its population and puts others in dread of rejection. For those who are in a good position to do the rejecting, it is easier to think of making amends by handing out food than to think of revising the rules that produce the unequal distribution. 'Cultural bias' explains how the paradox arises.

If a common theme runs through these essays, it is summed up in the first, 'Passive voice theories', and developed more fully in chapter 9, 'Cultural bias'. The first essay introduces accountability as an idea which humans always lay at the basis of their social arrangements. Sociologists write of external influences which mechanically constrain human behaviour. But in holding each other responsible in their dealings, humans attribute to each other voluntary, intended agency. By tracing areas of accountability and different ways of keeping tally, the active voice sociologist can do better justice to beliefs and behaviour. The passive voice implies that people receive whatever happens to them as so many buffets and blows, including their ideas about god and death; the active voice encourages a search for expectations held about human agency. This sounds a small verbal change, but it is in reality a far-reaching challenge. For example, the second essay argues that the focus of demographic inquiry should be shifted from subsistence to prestige. Let oysters and champagne stand for the celebration of outstanding achievements; assume that social and economic factors sometimes reward small families, sometimes big ones. Then an oysters and champagne theory of demographic change which paid attention to social incentives to limit family size, would give full credit to the will and intelligence of the populations in question. I am sorry that this is an essay that ought to be suppressed. First, I did not understand Wynne-Edwards's whole argument about the effects of social competitiveness on population control. I started by attacking him and ended by proposing a thesis quite compatible with his own. As Sir Peter Medawar kindly said at the time, *Animal Dispersion in Relation to Social Behavior* is a complex book and easily misunderstood. The more I re-read it, the more I realize it is a great book and the more I would like to recast my essay completely. However, the second problem is that the whole subject has developed a great deal since 1966. Paul Spencer has written more on Rendille demography, Asen Balikci and Milton Friedman have published more on infanticide among Netsilik eskimos. Historical and anthropological demography have become enormous disciplines. The idea of hardship among hunters has been scrutinized and discarded. The whole scene has changed totally. To rewrite would be a major work beyond my scope. I keep the essay only because I still like the out-of-the-way examples and because it indicates an active voice approach to population change that does not stop the inquiry when mechanical physical factors have been enumerated.

The seventh essay is on a comparison of economic backwardness between two peoples in the Kasai province of Zaire. To explain big differences in wealth, I searched carefully for differences in natural resources, but I could only find different cultural goals and different intentions. If I had not the good luck to have Jan Vansina researching on the other side of the river, providing me with comparisons, I would have been tempted to stop my inquiry at the physical factors. To have concluded that the Lele were poor only because the soil was poor would have given them no credit for the making of other aspects of their own culture. Even quite contrary estimates of seasonal variation in the same region seem to depend less on the weather itself than on a feedback from different initial choices about how to deal with social life. The people who were committed to strong monarchy and to accumulation of riches worked hard all the year round: to them the dry season was cool and agreeable; the people who were more committed to feuding did their heavy work in one spurt in the dry season, and thought it a terrible time.

Goods, money and food are here all treated as media in which people make statements about their life. Sometimes they know what they want to say and the statement comes out clear, in the active voice. Sometimes they want to say two things at once or to maintain two contradictory attitudes. Then the statements are oblique or confused. Then we have more problem in interpreting them. A helpful procedure is to look for a way in which to express what happened afterwards in the active voice. Not that they were excluded, not that they were misunderstood, neglected or misread; the exercise is to ask whether style and message did not combine to give exactly the effect that was intended and received.

Essays on Frazer and Halbwachs together with an old one on the scope of economic anthropology all refer to a particular problem of interpretation that arises with ambiguous intentions. A message may be composed to express willingness tempered by reserve, call it evasive friendliness or qualified hostility. It comes from a wish to communicate and a wish to restrict communication. In consequence of such ways of framing a message so that it says two different things, it is hard to decide whether it was understood or misunderstood. I would argue that Frazer meant what he said, was well understood by critics and followers at the time and by those who now reject him. But there is the teasing discrepancy between his light, almost flippant style and his grandiose matter. The style of an essayist in the *Spectator*, stretched over twelve volumes of heavy scholarship; did he write thus in order to trivialize the subject? I think he wanted to cool a heated argument. His style focuses and does not distract from his message. He meant the heavy part of what he said and he meant the light way in which he said it. Take the information about Halbwachs's work which Frederick Bartlett transmitted to the English psychologists or the idea of Halbwachs given to the phenomenologists by Alfred Schutz. They felt they had to mention him because of the importance of his voice, and did it in such a way as to block his right of entry to their conversations. In his turn, he did his own piece of exclusion, telling the French sociologists in 1948 that though Keynes made a significant contribution to economic thought, they would not need to bother with it. Often it is the excluders who get excluded, so the French were left out of an important conversation between world economists – so were the anthropologists left out, who complained of the irrelevance of economics and who tried to make their way in that subject without the labour of joining issue and contending direct with the main protagonists. They complained, but the caravans went on. It would mislead to use the passive voice, saying they were left out, whereas history shows they chose to leave the others out.

The chapter 9 represents work which is still in hand and to which I see no end. 'Cultural bias' is one more attempt to encourage active voice thinking in the social sciences. It proposes a typology of social environments, which is a typology of ethical systems. Starting from ideas about accountability, it focuses on different sources of bias in interpretation. Any of my current work that is not concerned with food symbolism is all focused on the programme sketched here.

Acknowledgments

Three of the essays ('Passive voice theories,' 'Maurice Halbwachs,' 'Judgments on Frazer') were written while I was working at the Russell Sage Foundation. I thank the President and the Trustees for the generous allowance of time and facilities and particularly for the help of Madeline Spitaleri. I also acknowledge and warmly thank the publishers of the following books and journals for permission to reprint: *The Review of Religious Research*, *British Journal of Sociology*, *New Society*, *Africa*, *Daedalus*, *The Times Literary Supplement*, Northwestern University Press, Oxford University Press, Royal Anthropological Institute, Universe Books, The Association of Social Anthropologists of the Commonwealth, Harper & Row and the Natural History Press.

1 Passive voice theories* in religious sociology

'Passive Voice Theories' include all sociological and psychological approaches which imply a passive human object influenced by impersonal forces. This paper argues that a sociology of religion which purports to take account of human intentions and do justice to individual beliefs can develop an active voice theoretical approach. This would proceed by tracing the accountability systems which individuals develop when they make claims against each other, and which they reinforce by appeals to unseen powers or attributes of the personality. Accountability systems rest on moral assumptions but can be investigated anthropologically by tested methods. They can provide a basis for objective comparison of beliefs between different cultures.

A wide range of criticisms of sociology and psychology agree in protesting against mechanistic procedures and naive determinism. One form of complaint is that the theoretical apparatus treats the human agent as a passive arena in which impersonal forces are alleged to contend. The passivity attributed to the agent gives me my title and focuses a question I wish to address about the relations between language and theory. Some of these critics maintain that if terminology were to be changed, right thinking would follow. I do not agree that a switch into the active voice in speaking about the human agent is enough; there still would have to be new theoretical approaches to match the new form of language.

'Sociological determinism' stands for an attitude on the part of the sociologist. We can treat it as a kind of belief, not one necessarily adopted by the sociologist personally, but an attitude which is implicit in the terms in which the inquiry is set. It assumes, for the sake of inquiry,

* The 1978 H. Paul Douglass lecture, *Review of Religious Research*, vol. 21, no. 1, Fall, 1979, pp. 51–61.

that some social forces external to the individual are acting upon him. The external agencies are active; the individual is a passive respondent. The sociologist's belief or attitude is itself like a passive response to a theoretical framework which requires it. By using this theoretical framework, the sociologist expects to carry out an important sociological enterprise. He intends to discover and measure the extent of social pressures upon belief.

However, by one of the several paradoxes inherent to the case, he cannot use the theoretical framework to investigate his own professional attitude. The machinery of analysis has these blind spots. It cannot study the validity of religious beliefs in the way that it is designed to study the validity of beliefs that the weather will change. The methods of natural science seem to have this disadvantage in religious studies: they cannot say anything about subjective experience. This gives the sociology of religion four famous disadvantages. It is intended for studying beliefs, yet beliefs are what it cannot study. It is intended to be objective, yet the observer's bias belittles the status of the belief. It tries to study meaning, by a method that reduces meaning to behavioural response. And, it eliminates the subject as an active agent. The dignity of the human subject and of the beliefs espoused by him are both reduced to epiphenomenal disturbances of a normal state. The social causes of beliefs are just as crude a bludgeon as the physiological causes of states of mind. In either case, the autonomy of the subject and the validity of the subject's statements is irrelevantly impugned by a whole system of causation: 'You don't really mean it, your indigestion makes you irritable;' 'It is not surprising that you should subscribe to the Episcopal church, given your upward social mobility.' Believers can certainly try to shrug off the insult, with a *tu quoque*, 'You only belittle the active human subject and distort beliefs because you are talking sociology.'

But mud-slinging will not save the sociology of religion. Too many serious thinkers worried by these well-known problems have given up the sociological enterprise altogether and turned to a literary mode for thinking more profoundly on the human estate. The result has been a shift of sociology as a rigorous explanatory discipline into a richly evocative literary mode, full of insight and beauty. However, the new mode completely shirks the initial project of discovering and estimating the power of social pressures upon individual belief. A century of sociological endeavour is rolled back and, instead of analysis, we are offered essays that are as absorbing and elegant as excerpts might be from *War and Peace*, *The Brothers Karamozov*, even *Pride and Prejudice* in modern dress. The old sociological questions about belief lie rustily on the shelf.

Proposal

If we are to stay with the original important problems – assessing social factors in belief – we need to change our theoretical stance and our language as well. The problem is not confined to the sociology of religion. Social psychology and the sociology of knowledge both study social factors in belief and both are without a strong theoretical approach. An agnostic or deterministic view does not undermine their work so drastically. They can honourably chip away at part-problems. But the trouble is much more acute for the sociology of religion than for any other branch of inquiry because it loses all its claims to serious scholarship unless it can surmount the several difficulties simultaneously. Nor can religious studies be greatly helped by those who believe that careful attention to an active voice terminology will be enough to turn the direction of thought towards taking into account the autonomous human agent in the analysis.

This belief, that language is strongly determinant of thought, addresses our problems in what can be called the passive voice. It is almost a parable for this essay. It assumes, implicitly, that to correct the language will correct the thinking: the thinker is reduced to a passive element to whom linguistic things happen. It is another exemplification of the error we are examining. The hidden assumption is that the speaker does not exert an independent control over his thought; it is channelled and directed by the structure of his language. Only one step removed from cultural determinism, speech determinism is an uncomfortable assumption with which to attack mechanistic, deterministic thinking in the social sciences.

I would like to take Roy Schafer's challenging book *The New Language of Psychoanalysis* (1976) as a model for this discussion. Schafer is fully apprised of these problems and has expressed them very forcefully. However, his own solution is to change the vocabulary. He maintains that if the form of words gives live agents the credit for their own actions, clearer thinking and better theorizing will result. Most of his examples of the use of the passive voice come from the psychoanalyst in the clinical context, when the patient is given a mechanistic model of the self struggling with extraneous forces. The analyst will say mildly: 'You broke through the internal barriers against your feelings of love.' Since Schafer does not believe in internal barriers, the new action language that he advocates would say instead: 'You finally did not refrain from acting lovingly,' thus pinning on the patient the full responsibility for his own emotions. Using passive voice language the analyst will say: 'Your chronic deep sense of worthlessness comes from the condemning voice of your mother.' But Schafer does not believe that the voice of the mother is really there. Action language would translate: 'You regularly imagine your mother's voice condemning you, and you, agreeing with it, regard yourself as being essentially worthless.' Passive analytic language says: 'You are afraid of your impulse to throw caution to the winds.' Schafer does not believe in impulses as entities to be afraid of any more than he believes in barriers, so his action language retranslates.

Schafer expects careful adherence to action language will pin responsibility where it belongs. It recognizes the human agency of will and purpose. It would accurately convey psychoanalytic thinking instead of condoning or colluding with the patient's wish to deny his own intentions. For example:

> If one looks at the idea of 'slip of the tongue' from the standpoint of disclaimed action, one notices several facts immediately: First, it is being maintained through circumlocution that it is the tongue, not the person, who (that) has slipped – as if the tongue regulates its own activity. Second, it is being maintained that what has happened is an accident – a slip – and not a meaningful extended action . . . In psychoanalytic practice we do not accept these disclaimers. We do not believe that there has been an accident. (Schafer, 1976, p. 130)

The slip is not a disrupted action, but a special kind of action in which two courses are taken simultaneously, corresponding to ambivalence in the speaker.

> Once action language is fully adopted, a range of picturesque metaphors will be dropped, because they misleadingly allow the speaker to split elements off from himself, to endow them with initiative and energy, and thus to disclaim his own responsibility. Anger can no longer be treated as a substance – liquid when it spills over, solid when it crushes or penetrates the consciousness, or gaseous when the challenge is to keep the lid on it. (Schafer, 1976, p. 281)

To love and act lovingly are the proper focus for rendering the idea of love in action language. Having thereby lost its status as an entity in this language, love can no longer make the world go round; it can no longer glow, grow, or wither; and it can no longer be lost or found, cherished, poisoned or destroyed . . . it is we who glow, love more or love less, love at all or stop loving. (Schafer, 1976, p. 279)

The reason for radical criticism of the current language in psycho-analysis is that physical science deals with forces, causes, determinants and effects. It cannot deal with meaning and with subjects entertaining meanings. The analysis of the human psyche needs to focus on *situations, meanings, actions and reasons*. These four terms co-define each other. No situation can be envisaged unless it is interpreted as such or given meaning; nor can it arise unless human actions have created it; nor can the human actions be explained except by the interpretation of situations which generate reasons for acting.

This same foursome which Schafer proposes to put in place of mechanistic causes and forces in psychology will do well for the equivalent switch in terminology in the sociology of religion. But Schafer allows himself to rest there, whereas sociology must go on. Schafer has only the limited aim of reconciling clinical practice with high psychoanalytic theory, proposing the same language for each. Benefits surely would flow automatically from any such reconceptual-izing exercise. But there must be real conceptualizing, not mere vocabu-lary change. Schafer thinks that if we change the sentences from the passive to the active voice, a new theoretical scheme will emerge. But this is surely a mistake. First, he only proposes to change the clinical practice of speaking as if to a passive patient. This will do nothing to change the high theory of which he is mainly critical. It also will create awkwardness and counter-productive strain in the clinical situation. For the passive voice corresponds to a particular social intention. Sociol-ogists who use mechanistic theories and passive voice language in respect of individual beliefs also have an explicit intention set by their theories. The psychoanalyst in his clinic has a social situation to deal with, which would get out of hand if he were to use active voice language for explaining to the hypersensitive patient the full extent of his own responsibility. An active voice theory of the relation of words to thought would take systematic account of the intentions of speakers who have chosen to use the passive voice to describe their own thinking. To hear Schafer subscribing to a passive voice theory of language convinces one that thinking the problem through requires more theoretical energy, more questioning and rethinking of the basis of the study than he is prepared to give at this stage.

Analysis

I will illustrate further the contrast between passive and active voice theories by drawing an impressionistic contrast between Müller's (1873) theory of the disease of language and Whorf's (1956) theory of the restrictions placed by language on thought.

Müller vs Whorf

Müller, the great philogist, has become an antique curiosity in the history of religion. His theory about how some peculiar religious beliefs originated is relevant here. Müller never doubted the human power to reach spiritual heights of imagination or to conceive abstract ideas. He was prepared to credit humans with such powers. In so far as the gods of classical antiquity were alleged to behave with justice and decorum, he felt no need to explain religious beliefs by any pathological tendency. But to explain stories about their more idiosyncratic and lusty feats, he developed his theory of mythology deriving from a disease of language. This disease he attributed to a universal human weakness, inability to retain an abstract idea as first conceived: a word once devised to carry a complex meaning would soon fall away from abstraction and spirituality and be used only to convey a crass, particular, material sense. This disease of language would always be leaving daily speech cluttered with great words demeaned. Empty of their original connotation, a host of hybrid anthropomorphic agencies poses puzzles for worthy lexicographers whose trade drives them to invent stories about them. In this way, the odder parts of Greek and Roman mythology would be seen as later additions to purely intellectual and moral philosophy.

The disease of language theory was dismissed for many reasons. Surprisingly, in the wider modern context, it was held utterly implausible. Yet other linguists who have proposed equally unconvincing theories about the relation of thought to language have been taken very seriously. Whorf speculated that syntactic structures would tend to limit the possibilities of thought. He presented thought as a kind of moving flow of traffic through the structures of language, channelled and restricted by the latter. The implication is that for each kind of language, only certain ways of thinking are possible. In Whorf's view, thought is limited by language. In Müller's view, thought is limited by itself; language can say anything that humans want to say but, unfortunately, their wants change. They do not always need the more difficult concepts for which they have developed words. This seems to have some long-run plausibility. Contrasted with Whorf, we can place Müller on the side of those who take meanings as prior and speech constraints as secondary. He did not see language itself as a barrier or constraint to thought and held failures in thinking responsible for a process by which abstract theogonies degenerate into mechanistic, material models. Psyche becomes a seductive girl; Zeus a lecher in comic opera disguises. Going beyond more speculative generalization, Müller actually proposed his rule as a tendency in language. He can be credited with a theory of downward semantic drift.

In like fashion, sociologists who mean to investigate the intellectual and emotional life of human beings have drifted away from their intentions. They talk about human agencies, meanings, and actions. They have not let their grammar lead their thought, but their thought has left their wider intentions stranded, doing justice only to their natural science assumptions and methodology. The use of natural science methodology and its terms have produced rich insights into religious sociology. But our failure to hold to the original complexities of the enterprise have left us with extraordinary entities in our dictionary, belittling of the believers and the beliefs which we would like to understand. We now have to cope with causes (such as relative deprivation, or upward social mobility) and effects (such as routinization and secularization). At the same time, there is no reason to suppose that we cannot throw out the distracting elements of our language and start with a new effort of will to reinstate Zeus and Psyche in their full majesty.

To justify Müller's idea further, we can easily find words which reify strange mechanical forces credited with anthropomorphic intentions. When we view these carefully, we recognize that the words are not doing something to our thoughts; out intentions have weakened and narrowed, our thinking has lost its sharp edge. We have fallen into inertia and exemplify the disease of language.

Ordinary speech attributes to other entities the agency which belongs to ourselves. In everyday locutions, we attribute spatial properties to the mind: 'It went clean out of my mind'; 'Murder entered my mind';

'Suicide was at the back of my mind.' These are examples given by Schafer. Recall also the legal formula which speaks of the mind as a machine with a definite equilibrium: 'While the balance of his mind was disturbed.' Then sometimes we refer to the mind as an autonomous agent: 'My mind plays tricks on me'; 'I wish I knew my own mind'; 'I am in two minds.' These phrases do not mislead the listener. They are couched deliberately as disclaimers of responsibility in which the speaker's goodwill is guaranteed, and guaranteed all the more because, by implication, what the mind will do is left in doubt and outside the speaker's control (Schafer, 1976, p. 132). There is nothing irrational about such disclaimers: 'A mad impulse seized me'; 'The words poured out of my mouth.' Everyday speech has good reasons for interposing another agent between the speaker and his own actions. It is more courteous to say: 'It must have escaped your memory' than to suppress the 'it' and simply accuse 'You forgot me.' Some care for the feelings of others justifies these polite disclaimers.

This sensitivity to our own everyday use of the passive voice gives a clue to the approach in the sociology of religion which I wish to propose. Many of the religions of the world have doctrines of multiple personality according to which the individual is divided between several more or less co-ordinated persons. These constituent persons of the person tend to have different intentions and capacities attributed to them. A person who has incurred blame is allowed to feel its force, softened by knowing that the action of which he was guilty can be attributed to one but not to all of his own constituent personalities. This time, the polite disclaimer comes from others in an ordinary context, instead of from the psycho-analyst speaking to the patient. The human subject almost disappears from sight, among a throng of other active spirits who are judging, willing, accepting, or rejecting on his behalf; the subject, indeed, in many religious doctrines becomes an object, a passive arena where bizarre forces contend. But we should not interpret this multiplication of personalities as a mistake, a form of inertia, or another case of the disease of language. If we take it as our principal assumption that nothing is done by mistake, that the subjects are in control of their own thoughts and their own language and have adapted the language to their thoughts, we can reach a better understanding of their stated beliefs.

Phenomenology

The active voice language is appropriate for a phenomenological theory. As sociologists, we have engaged on an investigation. We are determined that it be an investigation of religious behaviour which, fully sociological in its intentions, still insists upon recognizing the active independent agency of the people we are studying. Once, when I described these assumptions as necessary, a student asked me whether they achieved any better analysis, or whether they merely made me feel good. The claim is precisely that the analysis is improved.

At this point, I introduce the concept of the accountability system. As a concept, it owes much to the ethnomethodologists. As a method, it was developed by anthropologists for the comparison of moral principles. The method consists in setting people's beliefs back into the social context of their lives, by careful, intensive field research. With this method, no alleged belief in strange invisible entities is allowed to qualify as a belief until there is evidence that it is acted upon in some socially intelligible way. The moral judgments are supposed not to exist merely as noble sentiments; the interest lies in the way they are daily invoked as means of holding other people to their promises, enforcing contracts, extracting lenient remissions and so on. By systematic research into every kind of confrontation, the general principles by which people hold each other accountable can be laid bare. Accountability systems vary. The moral principles they invoke differ and the institutions into which they are incorporated differ to that extent. By fastening on moral principles and their use in building systems of accountability, the sociologist has a way of giving value to individuals' free negotiating activities. At the same time, from the limited but firm standpoint of a common cognitive enterprise, we can reckon what are the kinds of social institutions that are built upon different outcomes of moral judgment.

Each accountability system, to be sufficiently coherent to function, has to create explanations, and attribute qualities such as vengefulness, caprice, or kindness to invisible powers. Each accountability system is likely to call upon the malice of ghosts or on a High God's justice, or use other devices to make its sterner judgments acceptable. In modern industrial culture, we have developed a complex typology of personalities and talents to justify our procedures of exclusion or promotion. 'High IQ' is a concept that responds to our need to measure and scale criteria of admission. If we could agree a measure of mental stability, it would enter the repertoire of personality attributes. Sometimes the full responsibility is nailed to the culprit; sometimes the theory of causation will mitigate responsibility so that the offence which is being judged is softened into something that either might happen to anyone or the person could have committed unknowingly. For the sake of living together in peace, each society will combine the active voice and the passive voice in different measures, to make harsh judgments acceptable to unfortunate persons who ask why disasters have befallen them. Accountability systems vary, of course, in their internal consistency and completeness and in many other ways that reflect their use within social institutions.

The first elaborate examples of this method were Evans-Pritchard's analyses of Azande and Nuer moral and political systems. Haimendorf's comparison of Hindus and Buddhists in Nepal is another valuable exercise. The essence of the method is to trace beliefs in divine attributes to the moral values which are institutionalized and actionable. These beliefs are part and parcel of the social life, fully credible within it, subscribed to whenever a person in such a society wishes either to exercise his rights or to charge another with default. At that point, when insisting on moral claims, individuals declare their autonomy within society and reveal their own constructive efforts to maintain or change the local world view. Their active agency is a necessary starting point for the analysis. Moreover, the old sociological perspective is still in view.

African beliefs

Let me describe a comparison of two belief systems which could be submitted to the old style analysis of sociological determinism. The cultures of the West Coast of Africa have variant forms of a belief in multiple personalities. The thinking, willing, acting parts of an individual are split off from each other in various ways, culturally standardized in each case. One such set of beliefs has been described brilliantly by Fortes (1959) writing about the Tallensi in the Volta region of Ghana. Their cult of the ancestors and their belief in Destiny combine to give them explanations of misfortune which are much more than pure intellectual speculations. They channel the Tallensi ideas of moral responsibility and set them to work in the social context so efficiently that action, institutions, and beliefs are parts of one process. Fortes takes the Tallensi beliefs in their composite personality as seriously as they do.

He shows how their concept of the good person is inculcated through early training, and how it integrates the individual into the patrilineal lineage structure of their society, at the same time as finely adjusting the pattern of rewards and punishments (which the dead ancestors administer) to their moral ideas and to the social structure. Over and above the relation of the live individual to the justice and vigilance of his ancestors, the Tallensi have to reckon with a part of the personality which existed before they were born – their individual Destiny – which is thought to have accepted or rejected the moral requirements. If the Destiny is a bad one, then they will (not consciously) tend to behave in deviant ways, lacking in respect for their kinsmen, and so bringing down the misfortunes which punish the unfilial.

In a paper which should be read by every student of religious sociology, Horton (1961) makes a parallel analysis of similar beliefs. Among the Kalabari Ijo of the Niger Delta, words of Destiny spoken by the prenatal self explain the misfortunes of an individual. But in this case, the choices of the prenatal self are judged good or bad for different kinds of deviance. In the Tallensi case, the bad Destiny was chosen by the man who pitted himself again paternal authority and refused the prescriptions of Tallensi social institutions. In the Kalabari case, the bad Destiny is chosen prenatally by the person who has no taste for the rat race of an entrepreneurial, individualist society; their good Destiny is that of the ruthless competitive fisherman and merchant.

So here would seem to be a case for sociological determinism. Given the social institutions, the beliefs are differentiated adaptive responses. But Horton's essay is a vehement criticism of such argumentation. One of the staunchest upholders of the independent status of beliefs, Horton makes a programme for the comparative study of religion, which I seek to expand and to emulate. The simple question to follow is this: if the Tallensi and the Kalabari are given their beliefs as part of one packet with their institutions, where do the institutions come from? The usual ways in which sociological determinism answers this question are either by maintaining a thorough-going economic determinism which assumes only one possible adaptive strategy to physical conditions, or by allowing for blind chance in the particular set of adaptations made in any one case. The first solution carries all the limitations to any sociology of religion that denies agency to humans and validity to belief. The second, of course, is an abdication from explanation. I shall proceed on another basis. I shall assume there is a full programme for a sociology of religion: the interaction of human agents must be its subject; and in so far as they choose beliefs, they choose their institutional forms and try to make sense of them, justifying their choices at the same time.

Fortes's *Oedipus and Job in West African Religion*, and Horton's elaboration of its theme demonstrate what the sociological exercise could still do in its old comparative programme.

Writing of Fortes's approach to Tallensi beliefs, Horton says:

> A great virtue of this essay is that it is one of the few recent socio-anthropological works to take religious relationships seriously. By this I mean that it treats talk about gods and their involvements with men at its face value, rather than assuming that such talk is 'merely a way of referring to social structure.' Because Fortes accepts the psychological reality of such relationships so far as the people involved in them are concerned, he is led to explore their quality in Tale religion with a fullness and depth rarely seen elsewhere. Again, though he follows a well-worn path in correlating cult structure with social structure, his relation of religious notions specifically to features of the individual's passage through society is a new and exciting approach. (Horton, 1961, p. III)

When he makes a summary comparison of the two similar belief systems, Horton draws attention to the local ideas of personality.

> It is interesting to compare Kalabari ideas about the locus of these personality conflicts firstly with Tallensi ideas and then with the classical Freudian ideas themselves. In Kalabari thought, the conflict centres about the desire to engage in status competition: whilst the conscious self pursues and approves competition, the unconscious may abhor it. There is, however, no focus on conflict of attitudes to particular people. In Tallensi thought, by contrast, the conflict centres on a specific person, the father: whilst the conscious self submits to parental authority, the unconscious hates and rejects it. Switching to Europe, classical Freudian doctrines play down conflict over status rivalry and lay heavy emphasis on conflict over sexual drives; though it should be noted that the American school of 'Neo-Freudians' has rejected the overwhelming sexual emphasis of classical doctrine in favour of conflicts centering on status competition.

> These differences are revealing, for they reflect wider differences of cultural and structural emphasis. In Kalabari communities, structural arrangements are such that the people involved most

intensively in status rivalry at any one time are never in any set relationship to one another; this because in questions of accession to leadership of a group, great latitude is allowed for achievement irrespective of ascribed characteristics of age, pedigree, or relationship to other competitors. Again, whilst aggressive competition is formally enjoined in this culture, it is at the same time discouraged in fact, because current beliefs lay such heavy stress on the use of lethal sorcery by way of reprisal. Correspondingly, Kalabari personality theory features an aggressive Conscious and a timid Unconscious. In Tallensi communities, on the other hand, status advancement can only take place at the expense of a specifically related figure – the father. Hence the ambivalent attitudes described in Tallensi personality theory feature him in person; as where the *yin* ('Destiny,' Unconscious Wishes) of a son is said to be in chronic opposition to the *yin* of his father. Another point of contrast with Kalabari is that here amity and non-competitiveness are formally enjoined in all the most important relationships, whilst the culture makes no real provision for the frustrations of a son who remains a jural minor till the day of his father's death. In consonance with this, Tallensi personality theory postulates the reverse of Kalabari theory – an amicable Conscious and an aggressive Unconscious. (Horton, 1961, pp. 113–14)

The Tallensi use a passive voice theory of responsibility to help a victim of misfortune not take the full weight of guilt upon himself. At least he can believe that some limited part of himself entertained the initial ill-will from which his destiny sprang. The Kalabari use the passive voice theory of personality to focus a victim's will to conquer his fate: he is helped to identify that part of himself which is not fully committed to social competition. Horton goes on to call for a systematic study in West Africa, which would note the number of divisions of the personality, the desire attributed to each, and the power relations between them. The variations which emerge could be correlated with structural and cultural variables as demonstrated in Horton's comparison of Kalabari and Tallensi.

Conclusions

Whereas Horton suggests his programme modestly, as an improvement for ethnographic practice, it is also suggestive for the development of psychoanalysis at the point we left it after considering Schafer's linguistic reforms. Psychoanalytic theory seems too much like a ship at anchor, once fitted out for a great voyage, but sails now furled, ropes flapping, motion stilled. It is not as if theoretical winds were lacking to drive it. But the motive to go somewhere is missing. As Müller said, sometimes the will to hold to a great notion can fail. A mere linguistic switch from the passive to the active voice is not going to give psychoanalysis a purpose or plan. The grand conception must be recalled. The original enterprise of psychology was to chart the human psyche. But that can never be done without charting, at the same time, the range of possible social constraints laid by one person upon another or by hundreds acting in concert. For good success, the psychological approach to meaning surely will have to keep in step with the sociological approach.

We can agree easily enough upon a common language; the terms that deal with meaning, action, situation and reasons are good for both disciplines. But we still need to agree upon methods for using the language. We also need to agree upon whatever it is we want to say. We will not lie down passively under the constraints of a natural science language of causes and determinants. We believe we are free agents and so free to pick up and work at our original idea. In the sociology of religion that idea was to examine the social factors in belief.

This programme requires the investigator to trace the controls that the human subjects of his research are laying upon each other. If the sociologist investigator always checks the constraints upon action which appear as penalties and moral judgments, the investigation itself is protected from his own imported subjective interpretations. The Kalabari and Tallensi make different judgments of failure; they deploy different resources for explaining, reconciling and reinstating or washing their hands of less fortunate fellow men. This is the essence of the powerful method in which action terminology can be used. Never denying active human agency, we can trace how people work their institutions as well as create the conditions in which their beliefs get plausibility. The task of careful comparison is a heavy one. It can achieve the same ends as those for which the conceptual apparatus of sociological determinants of belief was devised. It is a much more exacting programme than anything that has been tried in the sociology of religion. But it is a programme for our times, both methodologically sophisticated and phenomenological in its assumptions.

References

Evans-Pritchard, E. (1937), *Witchcraft Oracles and Magic Among the Azande*, Oxford, Clarendon Press.

Fortes, Meyer (1959), *Oedipus and Job in West African Religion*, Cambridge University Press.

Haimendorf, Christoph von Furer (1967), *Morals and Merit: A Study of Values and Social Controls in South Asian Society*, University of Chicago Press.

Horton, Robin (1961), 'Destiny and the Unconscious in West Africa', *Africa*, 31(2), pp. 110–16.

Müller, Max F. (1873), *Introduction to the Science of Religion*, London, Longmans Green.

Schafer, Roy (1976), *A New Language for Psychoanalysis*, New Haven, Yale University Press.

Whorf, Benjamin Lee (1956), *Language, Thought and Reality: Selected Writings of Benjamin Lee Whorf*, ed. J. B. Carroll, New York, John Wiley.

2 Goods as a system of communication*

No serious writer on the problems of poverty would defend a grossly materialistic view – either of the condition or of the remedy. Poverty is not merely due to lack of goods nor even to lack of money. It is much more a matter of personal dignity. So William Morris set the scene of his *Nowhere* in a society of beautiful people, who worked for the happiness of service and craftsmanship; material possessions were not important to dignity. Somehow, in our society, material goods do affect it, but it is not clear why personal degradation follows from their lack. Paradoxically an isolated tribe whose culture is poor in material goods but rich in spiritual ones does not excite our compassion until it has been debauched by desire for our kinds of goods. Obviously there are ways of keeping dignity intact without a vast array of material things. So the evidence of poverty in the midst of plenty is more than a deep reproach to our civilization – it is an unsolved problem. Two of the most common ways of posing it fail to clarify the issue; one is the materialist approach by way of comparisons of real income and levels of subsistence, the other by subjective assessment of relative deprivation. A third approach considers poverty primarily as restriction of choice. This opens up the most scope to anthropological analysis, so I shall return to it after saying more about the other two.

Let me start by making a distinction between destitution and poverty. The word destitution will here be used to refer to the state in which the main problems are subsistence problems and the main choices to be made are choices about purchases of food, drink, and rent. The level of subsistence is always set by the particular technological conditions of the time. People may be actually subsisting, and likely to continue in such a

---

* Original title, 'Relative Poverty – Relative Communication', *Traditions of Social Policy, Essarys in Honour of Violet Butler*, ed A. H. Halsey, Oxford, Basil Blackwell, 1976, pp. 197–215.

condition, indefinitely, especially if relief is available to keep them alive at just that level. Private alms and public assistance are very properly channelled to the relief of destitution and for this purpose careful measures of real goods and the money income required for acquiring them have to be devised. But there is surely a complete break in the terms of the argument, a break in continuity between the problems of destitution and those of poverty. The questions have to be separated. The data relevant for the one have to be reconstrued to be made relevant to the other. Questions about subsistence are posed in material terms and physiological tests are applicable. When subsistence is at issue, it is proper to consider levels of heating, intake of calories and proteins, the dampness of walls and ceilings. If it were not for speedy relief measures, those living near subsistence level would sink below it and die. Thus subsistence problems are not only physical problems, they are emergencies. Considerable confusion has arisen from taking the measures which are proper to this field of thought and applying them to broader problems, such as poverty: hence, indeed, many of the difficulties in defining the latter. For one reason it is unlikely that a physiological and material concept which is implicitly static can be used for a comparison of social relations which are essentially dynamic. Brian Abel-Smith and Peter Townsend wryly point out the absurdities in trying to update the standards of physical subsistence to match changing conditions.[1]

> The subsistence standards used by earlier writers on poverty seem at first sight to lend themselves to comparisons over time. This approach allows a basket of foodstuffs and other goods to be defined as necessary to provide subsistence. The cost of purchasing these goods can be calculated for different years and the number of households with insufficient income to purchase the goods can be ascertained. Although the principle seems easy to state, there are problems in applying it in practice. For example, the goods on the market at the later period may not be the same as at the earlier period. The cumbrous garments which convention required women to wear at the beginning of this century were unlikely to be found on the market in the 1930s, let alone today. Electricity has replaced oil lamps and candles. Even food habits have changed. These are among the problems which face those who attempt to apply the same poverty line at different periods. Again, the choice of goods that are selected initially cannot be defined in narrowly 'physical' or 'nutritional' terms. In laying down what articles of clothing and items of food are

necessary for physical efficiency, those in charge of the surveys have been unable to prevent judgments about what is conventional or customary from creeping in to their lists and definitions.

This quotation serves to reveal the muddle. It is fair enough, perhaps, to write as if somehow scientific, physical, and nutritional judgments concerning poverty could be made more precise if they could be stripped of all the local conventional culture. For this is how the subsistence standards defined for national assistance purposes are intended. But how mad – there is a crucial difference according to whether the subsistence standards are to be applied by humans to pets or to other humans. For the first, the veterinary surgeons' criteria go. For the second, their own ideas about their own society must intervene. Our authors, after a little forehead-wrinkling, give up the task of devising a culture-free standard of living: 'Poverty is a relative concept. Saying who is in poverty is to make a relative statement rather like saying who is short or heavy.'[2]

The idea that poverty is to be measured by levels of physical subsistence goes back to Rowntree, of course, and has been made the main platform of our public policy for alleviating it. J. C. Kincaid soundly berates William Beveridge for using a standard of physical subsistence for the social security scheme which he pioneered.[3] But what he dislikes is not the intrusion of physical subsistence, but that the standard was set too low. He trips on the same snag that catches everyone who takes a strictly material idea of the standard of living: 'Obviously even those at the very foot of society in contemporary Britain enjoy a standard of living that is somewhat higher than that of the poorest in Victorian society a hundred years ago and much higher than the norm in many underdeveloped societies today.'[4]

In saying this, Kincaid only echoes a widespread fallacy. The Report of the National Board for Prices and Incomes on the General Problems of Low Pay makes the same comment: 'Poverty is now accepted as being a relative concept. People who in this country are reckoned – or who reckon themselves – poor today are not necessarily so by the standards of twenty-five years ago or by the standards of other countries.'[5]

In the proper context, there is much to be said in favour of developing the concept of subsistence and material standard of living. Destitution is a grave problem and must be measured somehow, though the scale be imperfect. By comparison, the relativist approach to poverty has flippant overtones. It tends to hang the weight of definition on subjective experience. By abdicating responsibility to define the condition, the argument can only say that people feel poor because they see others richer than themselves. Poverty is then over-closely equated with jealousy, a feeling which intensifies with the widening of the reference group (Runciman). Since the poor cannot protect the view from their windows or preserve their garden plot from developers, their street from thundering traffic noise, their diet from monotony and so on, they must put up with increasing intrusion, narrowness and despoilment, and will do so all the more passively if unaware of persons that they can identify with who enjoy a better condition. Apart from trivializing a serious matter, the definition based on subjective jealousy can be soporific, while at least the subsistence approach leads to soup kitchens and doles. As Kincaid says:[6]

> once a relative view of poverty is adopted, it follows that poverty cannot be abolished, since in any society where complete social inequality does not always prevail, the label of poor can always be given to the 10 per cent or 20 per cent of the population who come lowest in the hierarchy of income. If the absolutely poor need not be always with us, surely the relatively poor, by definition, cannot vanish.

Like many others, his solution is to remove inequality of income. Whatever the merits of that policy (and it should of course apply to wealth as well as to income if it is to achieve its stated goal), the relativist definition of poverty on which it rests ought to be improved. Those who espouse it are right to reject a material standard and right to emphasize that personal dignity is at risk when market forces are uncontrolled. But they need not found their case on a negative sense of unfairness and jealousy. An anthropological approach would start from assuming that goods are used in a system of communication. It should be possible to be objective about the quantity of goods and the kind of goods needed for entering the system and catching the message necessary for participation. Deafness is a relative condition; a person can be more deaf or less deaf than another, but this does not mean that the experience of deafness is purely subjective, that it cannot be measured or defined, nor the effectiveness of deaf-aids be judged. Poverty should be regarded as a social defect equivalent to physical deafness. It is capable of definition and remedy. The difficulties of establishing this viewpoint lie largely in the history of economics.

For one thing, there is the over-narrowing of the problem to the

individual's access to consumer goods. Since consumption is treated by economic theory as an individual matter, consumption goods being bought mainly to be consumed within the home, it is difficult to explain within that theory why one household's having more of them than another is damaging to the less well-provided – unless health is in danger. Hence the emphasis is on physical well-being. From this barren ground, Harold Watts tried to establish a richer theoretical basis.[7] He starts from the economist's central distinction between preferences and constraints: poverty is a property of the individual's situation, a severe constriction of the choice set. Second, he expands the time horizon for the choice set so as to include 'the value of the largest sustainable level of consumption, the sum of income flows from all sources evaluated at the normal rate they can be expected to maintain over the long run, instead of at the current level'. For purposes of calculating poverty, he would convert net wealth (assets minus liabilities) into equivalent life annuities for purposes of measuring the capacity to sustain a level of consumption. 'So the unemployed dishwasher would be counted as poorer than the unemployed plumber even though both had the same zero level of current earnings.' Third, recognizing that poverty is not a discrete condition, he asserts that 'constriction of choice becomes progressively more damaging in a continuous manner'. The rest of his argument is concerned with working out a family's 'welfare ratio' as the ratio of its permanent sustainable income to an arbitrarily established 'poverty threshold'; a technical exercise of some ingenuity but difficult application. The first three definitional points (poverty as a constriction of choice, with lifetime implications and cumulative effects) make the best start to analysing the relation that is too often taken for granted between choice over goods and the protection of dignity. Poverty means constriction of choice: that is surely obvious. That the restriction has lifetime and cumulative effects may need some illumination. I take it that he is recognizing here that the move to a cheaper house means living in a poorer neighbourhood, sending children to less well-equipped schools, and so on, the familiar degeneration of circumstances which is summed up by 'lifetime cumulative effects'. To the layman this has the ring of truth, but the theoretical foundations for such a statement are hard to find in demand theory.

Consumption is a peculiar idea, embedded in the history of economic practice. It derives from the contrast with production, as the object or end product of the latter.[8] In this regard it has an analogy in accountancy as the net result when all costs of production have been subtracted and double counting eliminated. In systems analysis it has a general analogy with output when all input processes of transformation are reckoned. However, it also derives from its use in contrast with saving, since saving is that which might have been consumed but which is put aside for future consumption. In that case consumption counts as part of the costs of production and the only net gain is the saving. The concept arises as part of an equation. In the national aggregate, consumption is equal to income minus savings; for the private individual it is his expenditure from income, part of that which the income has been earned to obtain. It is a concept which results from technical calculations. In the analysis of demand the assumptions about consumption have been so polished and refined that no false psychological ideas are entertained. In consequence, there are no other ideas for why people should want goods at all. For lack of a formal theory, economics falls inadvertently into the materialist mode of thought. It is easy to see that physical subsistence is a basic need and measuring real income is one of the things that economics can do. Hence many economists' writings on needs give confidently a mixed list which starts with subsistence and includes such ill-assorted motives as benevolence and thrill.[9]

For the anthropologist seeking a useful discussion of poverty the pitch is queered by lack of a systematic account of consumers' objectives. Hicks taught that the individual does not regard the commodities he buys as ends or objectives, as consumer theory would imply, but as means to the attainment of objectives. 'It would accordingly appear that we ought to think of the consumer as choosing, according to his preference, between certain *objectives*; and then deciding, more or less as the entrepreneur decides, between alternative means of reaching those objectives.'[10] Anthropology might be able to supply a systematic account of consumers' objectives, but hitherto none exists. If this first step were taken successfully, then two advantageous changes could be made in the present discussion of poverty. The first would be to treat subsistence as a cost, not as an output. The second would be to introduce some idea of scale of operations.

To treat subsistence as a means of obtaining other objectives makes some basic layman's good sense. For many of its practitioners, economic theory is primarily designed for understanding long-term stable conditions. The merits of adopting such an approach are described by G. L. S. Shackle in the introduction to a survey of theories concerning the rate of interest:[11]

in historical fact the cleavages between groups of theories have run along a few clear lines, which can for practical purposes be easily defined. These lines, of course, intersect each other and yield cross-classifications. One dichotomy is between equilibrium and development theories. Equilibrium is a test that selects for the economist one particular situation out of an infinity of situations and justifies his calling attention to it as something special. Just by the smallness of the ratio of what it accepts to what it rejects, no other test seems able to rival its selective power . . . on the most general grounds equilibrium has great claims as economiser of thought. To dispense with it has meant, in practice, to be reduced to mere factual enumeration.

Equilibrium theory does not claim that a sequence of actual economic states will terminate in an equilibrium state, but 'that no plausible sequence of economic states will terminate, if it does so at all, in a state which is not an equilibrium. The argument is straightforward; agents will not continue in actions in states in which preferred or more profitable ones are available to them nor will mutually inconsistent actions allow given prices to persist.'[12] If the branch of economics, central to the theory of demand, has been such a powerful organizer of thought, consumer theory would rightly expect to take advantage of these tools.

Equilibrium theory, being concerned with stable states, would be misapplied if it were to treat as stable a state which was in essence a crisis, a temporary emergency which must move either to stability or catastrophe. Whenever it is taken for granted that physical subsistence is the main and dominant objective of economic behaviour, the theory is being misapplied. Anyone whose dominant concern is to survive is in a parlous state which cannot continue. If the whole society has to treat physical survival as a prior concern, again, it is in a mess. Its problems rightly come under those of destitution, not of poverty. The theory of demand needs some statement of a normal set of consumer's objectives, which can be assumed to be held under stable conditions. For any selected level of physical subsistence deemed a prior requirement for achieving this set of objectives, the economist can work out a production function. Such a two-level approach would ask for an account of consumer's objectives, and second an account of the prevailing technology creating the cost-structure within which they have to be achieved. Thus subsistence, instead of befogging the definition of poverty by its implausible status as one objective of consumption among others, would be relegated to the status of a cost. By this route there is no need to look for a culture-free definition, either of human subsistence or of poverty: both have to be defined within the techno-cultural standards of the time. One last adjustment; consumer theory needs some concept of scale of operations. So far the dimension is missing, so that there is no way of comparing consumers' operating on larger or smaller scale, or of thinking of how benefits of scale might help in achieving the consumers' objectives. Without taking account of benefits of scale, certain features of consumption behaviour go unrecorded, but if they are taken into account, we can bring strong arguments to support Harold Watts's view that restriction of choice may be cumulatively damaging. For we will be able to show that in the field of consumption alone, without regard to other aspects of the economy such as the labour market, there is a selective bias working in favour of some and against others. This is a serious problem concerning relative poverty which is lost to sight. The subjective experience which looks like plain jealousy is partly due to fear of being unable to meet social commitments and partly due to the existence of a spiral on which the downhill run can seem disastrously fast to the consumer who finds the cost structure working against him. Whether the downward spiral leads to destitution or anywhere near it is a difficult matter to demonstrate. But the existence of descending and ascending movements in the ability to command goods and services is worrying enough when the normal consumption project is recognized to be not an absorption into the household of more and improved goods wanted for their own sake, but the creation of a network of interpersonal obligations.

Modern industrial man needs goods for the same reason as the tribesman. They need goods in order to commit other people to their projects. It is somewhat of an anachronism or solecism to use the words 'goods', 'consumption' and 'consumers' beyond the boundaries of capitalist industrial society. Yet something useful is served by doing so carefully. When I have developed an anthropological definition of consumption, the meanings will not be so stretched as they are now. Anticipating, the theory of needs should start by assuming that any individual needs goods in order to commit other people to his projects. He needs goods to involve others as fellow-consumers in his consumption rituals. Goods are for mobilizing other people. The fact that in the course of these rituals food gets consumed, flags waved and clothes worn is incidental. Subsistence is a fortunate by-product. Bodily subsistence happens to be served by some aspects of consumption activities, by the absorption of food, but the fading of cut flowers and the accumulation of dust on paintings, the dying chords of a song, these are other costs in consumption rituals which just don't happen to serve subsistence needs. For keeping the discussion on the right tracks, flowers might be a better favourite example to take of typical consumption goods than eggs and butter. In tribal society goods are used for paying compliments, for initiating marriages, establishing or ending them, for recognizing relationships, for all celebrations, compensations and affirmations whatever. Every ethnography has an account of how the channels etched by gifts and countergifts constitute the social fabric.

The tribesmen also pass judgments on each other in respect of poverty. Most unusually the man is reckoned poor who has everything he needs for subsistence for himself and his family but no more. The Turkana pastorialists of Uganda, for example, live on mixed herds of sheep, goats, and cattle with donkeys for transport. A family can live well enough with just sheep, camels and goats, and with less trouble, since cattle are delicate in this region and need special herding and watering care lavished on them. But without cattle a man has to accept inferior social status: cattle are needed for marriage payments and gifts to friends and allies.[13] For us to think of poverty in terms of more or less real income is to be less intelligent as economists than the Turkana. They would never try to remedy a man's lack of cattle by giving him more sheep and goats. This is how we are tempted to think of remedying poverty, by subsidizing food and other things necessary for subsistence. Unless we know why people need luxuries and how they use them we are nowhere near taking the problems of inequality seriously.

An anthropological theory of consumption will require some new assumptions. The first aim would be to define consumption activity in a way that would be consistent with a communications theory of the use of goods. In the opening pages of *The Elementary Forms of Kinship* in 1949, Lévi-Strauss distinguishes three forms of transfers which uphold human society; the transfers of meanings, transfers of women and transfers of goods, thus giving three branches of anthropology, mythology, kinship and economics. The pity was to have kept them separate. The present essay is an attempt to incorporate the three branches into one theory of consumption.

The need to define and better understand consumption activity has been fully recognised by consumption theories.[14] Their chosen examples often rise above the ingestion of vitamins to holidays and clothes and transport,[15] and yet I fear that the following propositions will be unexpected and seem far-fetched.

First, let us assume that the ultimate object of consumption activity is to enter a social universe whose processes consist of matching goods to classes of social occasions. Second, for entry into such a universe, the individual needs the services of fellow consumers. These services are either in the form of personal attendance at consumption events or of material contributions of goods (e.g. flowers) and their object is to create or confirm a grading of the occasion. For want of a better term, let me call these services offered by fellow-consumers 'marking'. This is in the spirit of the hall-marking of gold, silver and pewter, the signing and otherwise authenticating of work, the marking in the sense of judging and classing of performances in competitive racing, dancing, music, etc., or marking in the sense of setting up milestones, boundaries and benchmarks of all kinds. Goods are endowed with value by the agreement of fellow-consumers. In marking events and grading categories, fellow-consumers uphold old judgments or make new fashions in the value of goods. Now it is mainly dry wine that is classed high, then gradually the place reserved for certain rare sweet ones is expanded; now it is only Beethoven, and then Vivaldi gets a better place; now it is either late eighteenth-century architecture or steel and concrete, nothing in between. The marking is spontaneous and unpredictable since it depends on the mobilization of fellow-consumers. But it is unmistakable. The women's magazine says 'Prints are being worn at the races': one only has to go to the races to see the profusion of printed silk dresses to know that the marking process is just so.[16] These matters of taste formation stand explicitly outside the scope of economics, but must be brought in somehow and made quantifiable for there to be a workable idea of consumption activities. Perhaps it is convincing that there can be no social universe without a system of discriminations in which goods are involved. Equally important for the individual is his dependence on fellow-consumers for his own point of entry into the classifications. He needs fellow-consumers not only to create the social universe around him but to assure himself a tolerable place in it. Their presence at his funerals and weddings and their regard for his birthdays establish his significance and partly do so by the choice of goods used to mark the events. Thus it follows that the individual who can mobilize the largest number of fellow consumers to join in marking his occasions has the best chance of a good place in the social scheme. It works both ways – if he has a good place, he can mobilize more people; if he can mobilize more, he will get a good place. We shall show later that there is inevitably a competitive element, since no one can be in two places at once and since grading activities are also selective.

These propositions will enable us to develop a concept of scale for consumption activities and an information theory of consumption which could supplement the information theories of market behaviour. Therefore it may be worth summarizing them.

1   All consumption activity is a ritual presentation and sharing of goods classified as appropriate to particular social categories which themselves get defined and graded in the process.

2   An individual's main object in consumption is to help to create the social universe and to find in it a creditable place.

3   To achieve his main objective he needs to mobilize marking services from other consumers.

4   Successful consumption requires a deployment of goods in consumption rituals that will mobilize the maximum marking services from other consumers.

By this path, we can be free of the unintended materialist bias which clogs much discussion of poverty and free of the equally misleading over-spiritual outlook of some critics who suppose that all goods over and above subsistence are meaningless luxuries.[17] Quite to the contrary, this approach allows meaning to all consumption activities and makes it easier to judge whether particular meanings are acceptable to any chosen ethical standpoint. We have now sketched an account of consumption that shows it to be essentially concerned with the creation and propagation of knowledge. It is admittedly a certain kind of knowledge, very different from scientific knowledge, very like aesthetic judgment when this is based on perceptions of fittingness. The marking services which create the knowledge categories and sustain them are free and unconstrained. True, there are rules of reciprocity, but they are not legally binding. We are in an area of social relationships of long-standing interest to anthropology – the sphere of the gift.[18] When one recipient of a gift, by a turn of bad fortune, cannot reciprocate, his partner has always the choice of applying the rules strictly, and so withdrawing from the relationship, or of lowering the rate. For example, it is well observed by Evans-Pritchard that the Nuer expected symmetry between the amount required for marriage payments and that required for blood-debts. But when rinderpest decimated their herds, they allowed the traditional forty head of cattle to be paid by a prospective son-in-law to be considerably reduced – not so in the case of blood-debts, when every one of the forty would be extracted from the enemy, by force if need be. I think it is safe to generalize and assert that there is no society known to anthropology so far which does not divide its transactions into at least two spheres, one which closely corresponds to our ideas of reciprocal gift-giving, the other which is more strictly ruled by legally enforceable contract, which corresponds to our idea of commerce. These spheres are kept clearly apart. Usually the media of transactions are different in the two cases. It is incorrect for us to send fruit or flowers before an exam to one of the examiners, but correct to send them to a sick friend before an operation. The former gets his money fee in due course, the latter cannot have cash in lieu of a visit. Behaviour in each sphere is equally apt for transactional analysis. The principles of comparative advantage and benefits of scale apply to the gift sphere as well as to commerce. Even in Chicago where they say, 'There is no such thing as a free lunch', it is not permissible to send the dollar cost of a lunch in lieu of attending. There is a boundary, and arbitrage across it is resisted. Big discrepancies in prices on either side of the line are proof of this. For example, the lunch is low in cost compared with the deal that is to be negotiated across the table, or with the value of the information received. What we have said about the nature of consumption activity explains why. In essence, the sphere of reciprocal gifts and hospitality is the sphere in which goods mediate the forming of public judgments. The fellowship of consumers is by free invitation and free acceptance. Their rituals generate the categories of moral judgment on which society itself is constituted. If the owner of the biggest bag of shell money could move in and buy control of these rituals, enforce unwilling attendance of some and eject others from them at spear point, he would subvert the moral basis of society. Some things cannot be put up for sale; private integrity, political honour. Nor can they be legislated for; nor arranged by physical coercion. Gifts can never be under external compulsion, however compelling the internal rules of reciprocity for those involved in the gift-making.

Now we can consider the benefits of scale. It will be to the advantage of an individual to mobilize as many fellow consumers as possible who can render him marking services. This is obvious in many ways. I will mention a few by way of illustration. For celebratory occasions there are intimate and public grades, the first needing only a few choice supporters. But the gamut between intimate and public gives full meaning to intimacy to the extent that a large force is mustered for the public events at the other end of the scale. Many people are needed for big celebrations. Meanings are reduced if support cannot be mobilized. Then again, the support of fellow consumers is a source of information: the whole of consumption being defined as a knowledge system, some pieces of knowledge are disconnected and add nothing to each other; some overlap and reinforce, by eliminating uncertainty or by filling in gaps; the more varieties of knowledge over the widest horizon, the more the consumer is oriented confidently in his universe. This is one source of benefits of scale. A further one comes from the backing that the individual receives from fellow consumers. If his backers are in a position to control the knowledge system which is the social scheme where he hopes to hold a respected place, the large scale of their operations is such that their approval of him guarantees his main objective. Whereas if his support comes from a quarter where only small corners of the map are known, people who themselves are isolated and can only muster a few supporters each, then his main objective of securing a good standing is endangered. There is yet another sense in which benefits of scale make an overwhelming difference to the success of the individual's main consumption project. To expand this needs some further thought about consumption as a cultural process.

Consumption is a process in which goods yield services in the course of which they are consumed – more or less immediately. Consumer durables, houses and pictures, etc., yield these services over a long time; flowers and food more quickly. Consumption means nothing if it does not mean that some physical things in the end get consumed. But let us realize that the services they yield are of two kinds, one the enjoyment of physical consumption, the other the enjoyment of sharing names. Take football – some people actually play football; some go to all the football matches they can, others watch on television. The football fan internalizes inside his head a reel of names of historic matches, famous clubs, referees, inspiring captains and crafty managers, heroic goalies, great stadiums, good and bad grounds, good and bad years. Inside his heart, so to speak, are grades of passionate judgments passed upon them all. He has acquired this rich collection of names by investment of personal time and attention and some cash. When he meets an alleged fellow-consumer, a few sentences are enough to betray how much they really have in common and whether the joys of shared consumption will be released. Among these two kinds of satisfaction, the physical enjoyment is more in the nature of proving – as puddings much discussed are proven in the eating – proving, testing or demonstrating the reality which has been brought under control. In terms of time expended this is the minor side of enjoyment. By far the larger part of life is spent in sharing names that have been learnt, distinguished and graded. Real consumption is the consumption that physically destroys goods. But there is further enjoyment to be had from a shared activity which is not subject to the process of depreciation or diminishing returns: the names are multiplied and revivified. Each consumption activity has its own field of names. Each field has three dimensions:

(i) it can be broad or narrow in the geographical range over which its names are known, as between mother's apple pie and coq au vin, or pêche melba;

(ii) it can be deep or shallow in the time-depth in which the names can be placed chronologically in relation to one another;

(iii) it can be rich or poor according to the number and complexity of the criteria for grading the names.

By this approach we have laid underneath the process of consumption, as a prerequisite to satisfaction, something like a filing system inside the consumer's head. The consumer is actively scanning, judging and enjoying. Consumption has to be assimilated to culture in some such way as this to support the rest of what we have said about consumption activity as a ritual matching of goods to occasions. Some interesting comparisons arise now between the different aspects of consumption with respect to scale.

The physical testing or proving is limited as to the number of people who can share together. Fewer people can walk out and shoot a duck, or can sit down and eat a duck together than can sit down and talk about duck-shooting or eating. So at first sight it seems easier to share widely the enjoyment of names. But in practice, names have heavy learning costs. The greater the historical depth, the more costly in time to learn the names. So the fields which afford the greatest number of dis-criminated names in relation to physical testing, instead of being the most open and democratic, are the most closed and elitist. Those fields which afford the least physical testing and the most discussion of names are appropriately said to be 'rich' in 'spiritual values' or to represent 'higher' or 'human values' contrasted with animal or physical satis-faction. In any consumption field there are a few top names and many smaller ones; a top name, such as Shakespeare in the field of drama, is a constant point of reference and comparison for the rest of the field. Anyone who knows well a top name in a big field will know also and correctly grade a host of smaller ones connected with it, such as *The Merchant of Venice*, Shylock, and 'All that glitters'. So there are econ-omies of effort in learning names. And economies of scale; for the most spiritual top names tend to overlap and offer reinforcing information. Top names travel farthest. They are the most widely known and so have big geographical as well as historical range. More Papuans and Africans know more names connected with Shakespeare than with Andrew Marvell. One definition we could put forward of poverty is to be poor in the spiritual enjoyments, for these are the costliest sort. Schools are right to strive to make children instant possessors of the costliest names; instant Shakespeare and instant history, subsidized ballet. This gives the children a chance to collect more names later. But they will never have incentive to do it unless they can see themselves entering a community of fellow-consumers who also share those very names. It could be a good investment; it could be sheer waste of time, depending on the other costs of shared consumptions. For unless they are going to be able to transact allusions, jokes, quotations, reminiscences and reactions about the names they have got, they will not be able to use that source of enjoyment to further their main objectives.

So far I have said nothing about marriage or earning. So I have not connected up the transfers of meaning with economics and kinship. But it should not be difficult. Earnings are influenced by the scale of consumption. Since a wide network of beholden friends is a source of information about work, and of backing in credit-worthiness, and for jobs, there is a direct connection between work-seeking and income maintaining through a well-deployed consumption programme. Marriages too: there are two kinds of impossible son-in-law, one who has no income, the other who has no manners. Essentially manners represent his past consumption experience: if the latter is appropriate, someone on the bride's side can put him in the way of an income. If he has enough money but no manners he may yet make the marriage. But to have no money and no manners is a hopeless barrier. Thus consumption patterns do more than result from economic distinctions: they reinforce them.

Now we have sketched in a dimension of scale in consumption, we can return to Harold Watts's assertion that poverty is cumulatively damaging. A consumption system which is closely related to earning capacity, in which consumers are selecting among one another for furthering each his own lifetime objective for acquiring more names and mobilizing more marking services has all the makings of a competitive system. The possibilities of big economies of scale generate further advantages for those who can use them, and increase disadvantages cumulatively. If this argument supports Harold Watts's thesis, and if learning costs constitute a further bar for those with an initial disadvantage, then the distinction I would like to see clarified between destitution and poverty becomes more important. Those who start in poverty may be afraid of ending in destitution. Subsistence measures will be needed, all the more because there is no mystery about the existence of poverty in the midst of plenty. Consumption is itself an activity which generates cumulative inequalities and is by itself capable of driving some people down to destitution. This should be recognized by everyone who selects among his uncles and nephews and godchildren, to give personal services of backing or promotion to a well-placed favourite. As to policy, a spiral is only a spiral. It can suck some people up and it can suck others down. To determine what is the incidence of its force is a highly technical matter. To add the enjoyment of names to the theory of consumption gives it the chance of developing within information theory instead of looking to physiological needs for its base line. With an information theory of consumption we would concentrate more than ever on the general network of social relations which support the specialized endeavour of educationalists. By itself school education only gives a start. The child who leaves school will need a means of acquiring a wide range of useful names, access to specialized information services, a habit of seeking professional advice and means to pay for it, above all, a continual means of up-dating information as the technological base changes and everything else with it. Relative deprivation is like relative deafness: someone who is outside one conversation misses the clues and can't adapt quick enough to get into the next conversation, so the chance of making sense and the chance of playing a respected role diminish.

This is the line of reasoning which makes me very doubtful about the puritanical streak in some economists, rather well paid, highly respected and often old, who draw a moral line between luxuries and necessities and who feel that we could all do with less material things. Unintentionally they condemn other people to the affliction of social deafness. When an earthquake rumbles or a typhoon starts to blow, those whose ears are attuned may escape in time. Let us start to think of luxuries as signalling devices, transmitting from person to person information about the social system. Then puritan judgments seem smug. Advocates of egalitarian policies should not be ignorant about the uses of goods. The prophets of anti-growth depend implicitly on the idea that goods are primarily needed for food and shelter. If that were all, we could cut them down to a healthy level. But as they are for communicating messages, highly discriminated ones, their use is like a balloon: press it down here and it will billow out there, new goods and new names will be invented, especially new names. Whoever heard of the anthropology of consumption before now? The creation of totally new lists of highly discriminated names can be achieved in a few months. New clienteles with new centres of power and influence can shoot up and the possessors of lists of old names can find their value has leaked out overnight. Clearly more thought on the anthropology of consumption is needed before we can apply it to practical issues, but eventually it will supply an account of the main objectives of consumers and a better theoretical basis for understanding poverty. It starts from the lesson that human information systems cannot be stopped in their tracks, except at vast and arbitrary cost. Therefore, it is better not to think of consumption as that part of the economic process which fits a worker to offer useful services in the labour market, but to try to understand what the transmission of goods does in establishing marriages and mythology.

Notes

1 Brian Abel-Smith and Peter Townsend, *The Poor and the Poorest*, 1965, pp. 9–12, 57–67.
2 Ibid.
3 J. C. Kincaid, *Poverty and Equality in Britain; A Study of Social Security and Taxation*, Harmondsworth, Penguin, 1973, pp. 44ff.
4 Ibid, p. 75.
5 National Board for Prices and Incomes, *Report 169: General Problems of Low Pay*, London, HMSO, 1971, p. 6.
6 J. C. Kincaid, op. cit., p. 175.
7 Harold W. Watts, 'An Economic Definition of Poverty', Chapter 2 of *On Understanding Poverty*, ed. D. P. Moynihan, American Academy of Arts and Science, New York, 1968–9.
8 J. M. Keynes, *The General Theory of Employment, Interest and Money*, London, Macmillan, 1936.
9 F. H. Knight, *The Economic Organisation*, Kelly, New York, 1951.
10 J. Hicks, *A Revision of Demand Theory*, Oxford University Press, 1956, p. 166.
11 G. L. S. Shackle, 'Recent Theories concerning the Nature of Interest in "Surveys of Econ. Theory" ', *Money Interest and Welfare*, 1, 1968 (edited for Royal Econ. Soc. and Am. Econ. Soc.).
12 F. H. Hahn, *On the Notion of Equilibrium in Economics*, Inaugural Lecture, Oxford University Press, 1973, p. 7.
13 P. Gulliver, *The Family Herds: a study of two pastoral tribes in East Africa, the Jie and the Turkana*, London, Routledge & Kegan Paul, 1955.

14 Kelvin Lancaster, *Consumer Demand: a new approach*, New York, Columbia, 1971; Richard F. Muth, 'Household Production and Consumer Demand Functions', *Econòmetrica*, 1966, 34, pp. 699–708.

15 R. H. Strotz, 'The Utility Tree – a correction and further appraisal', *Econòmetrica*, 1959, 27, 3, pp. 482–88; W. M. Gorman, Separable Utility and Aggregation, *Econòmetrica*, 1959, 27, pp. 469–81.

16 Roland Barthes, *Le Système de la Mode*, Paris, Seuil, 1967.

17 J. H. Galbraith, *Economics and the Public Purpose*, London, Andrè Deutsch, 1974.

18 Marcel Mauss, *The Gift, Form and Functions of Exchange in Archaic Societies*, trans. I. Cunnison, London, Cohen & West, 1954 (originally published 1925, *Essai sur le don, forme archaique de l'échange*).

3 Money

The contempt of ritual*

Ritual has always been something of a bad word. It means the formal aspect of religion. 'Mere ritual', one can say, and 'empty ritual', and from there to mumbo jumbo and abracadabra.

Ritual is external, so it contrasts with the interior life of religion. It is formal, so it contrasts with content. It is like a screen which should mediate knowledge, but may only too easily impede it. It is a facade which is less valid than what exists behind it, so spontaneous expressions are preferred.

'Home made cakes, home made jam and home made prayers are always best', says the minister's sister in Mary Webb's *Gone to Earth*. Psychologists use ritual for the repetitive routines of the mentally sick whose actions have only a private meaning. Zoologists use ritual for the animal routines which start like a normal series of aggressive or amatory actions but which are checked halfway – they are not the real thing, only ritual.

Limits of language

The belittlement of ritual is nothing new, but central to our European tradition. Our present generation is specially concerned with the limitations of language and its possible distortion of thought. There is a coming of age in being able to stand apart from linguistic categories and to think of them as if they were independent influences on behaviour.

* From *New Society*, 31 March 1966.

Such a self-awareness about the conditions of experience represents a slow maturing.

To collect up all the old strands we need to go back to ancient theological reflection on the means of communication. There we find distrust of rhetoric, distrust of money and distrust of ritual. It was fully recognized that a medium can get away from what it is mediating and take on a life of its own.

Money has been a favourite image for the distinction between form and substance, appearance and reality. Woe to the man who goes after money and lays not up real riches for himself. And ritual has attracted the same opprobrium. Paul's thunderings against the judaisers have been basic texts of the Reformation: 'For Jesus Christ neither circumcision availeth anything nor uncircumcision: but a new creature' (Galatians VI 15); 'Let no man therefore judge you in meat or in drink or in respect of a festival day or of the new moon or of the Sabbaths, which are a shadow of things to come' (Corinthians II 16–17).

The Papists, in the eyes of Calvin, had gone after the shadow, after superstition and mere empty ritual. In the same anti-ritualist tradition, Robertson-Smith tried to win his Church of Scotland critics to a modern treatment of the bible. His inaugural lecture contrasted the intelligent, historical approach to the Book with magical superstition:

> The Catholic church had almost from the first deserted the apostolic tradition and set up a conception of Christianity as a mere series of formulae containing abstract and immutable principles, intellectual assent to which was sufficient to mould the lives of men who had no experience of a personal relation with Christ . . . Holy Scripture is not . . . a divine phenomenon magically endowed in every letter with saving treasures of faith and knowledge.

Here we have it plain: ritualism goes with obscurantism, superstition and magic. And what is magic but a manipulative and mechanical attitude to reality? Magic beliefs endow rites with saving powers which work without engaging the will of the performer or requiring him to become a new creature.

Since the English firmly believed in the belief in magic and as firmly despised it, it was not difficult for them to swallow Sir James Frazer's description of magic-ridden primitive cultures. Primitive man appears in *The Golden Bough* as a pantomime Aladdin crazily rubbing his magic lamps.

This was the nadir of the contempt of ritual. It foisted upon unwary anthropologists excruciating problems of definition (how does religion differ from magic? how does rite differ from ceremony?): all a fruitless exercise because of the assumption that religious behaviour is a special kind of behaviour which has to be demarcated by special terms. Thus some anthropologists use the word ritual to mean religious.

The most important book in anthropological studies of religion was bound to be the one which broke out of this impasse. R. G. Lienhardt's *Divinity and Experience, the religion of the Dinka* (Oxford, Clarendon Press, 1961) took all the rituals of the Dinka tribe from the most trivial and mundane to the most awe-inspiring, in a single sweep. He started with the peculiar little gestures of reassurance which in Dinka life correspond to our knotting of handkerchiefs and crossing fingers.

When a returning Dinka herdsman finds that he is going to be late for supper, he stoops and knots a tuft of grass. The knot represents a delaying, and the gesture expresses his wish that the women delay the evening meal until his return. But then he does not slacken his pace and saunter home confident that the rite will be effective of itself. He hastens with renewed purpose. The knot is a visible expression of a well-formed wish: it concentrates attention.

To interpret those little rituals the student needs to be very conscious about the little rituals he himself daily performs. An honest and sensitive introspection would end by bringing to bear on the problem of ritual the results of Pavlovian and Skinner type studies of learning and perception.

Lienhardt opens the way for this as he goes from grass-knotting to animal sacrifice and thence to something very near human sacrifice. As the interpretation unfolds, ritual is presented, not as a mask or dead crust over the face of living experience, but as that which creates and inspires it. It is form indeed, but inseparable from content, or rather there could be no content without it. It is appearance, but there is no other reality. Public rituals, by establishing visible external forms, bring out of all the possible might-have-beens a firm social reality.

To put it differently: any particular event could receive the impress of 20 personal interpretations, or 100. The same actors looking back on it could see its significance differently from mood to mood and as it is differently mirrored in events to come. There is no end to the kaleidoscopic shiftings by which an event turns out to be one of a quite different sort. A great public ritual (such as Churchill's funeral) cages it, ends the wriggling, clarifies and fixes an impression.

The fund of ritual possibilities in any culture is limited. For instance, an illness can be handled by prayer to the ancestors, confession by a witch, a big or little sacrifice. But once the rite has been selected and applied, a crystallizing of experience takes place – just as in learning there is a corresponding clarifying and fixing which follows a physical, external representation of what is being learned. Thus a reality is established out of the flux of possible forms.

A way of death

The function of ritual on this showing is something like the function of form in art, as Professor Gombrich described it in his *Encounter* article on 'Freud's Aesthetics' (January 1966). For some artists, the forms received from their predecessors are channels within which they are content to let their experiences run easily. For others they offer a challenging instrument, the mastery of whose range itself stimulates the great artist to explore all the combinations and to produce unforeseeable new forms.

Thus Dinka rituals provide the ordinary man with a way of living: but to the great man, the exceptional Dinka, they provide an extraordinary way of dying. In the self-immolation of an aged priest, who allows himself to be suffocated so that his breath never leaves his body, all the daily rituals of the Dinka find a high climax.

I cannot do justice to the marvellous insight into the conditions of Dinka experience which comes across as Lienhardt develops his theme of truth and reality created by ritual. If this is what ritual does for experience, the primitive who is able unselfconsciously to abandon his life to its ordaining forms is indeed something of an Aladdin, but not in Frazer's sense. His magical universe of incredible powers and treasures owes its reality to ritual. Without rituals moulding his experience from infancy there could be no belief, and without belief not only no treasure cave, but no self, no world, no human destiny.

If this has any moral for us today, we must start by recognizing the poverty of our rituals, their unconnectedness with each other and with our social purposes and the impossibility of our having again a system of public rituals relating our experiences into some kind of cosmic unity. We are witnessing now a great literary exploration of the effects of ritelessness. For this is how I interpret the current concern with the unreality of experience and with problems of identity.

We cannot have or wish for powerful primitive rituals. This is the price we pay for our emancipation from what Kant called the shackles of the subjective conditions of knowledge. But why 'shackles'? Why 'emancipated from'? We still seem to be looking at ritual and language in the spirit of resentment and condemnation with which the medievals looked at money. They saw it as a dangerous power from which it would be better to be free, but were not ready to see it as a medium of social experience whose autonomous behaviour had to be understood in order to be controlled.

By the Keynesian revolution money has to some extent been tamed and put to service. A parallel ritual revolution lags behind. Ritual has so far only been denigrated. It is time for it too to be grasped and its creative potential to be understood.

Raffia cloth distribution in the Lele economy*

The distribution of raffia cloth among the Lele[1] raises two questions. One, mainly ethnographic, is that of the various functions served in the course of its circulation from hand to hand. In answering this, the second question arises. In some aspects raffia cloth seems to perform monetary roles. Is it to be classed as a type of primitive money? In the widest sense it seems to be an imperfect type of money, performing in a restricted manner some of the main functions of money: it acts as a store and a standard of value; it is given as payment for services and sometimes used as a medium of exchange. It is now, however, the principal, or usual, means of distribution in the economy. I hope that a discussion of the shortcomings of Lele raffia as a form of money may be interesting to others working in societies which are similarly on the verge of a market economy.

Distribution of goods

Little in the environment or productive system of the Lele encourages large-scale collaboration. They live at a density of about four persons to

* From Mary Douglas, 'Raffia Cloth Distribution in the Lele Economy', *Africa*, no. 28, 1958, pp. 109–22. Reprinted by permission of the author and the publisher. Also in George Dalton (ed.), *Tribal and Peasant Economies*, Readings in Economic Anthropology, New York, The Natural History Press, 1967, Chap. 8, pp. 103–22.

the square mile (the figure excludes recent alien immigrants). There are no markets. Each village (average population 190) is largely self-sufficient in producing for its needs, and with one exception there is no teamwork or long-term collaboration within it. The exception is the communal hunt, in which most of the able-bodied men of the village combine. Normally work is individually performed, and the basic unit of collaboration consists of husband and wife, each performing the tasks traditionally allotted to their sex. The division of labour has the characteristic – common enough, but worth noting for its consequences – of reserving physically exacting work for the men. This puts the older men at a relative disadvantage, which is partially adjusted by raffia-cloth distribution, as I shall show.

As Table 3.1 shows, units of labour do not correspond to units of consumption, and, though for most goods the range of distribution is wider than the producing unit, it is still not very wide. For most things, the kin of individual producers living locally are the widest group claiming a share in the product. Only for meat and wine is the whole village the sharing group. It would not be difficult for the Lele to lead their whole economic life within the bounds of each individual village.

Inheritance is another way of claiming goods. A new group emerges here, the matrilineal heirs of the dead.

The inheritance group does not appear as a unit in the first table, as they never work together, neither feed nor live together. It consists of fellow clansmen of the dead living in the same village or in villages near by. The members coalesce as a group through their common interest in the distribution, not of goods, but of rights over women. None of the goods (detailed in (A) of Table 3.2) are as interesting as the rights over women ((B) and (C) in the table) that a man may leave, excepting such small stocks of camwood and raffia or money as may be left which can be used to acquire such rights.

As may be seen from these tables, goods are distributed mostly on the basis of status, and not by purchase. A man's claim to a share in the product of anyone's labour, including his own, depends directly on who he is (boy, husband, father, etc., i.e. his relation to others) and not on his purchasing power, or on his work. Ultimately, of course, his status is something which he builds up by his own efforts, i.e. by generously and effectively interpreting his obligations. But at any one moment his status is known, and determines his share of what is going. This means that, although many things appear to have a traditional price, in raffia cloth, there is no real price system or level of prices, since it is not offer of the

TABLE 3.1 Distribution of Goods

Productive work	Range of collaboration	Product	Range of distribution
Men			
Hunting:			
(*a*) Communal	Village-wide	Meat	Village-wide according to membership of cults, and according to kinship obligations of hunters
(*b*) Bow, snares, or pit-traps	Individual		
Clearing land for cultivation	Individual or 2 age-mates or brothers		
Raffia-palm cultivation	Individually owned and worked, except for sending junior for wine	Wine	Village-wide, a nightly men's club; father, mother, and mother's brother of tapper and his age-mates
Weaving	Individual	Cloth	Distribution detailed below
Oil-palms	Individual cuts fruit from wild palm for wife to process and use or sell	Oil and Cash	Man keeps cash, woman uses oil
House-building	Sons, brothers, age-mates, son-in-law may occasionally help	House	Man, wife, small children
Smithing	Individual leisure-time specialists, collaborating with charcoal burner/bellows boy	Hoes, knives, arrowheads, gouges, etc.; maintenance of these	By gift with small acknowledgment fee to kinsmen of smith; or sale to strangers
Wood-carving	Individual leisure-time specialists, with occasional junior help	Drinking-cups, bellows, bows, plates, pestle, loom, shuttle, combs, drums	As for smiths

TABLE 3.1 Continued

Productive work	Range of collaboration	Product	Range of distribution
Women			
Sowing, hoeing, harvesting	Wife alone, with occasional help from mother or sister	Maize, manioc, bananas, peppers, ground-nuts, calabashes	If stored, crops under wife's control; if sold, cash jointly owned by husband and wife
Cooking	" "	Cooked food	Wife gives to husband and his age-mates, to son and his age-mates; children and sisters and wifeless fellow clansmen
Fishing	"	Fish	As for cooked food
Firewood and water	"		For household use
Salt-making	"	Salt	" " " or given to kinsmen for small acknowledgment fee
Gathering relish, vegetable or insect	" or parties of children		As for cooked food
Basketry	Individual leisure-time specialists	Baskets for storage, transport, fishing, sifting, etc.	By gift with small acknowledgment fee to kinsmen of craftswoman, or sold to strangers
Pottery	"	Cooking-pots	As for baskets

TABLE 3.2   Inheritance

(A) *Goods*	
Crops	Matrilineal inheritance group. Crops used for maintenance of children in year of mourning.
Raffia palms	"
House	Generally destroyed if death took place at home; otherwise kept by widow, or allocated according to village needs.
Personal belongings, weapons, tools, drum, containers, &c.	Matrilineal inheritance group distributes to sons or sisters' sons.
Stocks of raffia, camwood, or money	Matrilineal inheritance group, entrusted to eldest man to be administered on behalf of group as a whole, after claims on dead man's estate have been settled.
(B) *Widows*	Matrilineal inheritance group; after year of mourning widows allocated to members, according to seniority, need, and incest regulations.
(C) *Rights over clients* (i.e. descendants of women paid in blood compensation)	Matrilineal inheritance group, administered on behalf of group as a whole by eldest men.

traditional price, but the status of the recipient, which entitles him to the goods.

Uses of raffia

Every man and boy can weave. The preparation of materials for weaving is long and the actual work of weaving is more arduous than might be supposed. After the loom is set up, a man has to work steadily to weave two or three lengths in a day. Five lengths is supposed to be very fast working, and most men make one in an afternoon.

Two lengths sewn together, with stitched, embroidered, or fringed hems, make a skirt for a woman or a man. Five to ten sewn lengths, without embroidery, make a semi-ceremonial man's skirt, *lapungu*. Ten lengths, with a richly appliqué border, is a dance-skirt, *mapel mahangi*. This is the joint property of the matrilineal clan section, the group of matrilineal heirs, and a highly prized heirloom. Worn in everyday use, for hunting and working, a raffia skirt lasts only about four months. They are often carefully darned and patched. Shabby dress is much despised. Lele love the sight of well-woven cloth, correctly folded and tied for presentation.

Informal gifts of raffia cloth smooth all social relations: husband to wife, son to mother, son to father. They resolve occasions of tension, as peace-offerings; they make parting gifts, or convey congratulations. There are also formal gifts of raffia which are neglected only at risk of rupture of the social ties involved. A man, on reaching adulthood, should give twenty cloths to his father. Otherwise he would be ashamed to ask his father's help for raising his marriage dues. A man should give twenty cloths to his wife on each delivery of a child which qualifies him for entry into a cult group or she may repudiate the marriage. He should bury each of her parents with a mortuary gift of twenty clothes; if she reports a would-be seducer, he should reward her virtue with twenty cloths.

Certain dues must be paid before a relationship or status is entered. Among these are age-set dues, which may vary from six to ten or so, according to the local rule; marriage dues, 50 to the father, 40 to the mother; entrance fees to cult groups: Begetters, 100, Diviners, 100, Twin Diviners, 40, Pangolin cult, 20. Then there are fees for ritual officiants who perform healing rites or give oracular consultations: these may mount from one or two for a divination to 100 for a major cure.

Fines are paid to restore status after an offence has been committed. Adultery damages are usually 100 cloths; fines to the village for ritually spoiling it by fighting may be from two upwards, according to the occasion. Finally, tribute to chiefs is paid in raffia cloths.

This list, though abbreviated, shows that raffia is used extensively for the payment of services and the acquisition of status. The high demand for it for these purposes probably creates a value apart from its intrinsic value as a textile. The heaviest charges fall in the early part of a man's life, and the raffia paid on most of these occasions goes from young men to old men. A man who has entered an age-set, married, entered the Begetters' cult, and become a diviner, will have disbursed a minimum of 300 raffia cloths, and probably spent many more in maintaining good relations with his wife, in-laws, his father and mother, and settling adultery damages. Cloths paid for admission to cults are distributed between existing members, so that a man, once he has joined a cult, can regard his own fee as an investment which will bring in a regular return when each new initiate pays for entrance. Similarly, a man with several daughters enjoys an income of raffia cloths from his sons-in-law.

The effect is that young men are constantly in need of large quantities of raffia cloth, and older men are constantly receiving it. Young men do not expect to weave enough to pay for their own needs, in fact, old men are said to have more time for weaving. So young men go to old men to ask for help in raising their fees and fines. Thus there is asymmetry in raffia indebtedness between young and old, which goes some way to redress the disequilibrium between the generations created by the division of labour. Old men have a fund of raffia from which they can reward juniors, bolster up their own prestige, and make up for their declining effectiveness in cultivation and in the hunt.

A man trying to raise large sums of raffia draws on maternal and paternal ties of kinship, but more heavily on the former. Investigation of this is difficult, for people tend to forget the help of men with whom they have later quarrelled. Raffia loans and debts have a *prima facie* suitability for quantitative treatment, but I found I could not rely on information about transactions I had not witnessed, and here I confine myself to reporting a few such cases.

A man may be able to collect raffia from several quarters: from his own clan, his father, and affines, from his lord if he is a clan-client,[2] and from his clients if he is a lord. This is obviously more relevant to a study of kinship behaviour, but here it is worth noting that one of the characteristics of raffia, divisibility into small units, makes it a suitable form of wealth to reflect certain characteristics of the kinship pattern: division of responsibility between maternal and paternal kin, and the freedom of the individual to affiliate to the kin group of his choice.

Examples

I describe here how a man and his two sons raised large sums for marriage dues and adultery compensation. I shall refer to them by letters, indicating clan membership, and numbers, indicating age-position in their local clan section. Both sons of B7 needed to raise their marriage payments at the same time. For the elder, A13, his father gave one she-goat worth forty cloths, and ten raffia cloths, and the boy's clan accepted responsibility for the rest of his dues. The boy himself was ill and was not expected to make a contribution.

A14 raised his marriage dues in instalments. For the first payment of ten cloths, he wove six himself, and his father gave him four. For the next payment of ten cloths, he wove three, his mother gave three, three of his senior clansmen contributed one each, and E3, a client of his clan, gave one, saying that his own mother's mother had been married to A14's mother's mother's brother. Then he raised 300 francs, the equivalent of thirty raffia cloths. One hundred francs was given by A5 who obtained them from a man of E clan on a promise of ten raffia cloths. It is noteworthy that the money was 'bought' on a promise of raffia, but it was eventually returned when A1 trapped a pig and sold the meat, so if the supplier of 100 francs hoped to get raffia for ten francs a piece, he was disappointed. Another 100 francs were given to A14 by his father, who had borrowed the money from a friend in the next village. Another 100 francs were given by the three men of clan C living in the village, on the grounds that their father had been A14's mother's brother. A14 also earned another 250 francs himself. The equivalent of 75 raffia cloths had been raised, but the full amount of 100 cloths would have to be raised before he could marry the girl, as she came from another village, and no existing ties facilitated the negotiations. His brother, by contrast, marrying a girl of the same village, had already been able to set up house, though only half the payment had been completed. His father was hoping to be able to raise another 200 francs for A14 by demanding a refund of the purchase price of a worthless dog he had bought from another village.

In this case, the wide range of kinsmen from whom contributions were taken is significant. A14 had great difficulty in levying anything substantial from his own clansmen, of whom there were 17 in the village. Men in smaller, more compact clan sections generally had more support from their clansmen. A5 had been on begging rounds for him, and reported that all but two had refused: the older men made difficulties because A14 had been fighting and was a disturbing element in the village; the boys junior to himself replied that they were young and had nothing to give. Refusals to help the young man with his marriage dues were intended as sanctions on his past behaviour, but the effect was to weaken bonds of clanship, not to strengthen them. The same old men later felt unable to ask A14 for services which they would have liked to command.

While these negotiations were proceeding, B7, the boy's father, was caught in adultery with the wife of their mother's brother, A5, who demanded immediate payment of 100 raffia cloths. B7 was not in real straits, because his own clansmen were involved in a factional quarrel, so they were unusually slow to co-operate with each other. He produced the equivalent of forty raffia cloths, as follows: a fellow clansman lent him a small bar of camwood, valued at twenty cloths; a man of clan C, not a kinsman, advanced to him, against a promise of payment, a smaller bar worth ten cloths; a man gave him 100 francs as an outright gift because his brother had married B7's sister's daughter. He was given time to find the rest.

It emerges from these examples that certain goods and Congo francs are acceptable in lieu of raffia. No doubt, as the economy becomes more commercialized, the range of these alternatives to raffia will increase, but at the time of my fieldwork they were limited to camwood, Belgian Congo francs, and goats. Certain objects, traditionally acceptable, had gone out of circulation: iron bells worth 50 cloths, copper bars worth 100 cloths, and slaves.

The adoption of goats in recent years, as a substitute for large raffia payments, is interesting, as their role is also almost purely monetary in the Lele economy. The Lele do not eat goat-flesh but accept goats as a store of value which can always be converted into francs by sale to Luba lorry drivers and plantation workers.

The following is a list of the main units and equivalences used in raffia negotiations:

The peculiarity of these units is the 10 percent margin allowed in making up a standard amount of raffia. *Ibok* is supposed to consist of ten cloths, and *lutuku* of 100, yet no one can haggle or complain if the exact

TABLE 3.3   Raffia values

Unit of raffia	Name	Equivalent goods
9 or 10 cloths	*ibok la bipolo* (bundle of cloth) or *ihangi la bipolo* (10 cloths)	Axe
	mabok ma pe (2 bundles) or	a 3-foot bar of camwood
18 or 20 cloths	1 *nghei* (trade salt)	a he-goat
	2 *mihei* (trade salt)	2 *mihei* or one she-goat or
40 cloths		a 5-foot bar of camwood
	3 *mihei*	3 *mihei* or she-goat with
60 cloths		young
	lutuku	*ikoko* (copper bar)
90 or 100 cloths		*ibondo* (slave)

number is not reached when the payment is in raffia cloths. But this latitude is not extended to the goods accepted as substitutes for raffia. If a bar of camwood does not come up to two *mihei* in quality or size, it is treated as a one *nghei* unit; the goat is always the number of *ibok* indicated by its sex, neither more nor less. The full money equivalent is always required. For example, if raffia is valued at ten francs a piece, for a payment of 100 cloths the full 1,000 francs must be paid, though if it is made in raffia cloth, 90 cloths will be accepted. Whatever the origin of this convention, it usefully expresses the higher value of raffia over any of the conventional substitutes.

Monetary role of raffia

Raffia cloth is bartered for the goods which are imported from foreign tribes. The Lele see themselves in their foreign relations as the great clothiers of the Kasai region. The Njembe from the south come with large calabashes, arrow-heads, hoes and knives, bells and other iron work; the Dinga on the river bank sell pottery and fish; the Pende to the east sell baskets, and camwood which they have obtained from the north, and the Nkutu sell camwood, all in exchange for raffia cloth. The Cokwe hunters accept it in payment for game, though they do not wear it, and intend to sell it.

Apart from its export as a barter commodity, raffia cloth is used in internal trade, whenever anything is bought from a skilled specialist with whom the buyer has no close kinship ties. In these cases raffia has a real monetary role, as a medium of exchange, for the seller accepts it in order to use it as payment for other exchanges.

This range of goods is very narrow, as people tend to go without, if they cannot obtain what they need from a kinsman. However, skilled craftsmen sometimes gain a great reputation for carving, and may supply drums, bellows, or drinking-cups to strangers from far off. They will charge as much as fifty raffia cloths for a big item. These charges are real prices, to be distinguished from the gifts made to a craftsman who furnishes objects to kinsmen. Baskets, fish-traps, fur hats, carved cosmetic-bowls, dishes, cups, loom, mortar – the producer of these things is likely to receive no more than one or two cloths from a kinsman, in recognition that both parties acknowledge their relationship.

I had great difficulty trying to buy ordinary domestic objects with francs. They had no traditional price, as they usually changed hands on kinship lines, with an 'acknowledgment fee' of one or two cloths. My friends, mistaking this fee for a price equivalent to the value of the goods, tried to persuade reluctant sellers that they ought to part with their things for ten or twenty francs, the official equivalent of one or two raffia cloths. However, even if I doubled the number of francs, they were still not willing to sell. For raffia cloth they would have sold willingly, but my ethnographic collection seemed doomed, since I could not buy raffia cloth for francs.

Relation to Congo francs

Although raffia cloth is only used as currency in a limited range of transactions, the analogy with money is the simplest way of describing its behaviour. In one sense the Lele were trying to work with a raffia currency convertible into Belgian Congo francs at a rate which under-valued raffia. The conversion of raffia into francs applied only to a few rare purchases (such as buying a drum from a distant craftsman), but it applied extensively in all payment of compensation, dues and cult fees, and fines. The older men, who were not wage-earners, needed francs for payment for taxes and fines, while many young men found it easier to earn money than to obtain raffia, so this arrangement suited all parties. Even at the Native Tribunal fines and taxes could be paid in raffia in lieu of francs, and an official rate of exchange was therefore recognized. In 1924 this was two raffia cloths to the franc (Régistre Ethnographique,

1924), and since that date the value of raffia has gone up by leaps and bounds, expressing the greatly increased circulation of francs in the region, the opportunities for wage-earning, and the development of retail shops. On my first visit in 1949, one cloth was valued at five francs; in 1953 it was worth ten francs. Even then these prices, fixed for the payment of fines at the Tribunal, did not at all reflect what raffia would have earned in a free market. The Lele adopted the official rates of exchange for all their dealings in raffia among themselves; they knew it was undervalued, but felt obscurely that a devaluing of the Congo franc would be against their interests. The result was that it was impossible to buy raffia for francs at the official rate, but to offer a higher unofficial rate was disapproved. Once I had acquired raffia I could easily buy goods which had been refused for the equivalent value in francs, but I could only obtain raffia by applying to the Tribunal, and even there the native clerks were reluctant to sell large quantities.

In their reluctance to sell for francs, and the readiness to sell for raffia, there is an element of what I can only call 'irrational producer's preference', which I believe may attach to goods produced for subsistence in any economy. For instance, in our own economy, the producer of garden flowers or home-made jam would similarly be unwilling to sell his goods for cash at the retail price, though he would be happy to give them away to a neighbour for nothing. Some things are classed as more suitable for gift or friendly barter than for sale, and the ordinary market price would not compensate the producer for his work in the same way as he would be rewarded by the prestige and satisfaction of making a gift.

This attitude is exactly the reverse of the producer whose goods are intended primarily for sale. To him money seems scarcer than the products of his daily labour, and he will cheerfully barter away the goods at less than the usual price, if by doing so he can avoid parting with hard-earned cash. This difference was suggested to me by Dr Salim's study of mat-weavers in Iraq,[3] and I suggest that the contrast between the attitudes of subsistence producers and exchange producers to the money value of their products may be widespread.

Although the Lele would sell small objects to me for raffia, but not for francs, this was not simply a preference for one kind of currency over another. The situation was, for them, redolent of the atmosphere of gift-exchange, not of trade, and the conventions of the former make one kind of exchange more acceptable than the other.[4] It is none the less true that the official rate undervalued raffia cloth. Why did a black market in raffia not develop? Or at least, why did the production of raffia not increase to keep pace with the demand for it?

Social pressures inhibited men from buying and selling raffia. I heard of men obtaining francs with the promise of raffia, but I rarely heard of the eventual repayment being made in anything other than francs. Wage-earners in the north would sometimes carry their money to the south where opportunities of wage-earning were few, and the demand for francs consequently so much higher that the official rate was probably satisfactory to all parties. In these cases, kin ties between the parties were not likely to inhibit the sale. Normally, for a man to be obliged to buy raffia with money would be felt as a failure of all the social bonds by which he could be expected to raise raffia cloth. It would be as absurd as the imaginary case of an Englishman reduced to buying Christmas cards to adorn his mantelshelf. In other words, there was no market in raffia, so there could not easily be a black market.

Men would never admit that the difficulty of raising fees deterred them from applying for cult initiation. On the contrary, they would boast of the sources they could hope to tap. For example, one man, who was the son of a village-wife,[5] said that his fathers (meaning the men of that village) would be delighted if he were accepted as a candidate for pangolin initiation, as it would give them an opportunity for contributing the whole of his raffia fees. Another man, who married the daughter of a village-wife, said that of course he had been obliged to undergo initiation into the Begetters' cult in her village, so that his fathers-in-law could stand the whole of the costs for him, and they would have been very hurt if he had been initiated in his own village. The very costliness of marriage with a daughter of a village-wife is an attraction, as it gives scope for proving social solvency. Less successful individuals, like B7 above, who have to weave, earn, and somehow scrape together their raffia payments by themselves, are assiduous in excusing their various kinsmen, or, if they criticize the living for meanness, it is because they compare them with some dead uncle or father whom they could have touched for as much raffia as they required.

Shortage of raffia

Every man and boy can weave, and every man and boy would like to possess more raffia than he does. But they do not try to satisfy their own demand by sitting down to produce it. The Lele would explain that they are short of raffia now because they have so many competing demands on their time, especially earning money for taxes, that they cannot weave as much as their ancestors used to. This may be true, but, if so, I believe it only aggravates a shortage of raffia which is inherent in a quasi-inflationary situation.

In capital investment Lele economy is as stationary as any other primitive economy. But from the point of view of an individual who starts lending and borrowing raffia, it appears as a temptingly expanding financial system. The 'enterprises' into which a man is asked to put his available raffia cloths are productive, not of material goods, but of prestige: helping a kinsman with marriage dues, compensation for offences, medical fees, fines, entrance fees. Ever since boyhood he has been drawing on the stock of his elders, and has been made aware of a sense of obligation when they helped him. As soon as he acquires any surplus stock of his own, he starts to create obligations towards himself by lending. He gets drawn into a social game in which, if he cannot give the impression of generosity, he loses not only prestige but the opportunities of obtaining credit when he needs it. A man's dignity as a member of a village, able to pay his way and help his kin, depends on credit, for the contributions of clansmen to one another's raffia needs are largely a matter of gifts made in the expectation that the recipient will be equally generous when their turn comes to ask his help.

Since it is desired, not as purchasing power, present or future, but for the sake of the prestige gained by parting with it, there is no point in hoarding raffia. Raffia cloths stored away are buried talents. The Lele would agree with the millionaire industrialist who said that the ultimate failure of a rich man was to die rich. The more famous and the more generous a man has been, the greater the number who expect to share in the division of his estate, but in practice, reputedly rich men tend to leave paltry possessions. The heirs are often disappointed to find that they are burdened with the debts of the departed. Needless to say, the men who had died after extracting the last jot of credit out of their acquaintance are those who are considered to have lived most successfully.

Lele are constantly turning over in their minds ways of meeting their financial commitments, counting their assets, and possible future expectations. Among the young especially there is a feeling like financial pressure. A man will make promises on the strength of his unborn daughter's future bridewealth; any insult or injury will be almost welcomed as possible subject for a claim. In the frequent conversations about the need to raise raffia cloth, it is a striking fact that men think first, not of sitting down to weave, but of pursuing any debts or claims outstanding. They hope to meet their demand for raffia by increasing the velocity of circulation rather than by increasing supplies. No one is expected to be anything but quick in making claims, or ruthless in pursuing debtors. The result is an inflationary pressure on the available supplies of raffia. It is a situation in which too few raffia cloths are circulating after too many debts and promises. Raffia is no sooner paid over than it is transferred again to liquidate debts of ten or twenty years' standing.

I cite one example to show how easily an I-owe-you situation can be transformed into a you-owe-me one. A diviner in South Homb was temporarily cured of his leprosy by another diviner from afar, who charged him 100 raffia cloths. It is held that a cured man will relapse if he does not promptly pay his doctor. The patient had raised the equivalent of thirty cloths by borrowing from a colleague, and was casting about for more credit when his healer fell ill with intestinal trouble. The former patient quickly dispatched a powerful remedy, and reckoned that if he obtained a cure he would charge seventy cloths, thus exactly discharging his own debt. In other cases, when there is not so much urgency, payments can generally be delayed for years, so that when the final reckoning comes, both parties have scores to settle with each other.

The village treasury

From what has been said, it will be obvious that no one keeps large stores of raffia, and also obvious that this was too delicate a subject to investigate. Individuals like to store a few surplus cloths with one of their sisters, so as to evade the demands of wives and children. A woman trusted in this way would generally justify her brother's regard for her discretion. A much easier insight into raffia distribution came to me through watching the public affairs of the village.

Each village has an official, named *itembangu la bola*, whose post combines the duties of spokesman and treasurer. He is a young man, chosen because of his *lutot* (eloquence) and because of his trust-worthiness for keeping the *bikete bia bola* (things of the village). As the village budget is run on a deficit, the last responsibility is a matter of accountancy, not of keeping valuables under his hand.

The village has a corporate personality. Like a man it can acquire wives, slaves and clients, sue for compensation for injury to these, and receive payments for a transfer of rights over them or their children. Corresponding to these abilities, it has liabilities to make all the usual payments a man is liable to make in acquiring wives, or in compensating for offences committed by their children, paying son's marriage fees, and so on. Whenever something is paid to the village, a meeting is called, and decisions are taken about how the new funds are to be disposed of.

Five daughters of village-wives of South Homb were married within a few years of each other. Three of them married within the same village, and their husbands were therefore required to pay over only half the amount that would have been asked if they had come from outside, i.e. two *mihei* instead of four. One man was blind, and though now married for eight or nine years, he had never been pressed to give more than the first instalment, one bar of camwood. This the village had put with two other bars raised from another source, and used to make the first repayment of a debt of ten bars of camwood (200 raffia cloths), owed to a man of North Homb who had died unpaid, and whose heirs were pressing for payment. Two other girls were married to a man of Bushongo, as a kind of gesture of welcome when he came to settle permanently in the village. He was subsequently installed as junior official diviner of the village, and the four *mihei* which he paid to the village for both girls exactly covered the fee which the village owed to the outside officiant who had performed the rite of installing him.

For one of the two girls who married outsiders, the groom paid up five bars of camwood. On receiving these, the village ignored outstanding claims against itself *qua* village, and quietly divided them amongst each of its five constituent clan sections.

For the youngest girl the prospective son-in-law paid up three *mihei* while I was there. The fourth was still outstanding. Of the sixty cloths paid up, it was agreed that forty should be given at once to the grandfathers of the girl herself as marriage dues for her mother. As the latter had been herself a daughter of a village-wife, four *mihei* or eighty cloths should have been given. At first the representative of the grand-fathers refused to accept the half payment, pointing out with some justice that it was already long overdue. The men of South Homb rallied him by asking why he had not brought the ten chickens with which it is proper for a father-in-law to acknowledge the receipt of marriage dues, and he finally agreed good-humouredly to take what was offered, and to go home to collect the chickens, giving South Homb time to collect the remaining cloths.

South Homb actually had an additional twenty cloths in hand, for their son-in-law had paid sixty, but it had been decided that this last *nghei* should be devoted to settling an equally long-overdue debt with the head man of the next village, Middle Homb. He required thirty cloths in damages for a charge of sorcery made against one of his wives, who had been cleared after submission to the poison ordeal. It was agreed at the meeting that 100 francs should be raised by levies on each of the clans of the village, and that these should be added to the twenty cloths, so that this claim of twenty years' standing could be settled outright.

At the same meeting, the old head of the village of South Homb put in a rather hopeless claim for at least thirty cloths as part repayment of the copper bar he had advanced to the village for the marriage dues of one of its (now quite elderly) village-wives. The claim was brushed aside, on the grounds that many big debts had to be written off now that it was no longer possible to settle accounts by the transfer of women. On this point I shall have more to say.

These examples illustrate clearly the importance of raffia in its social role, creating ties of mutual obligation, between individuals and their fellow clansmen, between young and old, between clans and villages, and between villages. If we recall that the scale of their economy is so small that each village could almost produce and consume its whole wealth in isolation, we can see that raffia circulation immensely enlarges and enriches their social life.

Rights over women

To take the monetary metaphor too literally would lead us to doubt the whole analysis of raffia distribution, for in a monetary economy the shortage of raffia would eventually stimulate an increase in supply. It is not enough to explain the continued shortage of raffia by the imperfections of the market, or the undeveloped mercantile spirit of the people. It has also to be appreciated that until recently any Lele man had always the means of liquidating at one stroke an excessive pile of raffia debts.

One hundred cloths were equivalent to rights over a slave or a woman. Slavery (following capture in war) had ended in the early 1930s. Rights over women, creating a form of clientship which was used to settle blood debts, could still be transferred, but the Belgian administration was trying to end the system. Anyone wishing to repudiate his status of client can now take the matter to court, and end the relation with a cash payment. This is a subject for a separate study. But it is essential here to know that the Lele think of raffia primarily as a means to acquire rights over women, and therefore, if they could not repay loans in raffia, could settle by a direct transfer of rights over a woman or a slave.

Raffia is indeed paid out for all the various purposes I have listed, but when a man receives raffia, he hopes to use it to acquire a wife, or to sweeten relations with his wife and her kin, or to help a sister's son to acquire a wife. It may be diverted into other directions before he can put it to these ends, but this is simply because other men have made successful claims on his stocks, which they also intend to use for acquiring and maintaining wives.

In a sense, raffia keeps its high value, not because of its use as a textile, but because it gives command over women, and, in a polygamous society, woman are always scarce. Consistently, then, if a man's debts of raffia threaten to overwhelm him, he can cancel them by relinquishing rights over women in favour of his creditor. When this happens, no comparison with bankruptcy could be apposite, for the social bonds of creditor and debtor have been replaced by kinship ties. Formerly, the 'inflation' which I have mentioned was not controlled merely by the limits of leaders' credulity. Under the old system, the man who advanced 100 raffia cloths to a friend did so against the security of the sisters and clanswomen of the borrower. If repayment were refused, public opinion would applaud him for taking one of them by force. It follows that the inflationary trend was transferred to rights over women, who were, even before their birth, pledged as backing for loans.

It is this final equation of 100 raffia cloths for rights over a woman which clarifies the difference between the system of raffia distribution as it used to be, and the quasi-monetary system it is becoming, and which also explains some apparent anomalies in the Lele attitudes to raffia values.

Conclusion

What has become of the view that raffia might be classed as a primitive type of money? The essential quality of money is that it gives its possessor purchasing power. Lele use raffia principally for payment of marriage dues, fines, blood-compensation, and cult entrance fees, which may be collectively called 'status-payments', not purchases. As a medium of exchange it functions only rarely, as this is not a market economy. A very great number of other forms of so-called 'primitive money' are used in these ways, in Melanesia and North America, as well as in other parts of Africa.

Primitive money is often discussed without reference to the degree of commercial development. To correct this tendency, I find the most useful theory of money is Menger's (Menger, 1892), which starts from the different degrees of saleability of commodities in general. Those which are most highly saleable tend, with the development of markets, to become generally acceptable media of exchange – 'money'. Improved market conditions increase the superior saleability of such goods, so that when such goods as are relatively most saleable become money, there results 'an increasing differentiation between their degree of sale-ableness and that of all other goods. And this difference in saleableness ceases altogether to be gradual, and must be regarded as something absolute . . . hence the difference of meaning attaching to "money" and "wares," to "purchase" and "exchange" ' (Menger, 1892, p. 250).

At first sight, Lele raffia seems to have a high degree of saleability. If markets were to have developed without European contact or the introduction of francs, it would have been likely to have become a medium of exchange. But its saleability, on closer inspection, is not something inherent in the internal working of the economy, but some-thing which strikes the outsider arriving to do business. If the outsider can acquire raffia, he can buy everything with it, so it seems to him pre-eminently saleable. But it turns out to be not buyable, and this is because it is not strictly saleable between members of the community, because of what Menger calls 'limitations imposed socially and politi-cally upon exchanges and consumption of that commodity'. On the criterion of saleability, Lele raffia has evidently not developed into a form of primitive money, because most of their goods are distributed without buying or selling.

This approach suggests why travellers in other societies have so readily reported that a favourite commodity, wampum, shells, or iron bars, is the native money: they observe that when it comes into their hands it has an altogether superior degree of saleability, and if they stay to trade they may never remark that between natives it was originally scarcely saleable at all, though with the introduction of markets it soon becomes so. The advantage of following Menger is that we can avoid the paradox of money without commerce, and the study of primitive money can be confined to its appropriate sphere, the emergence of market economies.

Primitive rationing*

A study in controlled exchange

If we contrast primitive money with modern money issued by a single national authority one difference is striking. Primitive money is restricted in its flow, there are ranges of goods it cannot buy or persons to whom it cannot be transferred. By contrast, modern money flows freely. In this perspective primitive money is evidently a very imperfect form of money. But I suggest that it is the wrong perspective for a useful comparison between primitive and modern money. There are many situations in which modern money is restricted, particularly at the international and at the purely personal levels. In these fields there are sharp discontinuities in demand that are expressed by control devices such as rationing. Therefore I argue that it is enlightening to approach money, both primitive and modern, through the idea of rationing and control.

This idea came to me from two sources. The first in time was from field research among the Lele of the Kasai region of the Congo. I do not regard the units of raffia cloth with which they paid fees and fines and tribute as money, since the raffia units did not normally circulate in a market context. Very clearly, they were standardized entitlements to a series of social prerogatives – a kind of coupon. This in itself would not have led me to generalize more widely about primitive coupons were it not for introspection on my own personal experience with money. Menger's account of the origin of money, which I quote below, arouses a deep personal response in me. As he puts it, money is essentially something which permeates and flows. As I know it, money's tendency to flow continually threatens to destroy the ordered pattern of my wants. So I am always involved in the attempt to reduce liquidity by blocking, earmarking, and funding it in various ways. My friends also try to impose crude controls on their own use of money, and these restraints resemble strangely those restraints on the use of some primitive moneys reported by anthropologists (see Firth, 1938, p. 95).

It is well known that there are so-called primitive moneys which are rarely used as media of exchange, which are accepted for only a limited

---

* From R. Firth (ed.), *Themes in Economic Anthropology*, 1967, Association of Social Anthropologists, 6, pp. 119–46.

range of services and commodities and are transferable only to a limited range of persons. Their rates of exchange do not express a price system – or if there is one it is very insensitive. If these are money they do not expedite the transfer of goods and services as our money does. Many writers find difficulty in admitting that they are to be classed as money at all (Firth, 1938, p. 95; Einzig, 1948, p. 328). I should like to agree with them and take the narrow, conventional view of primitive money, counting it as money only when the medium of exchange function is well developed. So-called primitive money that is used only as a means of ceremonial payment I should consider as coupons or licences in a system of control. But it is pedantic to worry too much about terms. In many cases both the coupon function and the medium-of-exchange function are performed by the same units. Moreover, the analogy either with modern money or with modern coupon systems only applies in a very broad and general sense. Modern money and modern coupons are highly specialized instruments functioning in highly differentiated economies. We can make worthwhile comparisons by looking for similar functions and not by looking for similar formal characteristics.

As I see it, money in its nature is essentially an instrument of freedom, rationing in its nature an instrument of control. Money represents general purchasing power over all marketed goods; coupons restrict and channel the purchasing power of money. Money emerges as a spontaneous solution to the need for easier trading conditions; it represents the opening of opportunities. It develops its uses with the development of the market. Restrictions on trade restrict the use of money. Protective legislation sets up barriers to its free flow. By contrast, coupons are essentially instruments of control. In so far as they seek to contain and bar the use of money they are anti-market in intent, the tools of restriction, of closing of opportunities. Money and coupons could hardly be more opposite in their beginnings and in their purposes. Money starts as a set of open possibilities of acquisition, while coupons start within the context of restraint. It is in the nature of money to flow freely, to be like water, to permeate. By their nature coupons represent closed doors, restriction, and control. In a sense they represent form and rational order, for they express society's overriding purposes which curb the drive of individuals. But confusingly this opposition of money and coupons in their basic nature is lost in their actual functioning at any time. For money can be used as an instrument of control, closing doors and blocking outlets for individual energies, while coupons can easily come to represent purchasing power and become barely distinguishable from money. Hence the confusion of the two in the field is very understandable. We have to recognize both the basis of the distinction between money and coupons and their close similarity before we approach the study of primitive distributive systems.

Money may sometimes have emerged from the barter situation which is described in the first page of textbooks on money. On this familiar argument, the inconvenience of barter and the difficulty of arranging credit lead to the adoption of a medium of exchange. The only objection to this supposed historical sequence is that credit is never difficult in a primitive economy; credit exists before market, and Adam Smith's tailor who wants to buy bread for his children should have no difficulty in arranging long-term credits with the baker for whom he has made a suit. In practice, while I readily admit that money can arise in these circumstances of inhibited barter, the evidence for primitive money suggests that this is rare, while the origin of money in a type of primitive rationing system seems likely to be more widespread. I shall develop my argument by distinguishing medium-of-exchange money from coupon money in primitive economies, and start by considering the conditions in which real money is likely to emerge. Karl Menger said that where barter is going on the commodity which is the relatively most saleable will tend to be used as a primitive medium of exchange.

> Their superior saleableness depends only on the relatively inferior saleableness of any other kind of commodity, by which alone they have been able to become *generally* acceptable media of exchange . . . when the relatively most saleable commodities have become 'money' the event has in the first place the effect of substantially increasing their originally high saleableness. Every economic subject bringing less saleable wares to market to acquire goods of another sort has therefore a stronger interest in converting what he has in the first instance into the wares which have become money. . . . The effect produced by such goods as are relatively most saleable becoming money is an increasing differentiation between their degree of saleableness and that of all other goods. And this difference in saleableness ceases altogether to be gradual, and must be regarded in a certain aspect as something absolute. (1892, pp. 249–50)

On this account, money emerges as the market develops. All the emphasis is laid (and surely rightly) on the medium-of-exchange function of money. It implies that perfect money would be completely able to permeate any situation, flow freely, be interchangeable with everything else, be more widely acceptable than anything else. There are a few examples of primitive currencies whose purchasing power is so unrestricted. But in general primitive currencies do not flow freely, they are acceptable in only limited situations, they are not highly saleable. Very often several currencies operate side by side in the same economy. Thus we arrive at the traditional idea of primitive money as imperfect money. But to stay with this approach is, as I have said, to overlook the rationing and licensing functions for which many kinds of primitive money appear to be well-adapted instruments.

Controlled and competitive economies

Modern economic systems are often classed as planned, unplanned, or mixed. These classifications are very broad. In the same way we can distinguish three types of primitive economy: controlled, freely competitive, and mixed, that is, with a certain degree of control over certain areas. My argument is that primitive currencies which are found in the more controlled economies are more like coupons than money, while true primitive money only flourishes in the freely competitive economies. The latter are relatively rare. There are instances of small-scale primitive societies whose internal economies are largely organized by market principles and which clearly make use of money in the full medium-of-exchange sense. I shall discuss these first, partly because (as Pospisil points out (1963, pp. 400 ff)) their existence is often overlooked in general statements about the characteristics of primitive economies, and partly because they are less interesting to my general thesis.

The Reverend Benjamin Danks, a well-known missionary writing at the end of the last century, described (1888, 1892) what he called a type of 'commercial savagery' in New Britain in Melanesia. Here shell-money (*tambu*) was needed for ceremonial payments, blood compensation, marriage dues, funeral gifts, and for burial with the dead. If it had been required only for these purposes we would not account it as money. But it was also used extensively for purchase, and he gives a long list of everyday utensils and foods and their prices in lengths of *tambu*. He mentions that purchase and barter had two distinct words in the language, and that some things had fixed prices while for others the price varied according to the demand and state of supply. For instance, taro and yam prices varied according to the seasonal supply. Furthermore, he clearly describes how the money circulated in the economy. It was acquired directly by trade. Fishermen and farmers sold fish and agricultural products; bananas, coconuts, breadfruit, and fishing-gear fetched good prices. He praises the all-pervasive power of commerce for making the people energetic and industrious. He describes the credit arrangements by which money was lent at ten per cent, or deposited with a banker; the latter had to be in a position to defend the stores of money in his house and by that very fact became a political leader, since his clients could be relied on to rally round him if he was attacked and their wealth endangered. This shrewd observer also noted how the market economy provided the framework of the political system, since, apart from the *de facto* power of bankers, brokers, and creditors, there was no constituted authority and little control over their behaviour other than that provided by the need to maintain confidence in their future dealings. By their control of Duk Duk, a secret society, these same rich men seem to have been able to terrorize the neighbourhood.

Such a circumstantial and intelligent account leaves one in no doubt that New Britain in the nineteenth century had a true monetary economy (see also Epstein, 1964, p. 56), for modern confirmation of Danks's view). There are other modern accounts as convincing, of which I cite only two. By Oliver's description (1955), Siuai, on the south shore of Bougainville, in the Solomon Islands, evidently had a well-developed monetary sector which was geared to the provision of utensils, containers, and luxury foods for feasts. Oliver's fieldwork was in 1938. A more recent report is Pospisil's account of Kapauku economy. Considering that Danks had already described the New Britain economy, and that Oliver had analysed his Solomon Island society as an 'exchange economy', and that Mead (1937, pp. 215–18) had described financial transactions as dominating the social life of the Admiralty Islands, Pospisil seems unduly surprised by his own discovery of thorough-going commercialism in a New Guinea island, but he also is very convincing and circumstantial in his documentation (1963, pp. 402 ff.).

> Kapauku economy is a true money economy. The cowrie shell and the *dedege* and *pagadan* necklaces function in Kapauku society as true money is expected to do. They represent a common measure of value of commodities and are a general medium of exchange. Sale is the most important form of exchange. . . . Except for human beings everything can be bought in this society for the shell currency. . . .

With the emphasis on wealth, money and trade, Kapauku combine a strong version of individualism which, I dare say, could hardly be surpassed in our capitalistic society.

We can abstract from these accounts the following general characteristics of primitive monetary systems. First, there is evidence of a price function which relates supply and demand and responds to seasonal changes in output. This is the proof that in these economies what seems to be money is really performing an authentic monetary function. Second, the institutions of market are well developed: a wide range of goods can be bought and sold, the role of entrepreneur is recognized, and his success is rewarded. Third, credit is available for the promising entrepreneur, and part of his success lies in knowing how to attract credit and use it to the best advantage. In each case leadership and the political structure of groups are not set apart from the sphere of commerce; the rewards of the successful entrepreneur are the highest rewards of power and prestige which the society has to offer; he cannot dominate the political situation without first dominating the market. Since the native ability to do this is unevenly distributed, and since in competitive conditions the entrepreneur risks ups and downs in his career and decline as he ages, in such systems leadership is open to challenge and change and the political structure is unstable. This kind of fluidity is not a matter of individuals' moving up and down rapidly from one recognized position to another. It is much more an instability in the relation of actual positions, since each outstanding individual creates his own leadership, and when he declines his position lapses and produces changes in the total social pattern. Margaret Mead describes this characteristic formation in Manus as

an uneven skyline, a few leaders standing out against the sky and giving form and definition to the immediate situation. The position of each leader is dependent upon the number of other leaders in the community. If the standard is high, his standard must be higher. Thus each leader goads each other leader, both as his partner in economic transactions and as a measure of his own success. No one is primarily interested in humiliating others, but only in maintaining his own position. . . . So each man is matched against the *pace* of the group; his position is a function of it. (1937, pp. 218–19)

Her image of a changing skyline closely corresponds with descriptions of the status pattern in Siuai by Oliver, in Kapauku by Pospisil, and in New Britain by Danks and Epstein. In general, it seems that the more that entrepreneurship, credit, and market principles govern social life in the conditions of a primitive economy, the more the pattern of status is likely to be fluid in this sense.

Since the comparison with Western capitalism is tempting (indeed Pospisil makes it implicitly), we should note the essential difference. These primitive economies dominated by production for exchange are as thoroughly commercial as any in Western Europe or the United States. But technologically they are not advanced, institutionally they are not highly differentiated, and above all the productive energies are not directed in any very notable sense to the long-term accumulation of real capital goods. As far as producers' equipment and stores of consumers' goods are concerned they do not produce anything which will yield over a longer time than the life-cycle of a pig. For all their entrepreneurial energy they are not so blessed with capital as any tribe of cattle-herders. Therefore, it is misleading to think of this as a type of primitive capitalism: it is only primitive commerce. If there was real capital being built up and conserved from generation to generation, the profile of status would be steadied by reference to valuable material assets. As it is, the changing skyline is typical of the status pattern in primitive societies using true money.

Much more common is the mixed economy in which some measure of control is exercised over certain key transactions. Then we find large areas of social life are protected from the challenge of free competition. Institutions of credit and the rewards of entrepreneurship are arranged so that productive effort supports and does not undermine the traditional forms of society. For a fixed pattern of status to survive at all, social policy must override divergent private concerns. This type of social system, status-oriented and therefore conservative, is so much more common in primitive conditions that it is understandable why Pospisil, describing the competitive commercial atmosphere of Kapauku life, felt that he was challenging all the established assumptions of anthropologists about the nature of primitive economy. In this he was exaggerating, perhaps. But he was right to the extent that his picture of the primitive commercial society is relatively rare, and that the other, non-commercial type predominates in the records of anthropologists. It is in the latter status-governed type that I propose that we should reconsider the functions of what has been previously regarded as a form of primitive money.

There are many different ways of channelling distribution and of making sure that access to scarce resources is under the control of those in authority. Which method is developed depends partly on scale. In a very small community consensus on ends and means may be so complete that no specialized institutions may be required. Again, scale may not be so relevant here as the sense of distributive justice. If the pattern of social rewards seems manifestly equitable it may be maintained without a special manipulation of the economy. I would expect primitive coupon systems to emerge where there is some danger that the effective demand for scarce resources may so disturb the pattern of distribution as to threaten a given social order.

Primitive coupon systems

The object of rationing is to ensure a fair distribution of necessities, necessities being a culturally defined concept meaning goods which ought to be and usually are freely available. Rationing is applied when something restricts the supply of necessities, so we have bread and meat rationing in the wartime economy. The idea of necessities also includes things which it is held ought to be freely available, even though they may in practice never have been. Education or petrol, for example, may be regarded as such a necessity in our own society, water in an arid country. If we define necessities as those things which ought to be available to all, there are some societies in which it is thought that certain minimum forms of prestige and civic status ought to be available to all members of the community and should be recognized as necessities. In such societies rationing is an appropriate model for interpreting institutions which seek to ensure an equal distribution of high status. For example, the Lele social system lopsidedly reserves most prestige to old men, and keeps their young men in a deprived status. Yet their gerontology is inspired by a basically egalitarian principle. It is not birth or achievement or the unequal endowments of nature which, under this dispensation, will bring one man more prestige than his neighbour. But mere seniority, relatively greater age, in the due course of time is expected to make up to each deprived junior for the privileges forgone in his youth. In the interests of this principle of distribution, the Lele put wives and the means of procuring wives under rationing control. In seeing their bridewealth as a system for rationing women, I am closely following Lévi-Strauss. Taking the case of petrol rationing, he says:

Certaines formes de rationnement sont nouvelles pour notre société, et créent une impression de surprise dans des esprits formés aux traditions de libéralisme économique. Ainsi sommes-nous portés à voir dans l'intervention collective, se manifestant à l'endroit de commodités qui jouent un rôle essentiel dans le genre de vie propre à notre culture, une innovation hardie et quelque peu scandaleuse. Parce que le contrôle de la répartition et de la consommation porte sur l'essence minérale, nous croyons volontiers que sa formule peut tout juste être contemporaine de l'automobile. Il n'en est rien cependant: le 'régime du produit raréfié' constitue un modèle d'une extrême généralité. Dans ce cas comme dans beaucoup d'autres, les périodes de crise auxquelles notre société était, jusqu'à une date récente, si peu habituée à faire face, restaurent seulement, sous une forme critique, un état de choses que la société primitive considère plus ou moins comme normal. Ainsi le 'régime du produit raréfié', tel qu'il s'exprime dans les mesures de contrôle collectif, est beaucoup moins une innovation due aux conditions de la guerre moderne et au caractère mondial de notre économie, que la résurgence d'un ensemble de procédés familiers aux sociétés primitives, et sans lesquels la cohérence du groupe serait à chaque instant compromise. (1949, pp. 39-40)

In his succeeding analysis of the controlled distribution of wives, Lévi-Strauss restricts himself to 'elementary structures', that is, structures which positively prescribe permitted classes of spouses. He does not apply the rationing model to more complex structures in which the rules of sharing are negatives which merely limit the range of possible spouses by forbidding certain categories. Yet it is in this range of kinship structures that the analogy with petrol coupons applies most fully. The man equipped with the right number of raffia cloths, spears, cattle, or whatever is the accepted commodity, can use them with a certain freedom, other things being equal, to acquire the bride of his choice. In a sense his use of the bridewealth coupon is very like the use of money. But this is the case with any coupon: it is a supplementary means of purchase, it makes purchasing power effective. What makes the situation more like rationing than like money is not the use to which the coupons are put but the conditions by which their acquisition is controlled. The essence of money is to be transferable. It circulates, but coupons when spent return to an issuing point and their acquisition is continually under survey and control. Admittedly, there is a big difference between modern and primitive coupons. In a modern economy paper coupons once spent are returned to the office of issue, counted, and destroyed. But primitive commodity coupons simply return at each transfer into the hands of the senior members of the community who become by this fact to all intents and purposes the issuing authority. This makes it almost impossible to acquire coupons without being acceptable to the senior old men who hold them. Coupons do not circulate; they are continually issued and returned and re-issued. The dynamics of this movement I shall discuss later.

We should first consider further some characteristics of modern rationing systems. Coupons can be combined with the use of money in various ways. They can even be substituted altogether for money. At the beginning of the war Colin Clark published a scheme by which the whole of the Australian economy could have been organized by means of coupons, which would have replaced money for the duration (*Sydney Daily Telegraph*, 18 March 1942). Such a scheme was never applied, but instead belligerent countries used money and coupons as two kinds of entitlement to purchasing power which had to be combined in the specified units for acquiring rationed goods. De Scitovsky (1942) distinguishes three methods of rationing: specific rationing, in which a specific coupon has to be tendered for a specified commodity; group rationing; and value rationing. In group rationing a class of goods which are in consumer's practice generally substitutable are grouped together and acquired by means of a transferable coupon. Thus the consumer's choice within a certain range of behaviour is not limited, and no minimum expenditure on any specific item in the group is anticipated. So there would be not hat or coat coupons but clothing coupons; edible fats fell into one such group and non-alcoholic beverages into another. The idea of group rationing, by which the coupons are freely transferable between different items in the group, can be reversed to make it applicable to certain primitive conditions. In many primitive economies it would seem that any of a specified group of valuables can serve as a coupon for obtaining a specified status. For example, the Yurok of Northern California, who import so-called shell-money, used standard lengths for settling claims against one another: damages for adultery or insult, marriage gifts, fees for initiations or medical aid. I argue that it is a distortion to consider the medium used for these payments as money, since it did not perform the medium-of-exchange function. It was much more a coupon or ticket for acquiring or amending status. But the coupon consisting of a standard string of shells had a fixed value in terms of certain other commodities, for example, heads of rare birds, rare pelts, obsidian blades (Kroeber, 1925, pp. 26–7). These fixed values introduce the same flexibility into the system of payments that group rationing does in the wartime economy. What appear to be prices are not exchange values; there seems to have been no real internal market in which pelts or knives were bought and sold for shells. They merely were rates of substitution by which a coupon of one kind was equivalent to a coupon of another kind in the rationing system. Instead of a grouping of consumer commodities there was a grouping of commodities serving as coupons.

Value rationing is used when the amount of the scarce commodity which anyone is allowed to acquire is controlled simply by setting a limit on the expenditure of money. Thus, instead of the impossible task of deciding how many stews, joints, or cutlets of meat a family was entitled to per week, the meat rationing left the choice of prime or cheap cuts of meat free, and rationed it by a restriction on overall weekly expenditure. Here the rationers used the monetary system as part of the system of control. When we read of economists' elaborate calculations of the effect of rationing on prices (Hugh-Jones, 1950), discussion which consider the coupons as a kind of second currency, we are close to the cruder reality of primitive money in which multiple currencies operate side by side in not completely distinct spheres of exchange. The Kapauku have several cowrie and bead currencies circulating simultaneously which are fully interchangeable at known rates. Since theirs is a commercial economy, their various shells function more like coins of different denominations. Thus they differ essentially from the multiple currencies of some primitive economies. In these, each type of currency is acceptable only for a limited range of goods or services. One of the most famous examples are the currencies of Rossel Island, of which the most valuable units are reserved exclusively for the use of men.

Some primitive currencies are perhaps more like systems of licensing than like rationing, and it is as well to be clear about the difference here too. Both are instruments of social policy, but whereas rationing is egalitarian in intent, licensing is not. The object of licensing is protective, and to promote responsible administration. The object of rationing is to ensure equal distribution of scarce necessities. One of the objects of licensing is to ensure responsible use of possibly dangerous powers, so we have licensing of guns and liquor sales. Licensing pins responsibility, so we have marriage licences and pet licences. Licensing protects vulnerable areas of the economy, so we have import licensing, and so on.

An important side-effect of licensing is to create monopoly advantages for those who issue licences and for those who receive them. Both parties become bound in a patron-client relation sustained by the strong interests of each in the continuance of the system. Modern rationing does not have this effect so strongly, though it sometimes ties groups of consumers to particular retailers. The emergence of patron-client groups around a licensing system recalls the groups which crystallize round the issuing of primitive coupons. I have mentioned the Lele bridewealth in raffia cloth as an example of primitive rationing of women in the interests of an equal distribution to all who reach a certain age. The raffia cloth units are hand-woven by the men of the tribe. Thus in a sense it is possible for every man to issue his own coupons to himself. This, of course, no more makes nonsense of the rationing analogy than it makes nonsense to speak of money when the unit of currency is freely produced and marketed. The cost of production merely affects the price of money and equally the cost of production limits the possibility of flooding the rationing system with new coupons. In practice the demand for raffia cloths at every turn of his career and every step in status so overwhelmed a young Lele man that he could not expect to produce raffia for all his own needs. He turned for contributions to the men who were on the receiving end of the system. These old men had themselves passed through all the stages of payment and could now reckon to receive levies of raffia cloth in large amounts. These senior men thus found themselves at the issue-desk, as it were, and did not fail to take full advantage of the patron-client opportunities of their situation. I have described in *The Lele of the Kasai* (see especially Chapters III, V, and VIII) how the effective kin groups of adult men were activated in this way, and also the dynamics of the movement of raffia from old men to young men and back again.

Having distinguished rationing from licensing as found in our own society, I am no longer concerned to maintain the distinction in primitive societies. For it is academic whether we consider a revolving fund of bridewealth, cattle, or spears as a set of coupons controlling distribution of wives or as a set of licences creating a strong patron-client interest. In the primitive social system these functions remain in an unspecialized matrix.

Primitive coupon systems can be recognized by the following characteristics:

(i) The coupons do not represent general purchasing power in the internal economy. Indeed, market conditions are very limited, if they exist at all, within these economies. The powers of acquisition which the coupons represent are highly specific.

(ii) Their distribution is controlled in various ways. For example, in the Southern Bantu tribes, cattle are transferred in bridewealth payments, and this function is so dominant that it is hardly possible for a young man seeking to marry to acquire cattle except through the marriage of his sister. Since cattle paid for her have passed into the hands of his father, their allocation to him for his marriage is in every sense a restricted permission or licence.

(iii) The conditions which govern their issue create a patron-client set of relationships. Those seeking coupons must first acquire the favour of those who control the allocation; thus arises a focus of social control.

(iv) Their main function is to provide the necessary condition for entry to high-status positions, or for maintaining rank, or for countering attacks on status.

(v) In general, neither the economy nor the social system in which coupon systems operate is competitive. The coupons function to reduce or eliminate competition in the interests of a fixed pattern of status. The coupons ensure that the distributive system of the economy will not bring about a pattern of control over goods and services which is at variance with the pattern of ascribed status. I will say more about this below. But first I need to note an apparent exception.

(vi) It is possible for coupons to be working in a system which shows the characteristics mentioned above in every respect except that their distribution is not under firm control. Something like a black market in status then develops: the weakest to the wall, and the highest status to the strongest operator. In such a case, so far from being non-competitive and working in the interests of a fixed status pattern, the coupon system itself is open to fierce competition.

This is how I see the use of Yurok shell-money and the shell-money of the Tolowa-Tututni peoples, their cultural neighbours on the Pacific coast of America. Cora Du Bois in her perceptive economic analysis of these latter (1936) points out that in so far as daily subsistence is concerned, there is no competition. Rules of neighbourly sharing and hospitality spread the risks in the way that is common in small-scale non-commercial economies. But the acquisition of prestige is ruthlessly competitive. Men demand compensation for every insult and are trained from childhood to be extremely sensitive in recognizing insults. They pursue their claims for debts, fees, and fines with complete single-mindedness and only respect a man who is rich and has followers who will back him in a show of force. The patron-client relation is highly developed and, though fluid, it is the only effective political grouping in the society. The system of debt collection is tilted so that the rich man who has adherents can exact more for injuries to himself than can his followers in the claims which they would have no chance of collecting if he did not back them. Shell-money changes hands frequently, yet without buying and selling.

The one respect in which this case does not show all the characteristics I have listed above for primitive coupon systems is that here there is nothing analogous to controlled distribution. Anyone can challenge anyone else, claim to have been insulted, and demand compensation. This important difference makes the Yurok and Tolowa-Tututni type of economy a hybrid case, for their political system, focused on the strong man and his followers, is very similar to the focusing on the banker-creditor in primitive monetary systems I have described. The only difference is that such advantages accrue to the man who starts with a lot of shell-coupons and men in his control that a fairly rigid distinction between rich and poor classes develops. It is difficult for the poor man to become rich, and in this sense it could be said that, in spite of the individualistic and competitive atmosphere, the coupon system upholds a steady status pattern as it does so much more obviously in other cases.

Like most other anthropologists I have been intrigued and baffled by Armstrong's account of Rossel Island currency, and pored over the ranked series of shell coins to which Armstrong gives numerical value. Lorraine Barić in a very stimulating essay starts from the fact that, though some of the shells can be used for day-to-day purchases and so have normal monetary functions, for the most part each type of currency is reserved for a special transfer which has essentially to do with ceremonial and status (marriage gifts, blood compensation, feasting, and so on). Borrowing was a constant necessity for Rossel Islanders to fulfil their social commitments. Loans had to be repaid according to rules which prevented a simple return of the original loan. Either a higher-ranking coin was due or a coin of the same rank as the original one borrowed had to be supplemented by another lower-ranking coin. Old men argued keenly about what return was appropriate for a loan of given length of time, and in the system there seems to be a general idea of interest being paid for use over time. But Lorraine Barić denies the possibility of equating the values of the different series of coins. She emphasizes instead:

> The uncertainty of interest, the impossibility of expressing interest as an exact ratio of the principle, the impossibility of aggregating coins of different categories as equivalent to one of a higher rank, the impossibility of saying that one category of coins was in any way a multiple or proportion of any other category. (1964, p. 47)

Since the economic background seems not to have been dominated by market forces, she is clearly justified in claiming that these coins are not money in any strict sense: a view in harmony with Raymond Firth's treatment (1938, pp. 95–6). More interesting to me is her implied suggestion that Rossel Island might have much in common with other non-monetary systems of creating solidarity through indebtedness. Thurnwald already gave this insight in his perceptive account of shell and pig transfers in Buin: 'The process of converting one kind of object of value into another, of pigs into *abuta* and *vice versa*, upon the basis of reciprocity is a means of intensifying and adding complexity to the social texture of the community and the intercommunal life' (1934–5, p. 140). This was a very far-seeing reflection, but until Lévi-Strauss had analysed elementary structures of kinship as artificial techniques for elaborating reciprocity, it was not possible to take the next step and see primitive currencies performing not a specialized economic function but a generalized social function. We can now more easily recognize the advantage to solidarity gained by a system of universal mutual indebtedness.

If we interpret the independent series of Rossel Island coins as coupon-licences we can learn more about primitive money in general. Imagine our English experience of wartime rationing and our present experience of licensing enormously extended. Recall that rationing and licensing are limited and specific permissions to do or obtain certain things. Since they are specific, a gun licence is no good to a man who is seeking a liquor licence, and a TV licence is no good to one who wants to sell tobacco or to buy a watchdog. To cope with this extended system of licensing one might decide to make licences transferable, thus making them rather more like money than like coupons. Exchanges could be arranged on a modified group-rationing system. For example, there could be a series of pet licences, weapon licences, work licences, and there could easily grow up a system of swopping between holders of licences in the same category, with a scale of compensation for those who accept obviously smaller licences in exchange for more substantial ones, and obvious difficulties for swopping between categories. How many gun licences would be worth one marriage licence or vice versa? One solution would be for the acceptor of a marriage licence to accept the obligation to return a marriage licence to his creditor when need arises. Another would be to develop a system of brokerage with commission. Both of these solutions were adopted on Rossel Island.

Discontinuity in the demand function

If an imaginary Kafka-like outbreak of bureaucracy in England helps to interpret Rossel Island currency, it also raises another question about primitive coupon systems. In our experience controls are imposed by a central authority: rationing and licensing may seem to be far-fetched as analogies for a system that arises spontaneously without central direction. I have therefore to explain how it can happen that people, while independently pursuing their own ends, can take private decisions which have the effect of creating a controlled economy. In order to do this we should recall first the common tendency of non-monetary economies to have distinct, impermeable, ranked spheres of exchange.

Hoyt describes this (mistakenly) as a characteristic of primitive economies in general. She lists examples of the custom

> by which certain things must always be exchanged for certain other things. For instance the Marindanim of Dutch South New Guinea will exchange articles of need only for articles of need, food for food. . . . In the Solomon Islands and Bismarck Archipelago, likewise, similar things must always be exchanged for each other: necessaries for necessaries; iron hatchets for stone hatchets; taro for tobacco. The famous traveller of the 17th century, Peter Mundy, was unable to buy cattle in St. Lawrence, Madagascar because the people would exchange them only for large cornelian beads, though sheep, hens, fish, milk and oranges could be bought with various trade articles.
> (1926, p. 84)

Many anthropologists have borne witness to similar restrictions on exchange (see Firth, 1959, p. 36). The best account is Bohannan's analysis of the pre-colonial Tiv economy in which he discerned three distinct spheres of exchange. In the domestic sphere chickens, baskets, and food crops could be exchanged. This sphere ranked lower in esteem than the trade and war sphere in which guns, metal rods, trade cloth, and slaves were exchangeable. And this ranked below the sphere in which men competed for rights to acquire wives. In the old days a man could not get a wife without being allowed by the lineage head to offer one of the lineage girls as an exchange. Each sphere was impenetrable from a lower sphere save in exceptional circumstances. Any man would be delighted to make a deal offering subsistence goods for trade goods, but what man in his senses would be so foolish as to 'convert down', as Bohannan puts it, and give up goods held in the high-prestige trade sphere in exchange for subsistence goods? Conversion was only likely to happen if one party was desperate, say, to feed his starving family in a famine. The Tiv case is instructive, for the breaks in continuity in the distributive system correspond to breaks in the status system. The path to high status was not based on economic achievement so much as on a shrewd manipulation of esoteric knowledge of genealogy, ritual, and law. In the days when the Tiv system flourished, a wife was a necessary condition of lineage status, but while old men were polygamists, young men were bachelors. The age of marriage for men was late and many men probably did not make marriages at all (Abraham, 1933, p. 145; East, 1939, pp. 109–10). If coupons for the acquisition of wives had been available to any industrious young man who did well in trade, the whole status system would have tottered – as indeed it did under the combined impact of colonial government and commerce (Bohannan, 1955). It seems only reasonable to expect to find restricted, ranked spheres of exchange in societies with restricted, ranked spheres of status. In the terms of our analogy with a modern rationing system, the restricted spheres of exchange result from individual refusals to do deals which will result in giving up a coupon valid for a low-ranking position. The restricted spheres emerge in the struggle of those in privileged positions to keep control of the issue-desk. As soon as the restricted spheres of exchange are allowed to interpenetrate, the structure of privileges must collapse. No official regulation is necessary to impose these restrictions on the free working of the economy. They develop out of each man's sound perception of where his own interests lie.

The existence of separate, ranked spheres of exchange within a primitive economy is the clue to the development of multiple currencies in some of these economies, and I find it helpful to compare them with the development of hard and soft currency areas in modern inter-national money. Disequilibrium in trading accounts may lead to some countries having overall deficits and others overall surpluses. The old

Tiv lineage head, well-endowed with wives and daughters, and with guns, slaves, rods, and cloth, is like a hard-currency area which demands that its claims shall be settled only in its own currency. He will not give up a daughter except in exchange for a wife, and nothing would induce him to give up guns or slaves for chickens in any quantity, since he has plenty of these in his own compound.

Controlled exchange

At this point I must temporarily drop the distinction I have been at pains to draw between primitive money and primitive coupons. By comparing international exchange and also our own intimate treatment of our money incomes, I hope to explain the bizarre aspects of primitive distribution systems by quirks in our own experience of money. So long as it is circulating within the control of a sovereign authority, modern money is nearly perfect in Menger's sense. It can permeate almost any situation. It is almost completely buyable and saleable, its flow is unrestricted. But in dealings between two or more sovereign authorities this is no longer so true. Political considerations intervene, social policy demands protective measures for vulnerable areas of each economy: the free flow of money is not allowed to go unchecked. In a true sense, money in the international economy is very like money in the primitive economy where no sovereign authority is in control. In its international aspect modern money is hardly more freely saleable and unrestricted than the most primitive coupon/money we know. And here the distinction between coupons and money for obvious reasons is no longer interesting. I shall develop the analogy with reference to international blocked currencies and double exchange rates. But first let me try to fill in a gap in my argument.

If we admit that we ourselves as private individuals living in a modern monetary economy try to restrict the free flow of money by earmarking, blocking, and hoarding, then it becomes plausible to argue that in primitive conditions individuals do much the same. This capacity that money has for flowing freely in all directions can be a great nuisance. There are some who read their bank statement without astonishment, but they must be exceptions. It is more realistic to suppose that failure in 'controlling and structuring the future in long-run consumption' is the usual case (Reuben Hill, 1961, p. 70). Many of us try to primitivize our money as soon as we get it, by placing restrictions at source, by earmarking monetary instruments of certain kinds for certain purposes, by only allowing ourselves or our wives certain limited freedoms in the disposal of money. Some people hate to pay cheques, thinking that money disappears too easily that way. For others cheques are the preferred means of settlement just because they offer a means of control. Money from different sources is sometimes personalized and attracts distinctive feelings which dictate the character of its spending. For example, a friend whose main income derives from investments also earns irregular amounts by writing. The income which comes from this voluntary, private, and creative activity she refuses to spend on what is compulsory, public, and routine. So she tries never to pay rates and taxes with the earned income. Another friend artificially creates windfalls for herself by putting aside 3d. bits. In this way she has a fund for what she regards as luxury purchases. All these practices are but clumsy attempts to control the all too liquid state of money.

In accounts of primitive economies we find many parallels. Danks said that the entrepreneurs of New Britain hated to break into a big coil of *tambu* which represented a capital sum. Rather than change it, they would pledge it and pay interest on the loan of the required small sum. This would almost be like our being prepared to lose something for the sake of having a sum held in an illiquid and untouchable form. Considering that the secular decline in the value of money threatens to cancel the increase in the value of Post Office Savings Certificates, I feel that the continued attraction of this kind of holding is very like the big coil of *tambu*. The fight to control the liquidity of money is the reason why the pastoral Massa of the Cameroons constantly seek to put their cash into 100 F. notes, a form which is more solid and resistant to petty inroads (De Garine, 1964, p. 122). The Kapauku, who are cursed (or blessed) with almost completely saleable-buyable money, when they want to put aside a sum for their sons to inherit are never sure that they can resist touching it. So the would-be saver places a terrible curse on himself should he ever break into his pile. How difficult it is to keep under review the hierarchy of our wants, and to impose a rational pattern on our spending. It would be easier if money came in vouchers tailored to our various purposes. If a husband who wanted to stop his wife from spending housekeeping money on clothes or cigarettes could issue her with vouchers for these items then he could successfully enforce his budget policy. The Rossel Islanders actually have a series of high-value coins which women are prohibited from using. This certainly suggests that primitive money may not be an ineffective means of fulfilling particular economic policies. I hope that I can take it as established that exchange controls can arise very spontaneously, and that we need not be surprised to find something like hard and soft exchange areas appearing within a primitive economy.

To return to the international exchange analogy, travellers have often been surprised to find a low official rate of exchange (whether for native and modern money or for barter goods) existing side by side with a much higher unofficial rate. The official rate is not necessarily very widely applied in the internal economy. It is often a mere standard of value against which other goods are measured. For example, among the Lele in the Kasai in the nineteen-fifties a big store basket was worth forty Belgian Congo francs or four raffia cloths. This did not mean that 10 Congo francs could buy one raffia cloth. I have described elsewhere (1963, pp. 59–67) the absence of a free market for raffia cloth. The official rate for raffia, though it gained steadily between 1924 and 1953 in relation to Congo francs, was applied only when using raffia as a standard measure for barter. The 'unofficial' rate was not applied in exchanges of raffia for other commodities, but was quoted only when the equivalent values were being worked out for other goods. For example, one camwood bar of a certain height, valued at 200 raffia units, could be exchanged for one female goat. If in these exchanges anyone came forward with raffia cloth instead of any of the goods valued in terms of raffia, the rate for settling in raffia was automatically lowered by 10 per cent (and sometimes even by 20 per cent) so that nine raffia cloths were accepted in exchange for an object valued at ten raffia cloths, 90 for an object valued at 100, and so on. The same practice was reported independently by Luc de Heusch (1955) working among the Songo, hundreds of miles north and west of the Lele.

On the other side of the Kasai river, the Bushong tribe seem to have had a similar convention. I surmise that the strip of raffia on which 320 cowries were sewn and which was a standard unit of money (Vansina, 1964, p. 23) was probably reckoned at 400 cowries, 20 per cent being discounted. This is not just a matter of giving a 10 per cent or 20 per cent discount for cash down or for the less liquid form of money, though I think these considerations are present. The main reason for the double exchange rate is to protect the pattern of wealth-holding within the economy. The old Lele men who held most of the rights in raffia would be foolish to sell these rights for Belgian Congo francs, which only the young men were in a position to earn. No one would convert raffia into francs unless he were forced to do so. The soaring price of raffia (in terms of francs) represented the blocking of one area of the economy and of the social system; an attempt to freeze a pattern of social relations.

I would now like to use the foregoing to explain two characteristics of primitive economies. One is the unexpected tenacity of primitive currency in the face of European money with greater purchasing power. The other is the reported inelasticity of prices in many primitive economies.

It seems on the face of it surprising that *tambu*, described in the nineteenth century, should be a medium of exchange circulating alongside European shillings in New Britain, and that manillas should have been forcibly suppressed in Nigeria only in the late nineteen-forties after many centuries of trade with Europe. My answer is that those types of primitive money which display vitality are those which have a coupon function in controlling status in the social system. Their medium-of-exchange function is easily displaced, and there are indeed many currencies used specifically for trade which have disappeared. To take *tambu* first, A. L. Epstein describes it as the linch-pin of the social order in New Britain. Wages there are paid in Australian currency, and no European or Chinese store accepts payment in shell-money. For paying bridewealth and other ceremonial dues only *tambu* is acceptable. Between the two extremes there is an area within which cash and shell serve as alternative media of exchange. There is no fixed conversion rate between the two currencies, cash and shell. *Tambu* cannot be bought in cash.

> Cash and *tambu* operate in an area of overlap but they relate essentially to different sets of social values, each of which is recognized as valid in its own sphere. Those who would like to see *tambu* replaced by cash seem to be those with least stake in the perpetuation of the old social system, that is, younger and more educated men, and urban workers. (Epstein, 1963, pp. 28–32)

In the Cross River area of Nigeria a similar situation maintained the value of manillas in spite of disturbing fluctuations in price. Exchange rates between manillas and West African shillings fluctuated according to seasonal booms in the palm-oil trade and on the long secular trend manillas increased in value in relation to shillings. Speculative hoarding increased still more the relative scarcity of manillas, which was mainly due to the increase in shillings in circulation as opportunities for employment went up. The government recognized that hardship resulted from a coinage with marked fluctuations in value, but its first attempt to suppress manillas failed. This was an attempt to buy them up, but I suspect that holders of manillas were not willing to part with them at prices which the government thought it reasonable to offer. Finally, the manilla problem was solved by legislation restricting its use in trade. It is hardly necessary to add that manillas were used in Cross River societies as coupons for bridewealth and so were more than mere media of commercial exchange.

We can also look at one of the many cases on record in which Europeans have gained access to large quantities of the local coinage. Inflation inevitably results and inevitably the primitive currency soon loses its purchasing power. Einzig (1948, p. 162) cites a case in which iron-bar currency in the Congo, thus inflated by Europeans importing it to pay their way, devalued to such an extent that it defeated the travellers' intention. The point was reached at which the amount that a man could carry was not valuable enough to pay his wages for carrying it. In Mt Hagen, in New Guinea, the Europeans brought in large quantities of gold lip shell, the most esteemed currency, in order to pay for pigs and for labour. Inflation worked against them so that the size of pig a gold lip shell could buy became smaller and smaller, while the Mt Hagen natives fully exploited their position in inter-tribal trade and acquired foreign wives and pigs in large number. But although thousands of gold lip shells were now circulating and seeping out of Mt Hagen in inter-tribal trade, when the Europeans tried to buy gold lip shells for money, they could only do so at 'exorbitant prices' (Gitlow, 1947). So even severe inflation did not alter the situation which tends to govern the relations between primitive and modern currencies when the former have a coupon function.

I now turn to the reported inelasticity of prices in primitive economies. Basil Yamey invites anthropologists to make suggestions about this:

> There are references in the literature on peasant economies
> suggesting that there is a long-term stability in the values of such
> economic variables as the prices of particular goods or services, or the
> rate of interest in particular classes of transaction. It seems as if for
> long periods particular prices, wage-rates or rates of interest remain
> unchanged, despite other changes in the peasant economy at large.
> The economist, with his firmly entrenched idea that changes in prices
> both reflect changes in economic conditions and also bring about
> adaptation to the changes, is perhaps somewhat suspicious of the
> reality of such inflexibilities. (1964, p. 383)

Equally puzzling reports about prices that are insensitive to changes in supply and demand are made about the primitive economies I have discussed here. The explanation of these may also apply to peasant economies, since the people living in the latter are often concerned to protect a traditional pattern of society from change (Wolf, 1955). I would seek the answer in the analogy with coupons, on the one hand, and with international exchange, on the other. To suppose that prices should be highly responsive to supply and demand is to assume that they are operating in a free and perfect market. But such markets are rare in primitive conditions. To understand the slow movement of prices in some sectors of primitive economies we should recall that the rates at which coupons and licences are exchangeable for goods or money are inelastic even in our own modern economy. The price of gun licences and pet licences is not closely related to conditions of supply and demand, nor are legal penalties for that matter. These rates tend to change only infrequently, and to move with big steps when they do move. Where the patterns of obligation and privilege are governed by ascribed status we should expect to find that certain prices tend to be controlled, either by discontinuities in the internal distributive system or by discontinuities in the demand for foreign currency. In either case, issues of social policy restrict the freedom of the market. The Lele operated three exchange rates for raffia: one applied to internal transactions when raffia was the standard of value but did not actually intervene; another rate, 10–20 per cent higher, was applied internally when raffia was used in settlement; a third was used when anyone sought to buy raffia with francs, but it was prohibitively high. Thus they kept internal prices in terms of raffia low and discriminated against Belgian Congo francs so as to prevent francs displacing raffia. In such transactions there is an appearance of centrally imposed control, but it is deceptive. No central governing body imposes the rates of exchange. The exchange control emerges by the decisions of individuals striving to hold to their position of advantage in a particular social structure.

Notes

1 The Lele inhabit the region between the Loange and the Kasai rivers, in the Kasai District of the Belgian Congo. My fieldwork among them in 1949–50, and in four months in 1953, was made possible by a fellowship of the International African Institute and with help from the Belgian Institut pour la Recherche Scientifique en Afrique Centrale.

2   I use the word 'client' for the status of men and women descended from a woman over whom certain rights have been transferred to settle a blood debt, and the word 'lord' for the status of the representative of the clan to whom these rights have been transferred. As the institution is complicated, with far-reaching effects on Lele social organization, it must be described in a special article.

3   Salim (1962).

4   Many instances of similar conventions restricting exchanges could be cited, cf. Bohannan (1955). See also many examples cited by Hoyt (1926, pp. 84–5).

5   'Village-wife' is a woman whose marriage dues have been paid by an age-set of the village, and who is for all practical purposes regarded as the communal wife of the men of the village.

References

Abraham, R. C. (1933), *The Tiv People*, Lagos, Government Printer.

Anonymous (1949), The Manilla Problem, *Statistical and Economic Review*, 3, pp. 44–56.

Armstrong, W. E. (1928), *Rossel Island: An Ethnological Study*, Cambridge University Press.

Barić, Lorraine (1964), 'Some aspects of Credit, Saving and Investment in a "Non-Monetary Economy" (Rossel Island)', in Firth and Yamey (1964), pp. 35–52.

Bohannan, P. (1955), 'Some Principles of Exchange and Investment among the Tiv', *American Anthropologist*, 57, pp. 60–70.

Brown, George (1910), *Melanesians and Polynesians*, London, Macmillan.

Clark, Colin (1942), *Daily Telegraph*, Sydney, 18 March.

Danks, Benjamin (1888), 'On the Shell Money of New Britain', *Journal of the Anthropological Institute*, 17, pp. 305–17.

Danks, Benjamin (1892), 'Burial Customs of New Britain', *Journal of the Anthropological Institute*, 21, pp. 348 ff.

Davis, James T. (1961), 'Trade Routes and Economic Exchange among the Indians of California', *Reports of University of California Archeology Survey*, 54.

De Garine, Igor (1964), *Les Massa du Cameroun, Vie économique et sociale*, Paris, Presses Universitaires de France.

De Heusch, Luc (1955), 'Valeur, monnaies et structuration sociale chez les Nkutshu', *Revue de l'Institut de Sociologie*, 55, pp. 73–89.

De Scitovsky, T. (1942), 'The Political Economy of Consumer's Rationing', *Review of Economic Statistics*, 24, pp. 114–24.

Douglas, Mary (1963), *The Lele of the Kasai*, London, Oxford University Press.

Du Bois, Cora (1936), 'The Wealth Concept as an Integrative Factor in Tolowa-Tututni Culture', *Essays in Anthropology Presented to A. L. Kroeber*, Berkeley, University Press of California, pp. 49–65.

East, Rupert (1939), *Akiga's Story*, London, Oxford University Press.

Einzig, Paul (1948), *Primitive Money*, London, Eyre & Spottiswoode.
Epstein, A. L. (1963), 'Tambu: a primitive shell money', *Discovery*, December.
Epstein, Scarlett (1964), 'Personal Capital Formation among the Tolai of New Britain', in Firth and Yamey (1964), pp. 53–68.
Firth, Raymond (1938), *Human Types*, London, Thomas Nelson.
Firth, Raymond (1959), *Economics of the New Zealand Maori*, (2nd edn), Wellington, New Zealand, R. E. Owen, Government Printer.
Firth, Raymond and Yamey, B. S. (1964), *Capital Saving and Credit in Peasant Societies*, London, Allen & Unwin.
Gitlow, Abraham (1947), *Economics of the Mount Hagen Tribes, New Guinea*, Monographs of the American Ethnological Society, 12.
Hill, Reuben (1961), 'Patterns of Decision-making and the Accumulation of Family Assets', *Household Decision Making. Consumer Behavior*, 4, ed. N. N. Foote, New York Press, pp. 57–80.
Hoyt, E. (1926), *Primitive Trade*, London, Kegan Paul, Trench, Trubner.
Hugh-Jones, A. M. (1950), 'Points as Currency', *Economic Journal*, 60, pp. 162–9.
Kroeber, A. L. (1925), *Handbook of the Indians of California*, Washington, Government Printing Office.
Lévi-Strauss, Claude (1949), *Les Structures élémentaires de la parenté*, Paris, Presses Universitaires de France.
Mead, Margaret (1937), *Co-operation and Competition among Primitive Peoples*, New York, McGraw-Hill.
Menger, Karl (1892), 'On the Origin of Money', *Economic Journal*, 2, pp. 239–477.
Oliver, D. L. (1955), *A Solomon Island Society*, Cambridge, Mass., Harvard University Press.
Pospisil, L. (1963), *Kapauku Papuan Economy*, Yale University Publications in Anthropology, 67.
Rapport Economique (1924), Régistre Ethnographique, Bosongo District.
Salim, S. M. (1962), *Marshdwellers of the Euphrates Delta*, London, Athlone Press.
Thurnwald, R. (1934–5), 'Pigs and Currency in Buin', *Oceania*, 5, pp. 119–41.
Vansina, J. (1964), *Le Royaume Kuba*, Musée Royale de l'Afrique Centrale, *Anales, Sciences Humaines*, 49.
Wolf, E. R. (1955), 'Types of Latin American Peasantry: A Preliminary Discussion', *American Anthropologist*, 57, pp. 452–71.
Yamey, B. S. (1964), 'The Study of Peasant Economic Systems: Some Concluding Comments and Questions', in Firth and Yamey (1964) pp. 376–86.

4 Food as a system of communication

Food studied as a system of communication*

In 1971, attending the International Biology Panel of the Royal Society, its sub-committee on Nutrition, I became aware of the gap between social concern and sociological information on the subject of nutrition. On the one hand, the Royal Society's committees and panels have been well served by biologists and medical researchers. A great deal of information about the physiology of nutrition has been amassed in response to the world-wide concern in the subject. But by contrast, when it comes to understanding the social factors affecting presentation and acceptability of new food, practically no work has been done and certainly no general principles are established. The scientific members of the International Biology Panel were ready to agree that the very broad and often irrelevant categories in which sociological information is collected caused the results to be of very little use to them in interpreting surveys. The idea that each culture and often each sub-culture has its own criteria of palatability and its own rules of permitted combinations is certainly accepted. But how to discover these criteria and rules and how to draw general principles for guiding foreign nutritionists or for forming a policy about new foods, this important part of nutritional science is barely in its infancy. I was much encouraged by the readiness of the biologists to recognize that food always has a social dimension of the utmost importance and therefore I prepared to put in hand at the first opportunity research which would open this neglected area. A grant from the Department of Health and Social Security to study food as a system of communication enabled a start to be made.

* Report to the Department of Health and Social Security, November 1973.

Methodological problems

Research into the social aspects of diet is normally hampered by three procedural pitfalls. One is failure to disengage the physiological aspects of nutrition from the social – subjects are asked about their judgments as to the suitability of different foods for various ceremonial and other occasions, but in the same survey they are likely to be asked their views about the nutritional value of the foods, consequently their answers to the first kind of questions are ready cued by the nutritional concerns of the investigator. Second, the economic aspects of nutrition are not disengaged from judgments about social and nutritional concerns. Certainly both physical needs and economic constraints are deeply relevant to a housewife's choice of food. But since no theoretical principles as yet exist to guide us in distinguishing one from the other, the result is only too often a mish-mash which reflects the investigator's prejudices rather than revealing the principles upon which the social requirements of a family combine with their physiological and economic needs. The third pitfall is the questionnaire method itself. However much care is taken to disguise the investigator's viewpoint, food is a subject so sensitive to social manipulation that inevitably the answers to a questionnaire on food are suspect. Market researchers are fully aware of this difficulty and have evolved techniques for counteracting or discounting the misleading effects. But the questionnaire has to be structured in advance and it cannot but reflect the structure of thought which the investigators carry to their problem. The chance of new insights is thus whittled down. The solution of avoiding the question-naire on food attitudes and actually joining in the meals of the subjects for a day or two has been tried by canny nutritionists who report it a failure since their presence has obviously distorted the pattern of food presented in the home. There seems to be no satisfactory solution to these difficulties. The procedure we adopted in this research is itself open to the same objections, but less so, we hope, in each important respect.

We met the first and second difficulty by disregarding those aspects of nutrition (physiological and economic) which have already been much studied. Our research was explicitly concerned with the social uses to which food is put. As far as economic variables are concerned, we aimed to stay as far as possible with subjects whose economic circumstances were similar: industrial working-class factory labour, families with children. As far as the physiological aspects are concerned, since this side of nutrition has been so thoroughly investigated, we did not presume to be able to offer anything on the subject. We set ourselves the modest project of developing a method by which the sociological dimension of food could be understood. If we have been successful, the method will enable future nutrition surveys in, say, Ethiopia or Pakistani or Cypriot communities in England to work out a foreign dietary system, locate those parts in which cheap reinforced food substitutes will be acceptable and those in which the population can be expected to spend more on better quality foods. This limited target enabled us to deal with the third pitfall more boldly. Instead of a worked-out survey, asking the public about their attitudes to food and about the contents of their most recent meal, we eschewed all interpretive and other questions completely. The researcher found four families in which he was accepted as a lodger and he stayed in them for varying periods (the shortest was one month), watching every mouthful and sharing whenever possible. Finding the families and gaining admission to them was the hardest part of the research. Establishing a role of student-lodger engaged on a history of British food was surprisingly less difficult. The rule of not asking questions was taxing at first, but since every time that it was breached in the smallest way the menu immediately showed a directly responsive change, the value of this rule was continually in our minds. Once the North London hostess was asked whether she liked frozen peas and next day they appeared on the table. One question about the relative merits of real cream and custard and next day real cream took the place of the latter. The period of stay was much longer than previously undertaken in nutritional research. We reckon that after ten days of such a discreet and incurious presence the most nervous and sensitive housewife, busy with her children, settles down to her routine menus, making special allowance for the lodger in ways that are perfectly obvious, a cooked breakfast, for instance. The second way in which this study tried to meet the problems of imported assumptions was by making our assumptions completely explicit to ourselves. Therefore what we imported to the research is clearly visible in the structure of our attention. We knew what we were looking for. In brief, we expected to find correlations between the structure of the food and that of the social relations between people who habitually ate the food together. We were looking for regularities that might appear between social and dietary behaviour. It is possible that the smallness of scope may have allowed us to imagine regularities which would have disappeared in a welter of new facts if the research had been more extensive or prolonged. To protect ourselves against this objection, each family study was followed by a street survey to control for idiosyncrasy. Our assumptions caused us to be specially interested in the capacity of food to mark social relations and to celebrate big and small occasions. Therefore we needed as big a gamut of celebration as could be achieved. It was an integral part of our method, required by these assumptions, that the researcher be present on feast days, Sundays, Bank holidays, Christmas, weddings and christenings whenever possible.

At this point it may be useful for nutritionists and others interested in diet to be introduced to some of the other assumptions which the anthropologist normally makes in analysing cultural regularities. Behaviour in respect to food is assumed not to be random. First, it is a prior assumption of cultural anthropology (and one that would underlie all sociological study) that human behaviour is patterned activity. Second, it is assumed that the tendency to fall into patterns is affected by economic and political concerns. Consequently, and thirdly, the patterns that are sufficiently stable to be identified in research are assumed to be adapted to an equally stable distribution of power in the social dimension. As the distribution of power changes so will the cultural patterns affected by it. When these assumptions which are almost too deep to be explicit in tribal studies are brought to the fore and applied to family life, they shed an unfamiliar light upon the family and its food. We assume easily enough that within given budgetary constraints and within widely agreed cultural standards of hygiene and nourishment it makes sense to speak of a family food system. That is, within these constraints, each family works out a regular pattern of food, mealtimes, children's food and drink, men's food and drink, women's, celebratory and ordinary food. To call it a food system implies that if one part varies, other linked variations can be expected. We find in discussion with nutritionists that this assumption is perfectly acceptable. But it raises questions about the relations of one family system to the rest of family life. There is no reason to suppose that the cut we make for analytic purposes between food and the rest of family behaviour is not arbitrary. Since the Department of Health has given much thought to dimensions of parenthood, it may be interesting to present this background to an anthropological study of the family food system. The assumption that there would be a correlation between the ordering of social relations and the organization of food marks the limit of our preconceptions. Beyond it, we were ready to find everything or nothing. We could have lit upon a family in which the husband, say, cooked a mound of potatoes once a week from which the others helped themselves at will, or upon a family which subsisted on weekdays on bread and biscuits taken individually but which sat down to a cooked meal at the weekend. They might have subsisted year in and year out on ice cream and kippers. No menu would have surprised us. But with an entirely monophagous and unstructured diet we would have been surprised to find a structured family life.

The family as a set of systems caring for the body

Food is here taken as the medium through which a system of relationships within the family is expressed. Food is both a social matter and part of the provision for care of the body. Instead of isolating the food system, it is instructive to consider it frankly as one of a number of family body systems.

1 The system of rest. This includes access to beds and seats and privacy. It is only too easily assumed that only the conjugal bed is to be shared. However, in any family with children there are conventions about whose bed the child who cannot sleep or has nightmares can go to for comfort in the night. Sometimes it is to one or other of the parents, sometimes to an elder or younger sibling, sometimes to the grandmother and sometimes to the nanny, if she is there. There are questions which also get settled about precedence and priorities between members of the family as regards respecting each other's rights to sleep. Whose post-prandial rest must be respected by tip-toe and whispers? Whose early bed similarly needs to be respected by hush in the rest of the house? The same allocation of the best seating spaces near or far from the window, the door, the television, etc. arise as a result of exercise of authority or simply by bargaining or force. These allocations are settled through a process of indirect bargaining and direct appeals to standards of physical needs: 'Babies need sleep' or 'The bread-winner needs rest.'

2 Care of the body. This would include washing, excreting, care over birth, sickness and death. With the increase of organization of the medical profession, birth, death and sickness tend more and more to be taken out of the family and into the hands of professionals in specialized institutions. However, the extent to which this tendency is followed within any particular family varies. In the cases in which sickness is treated within the family, the question of who is involved in the care of the sick and who is let off is also subject to variation. In some families every single member of the family, not necessarily those living under the

same roof, will be involved in a rota, in other families it would all fall upon one person. This may be the youngest unmarried daughter, it may be the mother or the father. As to the rules about regular bodily care, crises apart, there are questions of access to the taps and lavatories for washing and urinating. Who has priority, who has to queue, and in what order, how often individual preferences are respected and so disturb the pattern of priorities; how much do the categories of sex and age, parental and child roles get expressed in terms of these rules, these priorities are also settled by indirect bargaining between the members of the family. An evolving system of body care is provided within the family, and at the same time it expresses the relationships within the family.

3 Clothing. Here there are, again, conventions within the family which affect budgeting priorities as well as access to furniture of the home or control over time. Who has the most frequent changes of clothes and greatest variety of clothes? What kind of washing standards and ironing standards, etc. are applied for each member's requirements? Borrowing and sharing conventions vary from family to family, so that each family has a clothing system.

4 Family food systems. This is the object of our study. Important questions here will arise with the possibility of the family food system coming into conflict with the other systems outlined above. The distinctive character of the food system is that it is in the control of one person only, the mother. The other systems are the result of bargaining in different ways. How the mother exercises her control to support or counteract the pattern of privileges produced in the other systems will be particularly interesting for the individual's attitude to food. To this we shall return below (p. 101), but first it is better to consider the relation of the food system in the family to the wider cultural background.

The relation of the family to the British food system

Information about food is continually pressed upon the family by the media, advertising and friends. The family food system does not exist in a cultural vacuum. Theoretically, this would seem to pose a major problem for our research if it were held to be necessary to distinguish the family or street as a sub-culture from the main culture of which it is a part. But fortunately there is no need in this particular project to make any such distinction. The project is not concerned with discovering the food system of a hypothetical population that might be called the industrial working class. It is concerned with formulating a method of discovering food systems. At the outset we did not expect to find necessarily any great common ground between the dietary systems of our different families. On the contrary, wide variation between them would have been welcomed for the better scope it would afford to an exercise in method. It was a surprise to find that the variation between families was less obvious than the common pattern they followed. Our report has perforce ended by presenting the common pattern because this provides a sufficiently crude categorization for developing a method. Once the broad outlines of what is held in common are discerned, it would be feasible to elucidate each variant sub-system, but that is not necessary for our present purposes.

A caveat is recorded here against a possible interpretation of our results. The pattern of food-taking we describe is made to appear static from the very method of analysis and presentation. But we are well aware that we have seemed to hold still for inspection a process in flux. As Professor Aylward has well said:

> In looking for the reasons for the changes in Britain, it is easy to suggest points such as marketing techniques and television advertising but the underlying reasons are to be found in social and economic factors, some of which have promoted changes in food habits over the centuries and which have become of even greater importance over the years. ('Synthesis, preparation and presentation of food', *Chemistry and Industry in the 1990's*, SCI, 1970, p. 75)

He goes on to tabulate social and economic reasons such as changes in the technology of communications, demography, economy, patterns of employment, size of domestic unit and growth of the catering industry.

What is striking to the anthropologist, newcomer to this field of inquiry, is that enormous changes have taken place in society at large in the last fifty years, a period which includes a modern world war and great technical developments in every field. One would expect food habits to have changed commensurately. But the literature of dietary inquiry and market research emphasizes the very opposite. It seems to be taken as axiomatic that the Britich public is conservative in its food habits. The same seems to be true of any dietary system that we care to name. Those who would promote a new food are conscious of strongly entrenched attitudes. To read the reports one gets the impression that when everything else changes, food systems are stable. However open-minded a population may, after the event, prove to have been in its readiness to adopt new crops, clothes, transport, in matters of food it is said to be likely to display a die-hard conservatism (Elliston, Allen D., *British Tastes*, London, Hutchinson, 1968). If this is true, then food is a part of culture which is well-chosen for the study of stabilizing factors. But we would question whether the alleged conservatism is not an optical illusion caused by a twofold focus upon continuity. On the one hand, the eye of the investigator lights upon any continuity which enables him to perceive a steady pattern in the flux of material he is studying. Thus it is reassuring to find that the British traveller in nineteenth century Paris was disdaining foreign cookery and calling for plain fish and potatoes (Jean-Paul Aron, *Le Mangeur du Dix-neuvième Siècle*, 1973, p. 59). On the other hand, the housewife who is composing a meal and her family who will be sitting in gastronomic judgment upon it are themselves conscious of the need for past models to guide them as to just what it is they are supposed to be serving or receiving. Parts of the meal may in fact reflect new economies or daring experiment on her part, but usually the meal has to be recognizably a meal of a certain known kind. The variations take place within a known matrix. Within that framework there may be minor changes, but everything conspires to imply that at least the frame is steady. Impossible to start a meal in the British food system with Hungarian cold pink cherry soup. Pastel colours and sweet liquids and fruits are ending gambits in this system not starters. Unthinkable in the British food system to start with a potato, go on to another potato and end with another 'for sheer greed' like the supper of the Curé d'Ars. Variation and sequence are required but both are under the governance of some kind of restrictive patterning. To find a way of identifying that patterning was our task.

Van Gennep described the patterning that governs initiation rites by noting that rites fall into three parts, a beginning, a middle and an end: the symbolism of the beginning is counterpoised to that of the end: the middle is an intermediate state in which the initiates who have first been separated from society and who will eventually be reintegrated into it live for a little while in a society of their own (*Les Rites de Passage*). A travesty of what Van Gennep said, this is also a tempting travesty of the structure of a meal which is by native informants described as 'dinner', prefaced by optional 'starters' and concluded with 'afters'. It could be that experimentation is permissible with the 'starters' and 'afters' so long as the dinner is recognizable; it could be that a three-fold structure of beginning, middle and ending is enough to give the impression of a repeat performance even though very different items may be inserted into the slots. We found that a much more precisely formulated structure still allows of variation.

Procedures

To elicit the rules of patterning we tried two techniques. One was frankly copied from the linguists and quickly abandoned because it proved too delicate in its necessary discriminations, too cumbersome in its yield of rules, and too weak in predictive power, and too dependent on the verbal and packaging criteria of items. A supplementary part of the research which was tried in the first year was a questionnaire to twenty anthropologists who were asked to record the food habits of populations they had studied. Their replies were useful in clarifying our ideas about how staples are used in meals. Since many different meanings are attached to this term, it was necessary to choose a usage. Staple in this report is taken to mean something more than the basic element of diet. Here it is related to the defining characteristics of two grand classes of meal, potato events versus bread and cake events. The dietary system under study is based upon two staples, potato and cereal. In this respect it is distinguished from upper- and middle-class English diet which tends to make use of a wide range of cereals, beans, pulses, roots as accompaniments to fish, eggs and meat of which the variety is such that it cannot be said that it is based upon one or two staples. Heavy dependence on staples diminishes with increased relative income. The same appeared to be the case of the Chinese food systems reported to us by Dr Barbara Ward. Similarly the hunting and gathering Hadza of Tanzania reported by Dr J. Woodburn could not be said to have a staple element in their diet of meat, roots and berries.

The most successful technique was to fasten attention upon sculptural and sensory qualities of the food and to compare its arrangement in the following dimensions which seemed regularly used and valued: savoury/sweet, hot/cold, liquid/dry. Under this grosser classification, the food served on the table was able to be correlated with the kinds of regular social events which marked a meal.

The researcher, Michael Nicod, introduced and defined for his purposes certain terms: food event, structured event, snack, meal. A food event is an occasion when food is taken, without prejudice as to whether it constitutes a meal or not. A structured event is a social occasion which is organized according to rules prescribing time, place and sequence of actions. If food is taken as part of a structured event, then we have a meal. The latter is distinguished from the snack according to the following definition: A snack is an unstructured food event in which one or more self-contained food items may be served. The event is unstructured in so far as there are no rules to prescribe which items should appear together and there is no strict order of sequence when more than one item appears. Snacks may be sweet or savoury, separable from but capable of accompanying a drink. The meal, by contrast, has no self-contained food items and is strongly rule-bound as to permitted combinations and sequences. Together with the distinction between special and common food events, these terms constitute the tools of the analysis whereby the structuring of social relations was found to be related to the structuring of the food. Simple Venn diagrams were used to record which members of the family and which categories of visitors were present for each kind of meal.

The structure of food

The food system that we discovered poses problems of notation. The full report describes the daily common menus and the special menus of each of the families and summarizes the response to the street questionnaires. When it comes to abstracting from the full report a set of rules we are conscious of creating our own conventions and anxious not to reify what are in fact no more than practical devices.

Between the week and the weekend different kinds of meals are taken regularly at different times of the day. Ignoring the names for the meals, and concentrating only on what is served, there are three kinds of meals: the major hot meal, at roughly 6 p.m. on weekdays and early afternoon at weekends; the minor meal usually follows this, at 9 p.m. on weekdays and about 5 at weekends; a still less significant meal, a tertiary food event consisting of a sweet biscuit and a hot drink, is available in the system to be used at different times, say at 4 on return from the factory on weekdays, at bed-time at weekends. Breakfast does not enter into the system as a meal. If asked, our subjects said they never had breakfast, just a cup of tea, just a piece of toast, etc. But this research has so much eschewed the evidence of question and answer that it has to rest upon observations and its own definitions. Breakfast stands as a snack according to our definition of the word. The three-meal system is broken by a major division between potato and cereal. The important

family meal is centred upon hot potatoes and their accompaniments.
This is more plentiful and more ceremonious than the other meals. The
minor meal starts with bread and may go on to cake and biscuits
accompanied by tea. The tertiary meal consists of biscuits and tea or
coffee.

The structure of the meal system starts to emerge with criteria of
ranking: A is the main meal, B the second meal and C the third meal on
the criteria of complexity, copiousness and ceremoniousness. The latter
is expressed by plate-changes and extra utensils, spoons, forks as well as
knives. Inversely correlated with rank is the progressive segregation of
liquids from solids as the meals become less important. On weekdays
this clear ranking in order of importance does not govern the times of
serving. At first sight the sequence of meals is a matter of convenience.
On an ordinary weekday when the family assemble after work, they sit
down to meal C at 4.30 p.m., have their main meal soon after 6 p.m. and
meal B at 9 or 10 p.m. On a Sunday, however, a match between the time
sequence and the rank order is to be seen. Table 4.1 shows that the
pattern has to be observed at least across the week and does not appear
in any weekday sequence in its full significance, still less in any single
meal.

TABLE 4.1

Week	12.30 p.m.	4.30 p.m.	6.30 p.m.	9.30 p.m.
	B	C	A	B
Weekend	1–2 p.m.		5–6 p.m.	9.30 p.m.
	A		B	C

TABLE 4.2   First correspondence
Temporal order corresponds to meal rank order on Sunday

1st	2nd	3rd	Sunday time order
A	B	C	meal rank order

In one of the four families the father came home for his midday meal, but
whether he did or not it is interesting to see that the family crams the
whole of the Sunday meal system into the last part of its day, after return
from work. In some parts of England it is being reported that the

working-class family which enjoys a hot potato meal at the canteen is less and less inclined to cook one again for itself in the evening. This just happened not to be the case in our four families. The weekday meals repeat the Sunday sequence in a modified timetable. A close correspondence between the structure of the Sunday dinner and that of the weekday main meal 'A' is very evident. Take the main course, which is generally called the dinner. It always consists of a serving of potato, a 'centrepiece' which on Sundays is always meat, 'trimmings' (which word designates one or two green vegetables) and a sousing in rich brown thickened gravy (here called 'liquid dressing'). The difference between this course in a special meal (say Sunday or Christmas Day) compared with a common meal (say a weekday evening) is that the number of trimmings are increased. So the rules of combination are the same: one staple, one centrepiece, one liquid dressing, one trimming in all cases; the special meal may have more than one dressing and more than one trimming. Architecturally speaking, it is as if the difference between the doorway of a humble home and that of a grand mansion when it consists always of two uprights and a cross-beam is entirely in the decoration on the main structure. The first course is the main course and it is always hot and savoury. The rules of sequence require this. When the second course is examined we find a repetition of the rules of combination for course one, except that everything is sweet. There is more freedom to serve one element and omit another from the three prototypes of Christmas pudding, trifle and fruit tart. The puddings vary very freely upon the theme of cereal, fruit and cream: on the one hand the fruit may be diminished to a thin layer of jam or a streak of colour in the jelly of a trifle which consists mostly of juice-soaked cake and custard and it may disappear completely in a rice pudding, on the other hand the fruit may dominate over everything else as in the fruit pie, or the cereal may be omitted as in tinned fruit and custard. Whether the cereal be omitted on a weekday second course or not, the Christmas Day pattern is staple, centre (fruit) and two dressings (brandy and cream) and in the case of a common meal the most simplified formula is centrepiece and dressing. The liquid dressing, the custard or cream, is poured over the plate in the same way as the liquid dressing, gravy, is used in the first course. When this course is nearly finished preparations are made for the third part of the meal, the hot drink and biscuits. Hitherto only cold water has been drunk with the food. The variations of liquid and solid are carried out upon the plate of food. Now, in the third course, a total segregation of liquids from solids appears: in the cup is the hot brown drink, on the plate the cold dry solid, a reversal of the hot-cold pattern of the first course, when the cold drink is in the glass and the hot food upon the plate.

TABLE 4.3   Meal A. Second correspondence
Course two repeats structure of course one in different materials

	Mode	Structure	Elements
Course 1	hot	staple	potato
	savoury	centre	meat, fish, egg
		trimming	green vegetable, stuffing, Yorkshire pudding
		dressing	thick brown gravy
Course 2	hot or cold	staple	cereal
	sweet	centre	fruit
		dressing	liquid custard or cream

The rules for structuring course one are absolutely strict. There is no possibility of recognizing the event as a meal in the system unless its first course is constituted on these rules. Some elements can be duplicated, but none omitted. It is impossible to start with something sweet, say grapefruit. There is more scope for fantasy in the composition of course two. It is possible to serve a sweet cake with custard, doing homely weekday service for the trifle, or to serve a tin of fruit in its syrup, with cream, in the one case leaving out the fruit, in the other leaving out the cereal. This scope for fantasy in the pudding course allows a formal pattern to be imposed upon the elements before they are served on to individual plates, an option which is not necessarily taken up on weekdays. Another difference is that the second course is served from the table whereas the first course is always served straight from cooking vessels on to plates. Pattern-making is not at all required or even appropriate for the first course. A third difference is that the liquid dressing of the second course is thicker than that for the first. We find that these three differences between course one and course two themselves become reinforced in course three so that their effect is of themes which extend over all the courses.

TABLE 4.4   Meal A. Third set of correspondences shows overall pattern

1	2	3
savoury	sweet	sweet
potato staple	cereal staple	cereal staple
no discretion to omit elements	some discretion	solid optional
liquid dressing runny	liquid dressing thick	dressing solid
other sensory qualities of food dominate over visual pattern	visual pattern dominates until serving	visual pattern dominates until eating
solids not segregated from liquids		solids and liquids segregated

It is no surprise to the native Englishman that the distinction between hot and cold is much valued in this dietary system. For the third course the teapot is heated before the water is poured in, actually on the boil, the plates for the first course are kept stacked on the rack above the cooker so that they are carried to the table warm. Apart from bottled sauces, no addition of cold foods to a hot plate is permitted, nor vice versa.

TABLE 4.5   Fourth correspondence. Meal B repeats meal A in course sequence, but keeps to the staple of course two

Meal B	course 1	savoury, hot or cold	staple	bread
			centre	meat, fish or egg or baked beans
			trimmings	optional
	course 2	sweet, cold	staple	bread
			centre	jam
			trimmings	butter
	course 3	hot sweet drink	optional cake for Sundays or biscuits	

Looking again at Table 4.3 we can see that the three courses of the main meal, in their due sequence and rules of combination present the same structure as do the three meals of Sunday. This becomes clearer when we consider the rules governing meal B.

The rules which govern the main meal acquire more significance when we find them governing the second meal and even more when certain of them carry through systematically over the two meals. The regularity of the pattern is so strong that it can be made to bear some weight of explanation. For example, before seeing the structure laid out, one could have asked reasonably why they never serve potatoes in meal B. The answer now would be that potatoes are the staple for meal A course 1. That part of the pattern would lose its distinctiveness and the pattern would lose its shape if potatoes were served in course 2 or meal B.

TABLE 4.6   Fifth correspondence. Rules controlling relation of meal A and meal B

Between meal A and meal B through courses 1, 2, 3, the following
rules hold: (a) increasing segregation of liquids
             (b) increasing dominance of visual pattern
             (c) decreasing scale of quantity
             (d) non-reversibility: (i) of staple order
                                     (ii) of savoury/sweet order
                                     (iii) of desiccation order
                                     (iv) of scale order

On to the three courses of the main meal are mapped the sequence, ranking and rules of the three meals of Sunday. First the potato meal, second the main cereal meal, third the last cereal, sweet and dry. Scanning the diagrams in the report we see that the last course of the first two meals and the only solid of the third meal is exactly the same item except that it is progressively drier. The lavish liquid dressing of sweet custard has been poured over a cake, whether plum cake or jam sponge, and dried in the form of icing sugar. The option to select any of the possible ingredients of a second course in the main meal is given even more latitude in the minor meal, but working through the menus, week by week and month by month the prototype puddings and custard in the second course of the main meal are recognizable in the minor meal in their dry forms as plum cake and jam sponge cake. When it comes to the final course of the main meal or the last meal on Sunday night, the range of sweet biscuits reveals the pudding again, in its most desiccated forms: currant biscuits, sugar-coated biscuits, jam-centred biscuits. Nowhere else in the world is there a steady demand for small geometrically shaped sweet biscuits with a layer of jam or cream in the middle and coated with icing, at a sufficiently modest price to permit them a regular place in the daily menu. In so far as the sweet biscuit eaten last thing at night on Sunday is a dry version of the cake, and the cake a dry version of the pudding, we can regard it not merely as a coda, nor as an irrelevant conclusion, but as a summary form, literally, of those courses. The biscuit is capable of standing for all the sequences of puddings through the year and of wedding cakes and christening cakes through the life-cycle. Our analysis is beginning to reveal in the dietary system, with undeniable economy of means, the mimetic and rhythmic qualities of other symbolic systems. The capacity to recall the whole by the structure of the parts is a well-known technique in music and poetry for arousing attention and sustaining interest.

The same recurring theme is visible in the sequence from thick gravy to thicker custard to solid icing sugar. One of the structural rules of this food system is progressive desiccation and geometrification of forms through the day. The first course of the main meal is presented in what appears to the uninitiated as a slushy indistinguishable mixture in which it is difficult to distinguish the trimmings and solid dressings from the meat and potatoes under their lavish coat of rich brown gravy. The second course, though still wet and viscous, has an undeniable sculptural form, whether it be the sphere of the Christmas pudding, or the trifle decorated with fruit.

We can summarize the rules transforming the elements of the sweet part of any meal, through the sequence of meals (Table 4.7).

TABLE 4.7   Course three under transformation

	Course 1	Course 2	Course 3
meal A	wet	wet	dry
meal B	less wet	less wet	dry
meal C			dry

This progressive desiccation allows of the shift from forks and spoons to fingers.

TABLE 4.8   The biscuit as a condensed symbol

	meal A	meal B	meal C
			biscuit
Course 3	pudding	cake	
			wedding cake

The movement from wet food to dry food through the day involves a shift in utensils; fingers can take up dry food, but forks and spoons lift wet food to the mouth. The axis between wet and dry, used in this way allows of a correspondence between intimacy and distance, thus linking this aspect of the food system to a dimension of the social system. The main course of the Sunday dinner is for the intimacy of the family circle. When this circle is greatly enlarged, as for the weddings, New Year party, twenty-first birthday or christening celebrations that Michael Nicod attended, dry foods are suitable. Thus the third course and the third meal have a further dimension of usefulness in summarizing hospitality when the intimate mode is not appropriate or possible.

Symbolic systems

The above may seem trivial to anyone who is not interested in problems of identity and analogy. In the very simplicity and economy of the working-class dietary system we are able to see at work universal principles of recognition and stable structuring. If we are able to answer the question, 'what is it that makes a meal a meal?' we are also hoping to contribute to the wider philosophic question of what makes anything a member of a given class? What is the basis of synonymy?[1] The answer is that the housewife can serve a meal that will be acceptable to her family so long as she works within certain restrictive patternings of sequence and combination. Novelties introduced within the pattern present no problem to the entrenched conservatism of the consumer. The pattern is not something which can be discerned in any one meal or in a day or weekend. The most basic rule is that each significant unit in which food is served must be complex enough to show in its structure the pattern of all meals. In spite of, or rather because of, their strict simplicity of resources, the sequence of meals forms a single recognizable system. We have written as if each part recalls the whole. But it is as true to see the whole as structured upon the parts. This lays bare the basis of conservatism in taste and explains its exclusion of novel units from its structure. The section in the report on snacks is particularly interesting. Michael Nicod divides the sweet common snack (chocolates) from the special snack, a savoury item, bread with a small slice of ham and a pickle on top. The special snack is a self-contained item, able to be served alone. But it is generally used for celebratory events. Common snacks are devised for solitary eating. No one goes off and eats a cocktail canape alone. We suggest that its capacity to do service at grand occasions derives in part from its metonymic reference to the whole meal system.

The principle that the whole is to be found in the part also explains the attachment of the British housewife to the round of beef, that ever-dwindling portion of meat which the British butcher knows how to prepare for roasting on Sundays. Whether it is chicken, leg of lamb, turkey or round of beef, the culinary treatment is the same: oven roast, and the hot, crackling, round morsel that comes out of the oven as a single whole for carving looks much the same, whichever cut or animal is used. The principle is that at this high point of the week's menu, Sunday dinner, the meat is produced as one unitary piece which is not to be cut into until the meal is assembled; stew is impossible on Sundays.

Social categories defined by food

Food preferences seemed to be important as the basis of transactions within the family. In order to understand the very delicate transactions which we discovered were taking place between members of the family in terms of food preferences and concessions of likes and dislikes on the menu we found it useful to introduce a distinction between the family food system and national food systems which appear now in restaurants. The working-class food system has its weekly menu closely anchored to the idiosyncratic likes and dislikes which are the subject of transactions between members. Thus the menu itself has strong relationships with the social structure of the family. By contrast, the menu in a restaurant or the menus suggested in magazines or in cookery books describing classical French or haute bourgeoise cuisine are menus which have to be by definition independent of such local social structuring and its pressures, though they are orientated to the standardized demands of their own clientele. It is tempting to make the comparison between food as a medium of communication and speech, on the basis of the distinction between restricted and elaborated codes being used in the Institute of Education Sociological Research Unit. Some food systems are independent of the local social structure and the variations in the menu can only be explained, and can fully be explained, by reference to the food system itself and its budget. For example, in such a system the reason for one dish's appearing in the weekly menu would partly be that it had not appeared so far in the slots in which it was available as a choice, while a good reason for not producing it on a given day would be that it had appeared on the menu the day before or the meal before. All the working-class family food systems, and we would hope all family food systems, are to be compared to the restricted speech code. The possible patterns by which food preferences are introduced into the structuring of the menu are as follows:

(a) the mother decides without reference to any individual preferences (no case was recorded).

(b) The mother decides but takes a negative account of individual dislikes only, ruling them out of the menu. In this case, some individual favourite foods are bound never to appear.

(c) A strong feedback from individuals to the mother forces her to include the favourite foods of each or of some and to compensate others by alternative dishes.

(d) The same as (c) above, except that bargaining between members and mother achieves a sequence of favourite and non-favourite foods in which each has a regular turn, creating a set of deferences to each other's preferences and incorporating a regular structure of individual preferences in the weekly menu.

For all these cases, the question is how the formal family hierarchy of father, mother and children, is expressed in the resulting menu. We noted that the mother is usually out of these transactions, her responsibility for variety, if this is valued, and quality, if this is valued, being rewarded explicitly by family consumption of what she has prepared, and punished by their rejection if she has not performed her part adequately. So the transactions are considered as taking place between other members of the family in relation to the mother. For example, the father can be privileged or he can be ignored, and either a grievance or an established precedence may result. The family food system must relate to the rest of the family social system as described above. This relation can be compared according to the degree of social differentiation expressed in the food system, and according to the harmony or disharmony between social differentiation given in the food system and that given in the rest of the social system.

Much social differentiation in the food system

	B	+	C
Harmony with the rest of the social system	**B** Food as a symbolic system expressing and exacerbating conflict in the family arising in the other body-care systems		**C** Treatment of food provides a richly textured symbolic system supporting developing family relations In other body-care systems
−			+
	A Food provides poorly textured symbolic system and one which is irrelevant or contrary to developing family relationships in other body-care systems		**D** Treatment of food provides poorly textured symbolic system but not conflicting with family relationships in other body-care systems

Little social differentiation in the food system

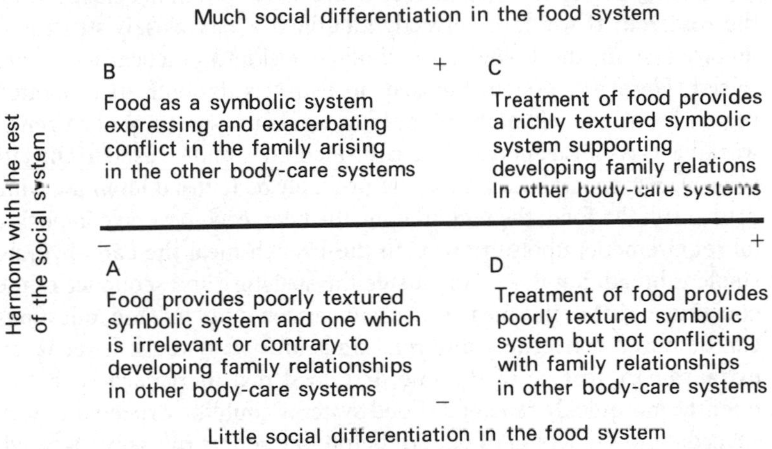

FIGURE 4.1

On the basis of this comparison we would predict:

1 That hospitalized children are always likely to be full of food fads when they first are admitted because of the missing dimension of social meaning in the food menu of a hospital, but that children from group D in Figure 4.1 are less likely, and children from group B are more likely to continue as food faddists.

2 Obese and obsessional feeders are likely to be drawn from groups B and A. The conflict between the family food system and the members' ideas about what the family social system should be ensures that meals are never satisfying events.

3 Old people from C and D are likely not to want to eat at all when they are alone.

4 Cultural minorities can never get used to food systems based on different social structural principles.

5 It might be more important for social workers to emphasize harmony of family systems than good food even from the strictly nutritional point of view.

Innovation

Michael Nicod's report describes the food system in detail. Here it is worth considering for nutritionists some of the problems arising from the research. If we have correctly identified a very closely structured dietary system, the following methodological and practical issues are raised. Here is a system focused on two cereals, both incorporated regularly into the rest of the food. How would the structure of a French working-class meal appear if the same method would be used to elicit it? Or a Danish meal? The first would probably be focused upon the wine drunk with the food, the second upon the beer, each beverage imposing its requirements upon the rest. In the French meal the carbohydrate staple is bread, but this stays outside the structure and sequence of the constituent dishes in a meal. Once comparison is put in hand, questions can be raised concerning different kinds of food systems. It seems an extraordinary feature of the one described that its pattern is so frequently and quickly repeated. Food systems could be expected to vary according to the length of pattern before the repeat rule is recognized. They would also be expected to vary according to the strength of the pattern, the tolerance or intolerance of unstructured elements, the prevalence of snacks, in our terms, over meals. We would risk hypotheses about the concomitant features of social relations in the family. For it would seem *prima facie* plausible that a very stable, tightly organized symbolic structure is only possible in a stable social system. Vice versa, correlated hypotheses can be tried for more open social structures and scope for successful innovation in food. Within a closely structured system there are less organized areas and here again, innovation would be easier than within the main structure.

Some examples may make this plain. The British system we have described, for obvious economic reasons in an industrial society, is organized upon carbohydrates whose entry into the menu and whose garnishing is strictly rule-bound. The system itself makes certain variations impossible. It would destroy the pattern to introduce whole raw fruit as a course. Fruit can only appear in the pattern within the pudding-cake-biscuit series as stewed fruit and custard or strawberries decorating a trifle or cut up bananas covered with custard or squashed into jam or jelly. For the middle-class dietician to appear on television and tell the great British public that its mothers can cope with rising prices by serving an apple per head instead of pudding is entirely unrealistic. There is no place for the ungarnished apple in this pattern.

For her to suggest Irish stew instead of the Sunday joint is likewise unrealistic. The system cannot be seen to replicate itself in small if such major dislocations of its pattern were regularly to intrude.

We have worked out two hypotheses for predicting kinds of innovation that are likely to be accepted within any dietary system that is as clearly structured as this one. Cheap labour-saving substitutes for or additions to a diet can be introduced in the unstructured parts of the system. Thus in the diet we have been studying, children's food, breakfast, women eating alone are points at which cereals and snacks are admitted. In these areas the diet has seen great changes in the last twenty years, but they are changes which have no effect on the dietary system as such. By contrast, the most highly structured area is the Sunday dinner and all dinners elaborating upon or modifying it. The main meal combines formality and intimacy: its range extends from Christmas Day to the weekday six o'clock evening meal. Innovations within this meal over a period of rising real income for the working class have been to up-grade the more modest forms to a closer copy of the best: more meat, better meat, less processed and more carcass meat, more trimmings vying with the staple potato in quantity and capacity to satisfy appetite, more varied vegetables, richer gravy, more dressings, mint jelly, red-currant jelly, apple sauce. We would suggest that in the most highly structured areas of the dietary system taste discrimination is most developed and standards of presentation strictest. This is why powdered potato never threatens the full place of the cooked potato in the working-class diet in spite of the heavy demands that the latter makes (in cleaning, peeling, cooking and pan-washing) upon the housewife's limited time.[2]

The new potato seems almost to be a symbol, a reminder of all the new and young things of summer. The very young potatoes were described as being like a new baby – 'just new'. They evoke very strong emotional response and are seen as being quite different in kind from the old, or everyday potatoes. . . . Dried potatoes: These were used by some women in winter when potatoes are bad, because they are economical. An advantage is that there is no wastage, but they are not thought to taste as good as fresh. Some claimed that their families could not tell the difference between dried and fresh although they credited themselves with better powers of discrimination. It was also seen mainly as a holiday or emergency substitute.

To sum up the implications for attempted innovation: in any dietary system the local food habit can be divided between highly structured and less structured food events. The food items which habitually enter into the former tend to be as closely bound together as if they were complementary foods. Potato and green vegetables may be complementary in the ordinary sense, since when one appears on the plate, the other will appear too as surely as mustard with beef. But over a longer series of meals meat and fish are also more of a complement than a substitute for one another since they occupy the same slots in the meal structure and the rule that calls for variation over the content of these slots implies also that the demand for any one of these items over the year will be the same as for any of the others in that slot. For commodities in the more structured parts of the food system, the elasticity of demand with respect to changes in income will be high, but as far as price changes are concerned, demand will be inelastic. The higher the income, the more discriminating the demand for more of better quality items. Taking potatoes, meat and gravy in our system under study as examples of related goods in a highly structured part of the food system, we have seen how quality counts and how there is little demand for innovations when they lower the price and save on work. This has been the fate of Cadbury's Smash in our four families. On the other hand, consider items from the less strictly structured part, cake and biscuits for instance. Discrimination is less strong here; so long as the items conform to the visual pattern which makes them capable of consistently completing the whole symbolic food system, there is a steady demand for them, very responsive to price changes. Finally, for the fresh fruits, apples, bananas, which have no place in the structured system and which enter the diet with chocolate and nuts as additional snacks useful to pack with the sandwich working midday meal, or as breakfast cereals given to the children, price elasticity will be high, and substitutes will be acceptable. To test these predictions is beyond the scope of the present study. The concepts of necessities, luxuries and inferior goods hitherto are identified in economics empirically by response to price changes and income changes. If the approach used in this study is valid, it will be eventually possible to give a cultural definition of the place of such broad groups of commodities in the social system in which they are used, and from that point, predict their demand elasticities.

Food as an art form*

Introduction

One of the differences between anthropology and sociology is that anthropologists have always been particularly interested in what they call material culture and in the point at which social interaction makes use of material things. Thus there has never been a period when anthropologists have not had a currently fashionable approach to the materials and art forms of the civilizations they study. The present one is structuralism. Having been so well established as a form of analysis by Lévi-Strauss and Roland Barthes and a multitude of others, structuralism is now being considerably widened and refined in order to take into account more fully the relation between art and society. What follows is a mere introduction to its hitherto untried possibilities for the interpretation of food as an art form.

Imagine a competent young anthropologist arriving on this planet from Mars and setting out to study the culture of the English natives. He would try to attend all their ceremonies. Sooner or later he would start being invited to weddings and there he would be perhaps baffled to make up his mind whether the central focus of the ceremony was the marriage or the cake. He would of course have read about Kava ceremonial in Tonga and tea ceremonial in Japan. Their complexity of ritual would pale into insignificance compared with the ceremonial surrounding the cutting and distribution of the wedding cake. At military weddings he would see the bride try to cut the cake with a sword, unable to succeed without the help of her spouse. He would see in photographs the bride standing near the cake about to cut it. He would observe the bride's mother in tears, the cake being parcelled into minute portions to be distributed around the room; a large section of the cake being distributed even more elaborately in small postal packets to be eaten by absent friends. Asking about the mythology of the cake, he would hear that those young maidens who receive a portion should sleep with it under their pillow and dream of their future husband, and also that the top portion of this towering three-tier confection should be put aside and kept for the christening ceremony of the first child, etc., etc.

* The substance of this paper was delivered as a lecture for the Royal Anthropological Institute, London, on 30 May 1974.

Taking an old-fashioned diffusionist approach, he could trace this cake through the history and geography of weddings in Europe. He would conclude that he had seen the apotheosis of the cake form, something as worthy of study as the American Indians' sun dance. He would have no difficulty in getting pictorial records of the cake for he would find that no bakery that produces wedding cakes is without its album of photographs of famous cakes that it has made. If he had Marxist leanings he might be worried to see the extraordinary uniformity of the wedding cake formula across the class structure. Although there will be many discernible differences in quality and price between one cake and another, for any guest standing at the other end of the room it is hard to see the difference; the wedding cake seems to be relatively classless – perhaps a symptom of the embourgeoisement of the European workers or perhaps the reverse process. When he had completed filling in the diffusionist and sociological background of the cake ceremony, the researcher would embark upon the structural analysis which I shall not describe in detail. Essentially this technique of study would require him never to consider the cake as a genre, still less the wedding cake alone apart from the food system in which it appears. The food system would be seen as a series of events using a defined medium combined according to clearly understood rules. He would have to set all the cake forms that he could record into the context of all other food forms habitually used by the people under study. This approach allows a very different set of questions to be posed, neither diffusionist nor sociological.

If food is to be considered as an art form it would be necessary first to choose questions which could be asked equally well of other art forms and then to identify an area of problems which are specific to the food medium. Having first distinguished what kind of art form food is amongst the others in that culture, it would then be right to ask how does the local food art compare with other food arts in other cultures.

It can be assumed that food is taken partly because it serves a biological function, nourishment. It shares its part-instrumental part-aesthetic place in the range of all art forms with clothing, architecture and utensil design. With these it belongs to the group of applied arts which is instantly distinguishable from the pure, or fine arts such as music, sculpture or visual arts. Therefore the questions which are suitable to address to the applied arts should also be addressed to food. In most of the applied arts there is a tension between the requirements of function and the requirements of design; one can find the utensil or building badly adapted to its function in the interests of design but one does not normally expect to find these things created with no intention of serving any function at all. However, this is not quite true of food. Curiously, there is no difficulty in thinking of examples of food that is produced entirely for display, so that food can be separated from its nourishing function and be associated with the decorative arts, flower arrangements and painting. This line of enquiry suggests that one might ask how much its adaptation to the biological function is deformed by its structuring into an art form. For example, there might be a direct correlation across cultures, the more developed the aesthetic the more the biological function may be subordinated and ill-served. This is one of the questions that we shall raise, but be unable to answer. Quite conceivably the correlation could go in the opposite sense: the more developed the aesthetic side, the better calculated to make the digestive juices flow and the better nutritional needs would tend to be served. I would like to know what systematic work has been done to resolve these issues which are obviously of supreme importance for the current concern with the feeding of our planet.

Obviously there is scope for argument in the identification of the aesthetic elements in food. My own preferred approach would be to take the aesthetic as distinct from the nutritional aspect of food to be that part which is subject to pattern-making rules, like the rules of poetry, music or dance. The explanation of any one such rule will only be found in its contribution to the pattern which it helps to create. Consequently rules which are explained with reference to pathogenic dangers such as indigestibility, bacterial transmission, toxic elements, etc., would be counted as rules concerned with nutrition and not with the aesthetic side. It is an arbitrary and difficult separation to maintain but essential for this kind of investigation. If it can be accepted that there is a field of behaviour which consists in making patterns which are in themselves the only justification of the elements which go into them, then this approach to the aesthetic aspects of food suggests various dimensions which can apply to food and the other applied arts.

The dimension of autonomy

One can ask whether the rules which govern the presentation of food are similar to those which prevail in the other applied arts in that culture. In other words, is food just treated as another medium in which the same patterns are worked out? For example, I once had the pleasure of attending the Dublin cattle show. There was a big tent with cake stalls and stalls for other handcrafts on sale. The latter included those thick creamy-looking Aran sweaters, with cable-pattern knitting and regularly spaced knots and twirls on a very bold and chunky scale. Turning to the crochet, embroideries and tea-cosies and hot water bottle covers I noticed that these too conformed in style to similar rules although carried out in a different material. Turning further to the cake stall, the Aran sweater cable-stitch was replaced in icing sugar and cream. A well-trained Martian ethnographer would have gone out to the churches and graveyards and found similar plaited twirls carved in Celtic style in the stone monuments of the region. But I forebore to pursue my research. The Irish cake is an apt illustration of common rules being shared between several media. It will serve to illustrate the range between complete autonomy and complete permeation between the different media. But it is a thoroughly bad example of structural analysis because it takes one item of food, the cream cake, one item of clothing, one tea-cosy and one hot water bottle cover. The arbitrary selection is inexcusable. It would be less arbitrary to compare food to a medium which had a sequential development over time, music or poetry, because food has an important temporal dimension. Even among the applied arts it is not the only one which develops its rules over the course of a day. Clothing also has a range from night to morning to afternoon to mid-day to evening, as well as seasonal rules. But food can develop its sequence and display its structure over time more quickly than can clothing. Like the fruit fly which is so useful in genetics because of the speed of its reproduction processes, food is very well adapted to this kind of analysis. This introduces another set of dimensions which can be proposed for comparison between applied arts.

The temporal dimension

Does the food system unfold the rules which make its patterns in a short or long time? How quickly does the pattern repeat itself? Is it more like a poem consisting entirely of rhymed couplets with a fixed metre? Or does it develop like a great epic poem, with galloping rhymed couplets when the narrative is jolly, blank verse when the theme deepens, and all the chapters symmetrically concluded with sonnets in the strict ab, ba form? Although food is capable of developing all its patterns in the course of a day (as we have seen from the example discussed above) it need not necessarily do so. Indeed the real sequence of patterning is only concluded at the end of the life-cycle when we have moved from the christening cake, to the wedding cake, to the funeral baked meats. This potentially great span makes it difficult to apply to food the kind of analysis which can be imported from linguistics. A verbal sentence which may take years to analyse but two minutes to speak is completely contrasted at the other end of the pole to the food sentence which might take a lifetime to complete. The food system of some working-class families that we studied in 1972 was very compact; the patterning of the rules was very strict and very quickly the pattern was repeated and repeated, the whole being represented in all the parts. But this does not necessarily hold for other food systems. A colleague described to me his experience of a French village in which domestic food is eaten without ceremony on a practically monophagous basis throughout the year, in great contrast with a communal village feast which is held annually. The villagers form a committee six months before the feast and three months before the committee is named the life of the village is entirely dominated by speculations as to who would be a good committee member. Once it is named, the work of choosing the menu and organizing the feast dominates village life until the feast itself is prepared and enjoyed. After this the next three months are taken up comparing the feast with previous feasts, criticizing and praising, until it is time to start thinking about the election of the next committee. Different in every way from the food system we are used to, by its apparent neglect of food in the domestic unit, this system is particularly interesting for its different phasing in the temporal dimension and opens up to us the possibilities of variation which we can expect to find once this kind of research is put in hand on a proper comparative basis.

The unities

Under this head I consider a number of questions which relate to the rigidity and the simplicity of the rules of the food system. How eclectic is it in regard to the range of materials it permits? Are there some parts which are very stable and others more experimental? This could be important for the nutritionist hoping to introduce new reinforced foods. How much is food of one kind always restricted to this or that particular setting? Take the example of the wedding cake – our researcher from Mars will be disappointed if he thinks he can find three-tiered cakes at

funerals or Sundays and birthdays. The wedding cake is highly specialized for one social function. But not all food systems will have such rigid
specialization of forms for restricted meanings. How much is the
preparation of food made visible? How much is it kept off-stage? What
are the rules for the processing being done in the home or outside the
home?

Sensory qualities

Any art form would have to be analysed according to its use of sensory
discrimination. The rules for presentation might take no account, or
little account, of whether the stuff is hard or soft or rough or smoothly
textured – or it might take a lot of account of these qualities. The same
goes for colour and smell. We might have here a criterion for deciding
whether the aesthetic aspects were dominating over the nutritional. For
example, would it be plausible that a food system which paid no attention
to colour and none to smell or texture left more scope for concern with
nutritional standards? Judging from the way the nutritionists write about
what is good food and bad food this would seem plausible, but on the
whole I fear it is a dubious conclusion. The subject is much more
complicated and needs to be divided up. For one thing, there is the
question of autonomy again. It seems possible that a food system could
use smell, colour and texture according to its own set of rules, which did
not correspond in any way with the rules for smell, colour and texture in
other media. Take colour, for example. There might be a restricted set
of colours, with fine gradations and permitted combinations, in sequence and simultaneously, a set distinctive of food colours and not
found in any other activity. If such a distinctive register for food colours
and textures were developed by a gastronomic community we could
compare it with the lexical register for balls and bats in distinctive sports.
Just as you cannot talk of a tennis bat or a polo bat you would find no
colour combinations on your plate which could possibly appear in any
other context. This, I suggest, is a case of complete autonomy of the food
system for establishing its own sensory range. It would be surely likely to
go with very elaborate aesthetic rules governing permitted combinations
and sequences. At the other end of the spectrum, food might never look
or smell like food but always be disguised to look like candles or smell
like flowers or given an impression of wild animals lurking in green
forests or about to eat fruit; cakes might be carved to look like toy trains

or soldiers, ice-cream to look like lilies, puddings like fairy-tale cottages. I just don't know whether the seeping into celebratory food of themes and imitations from the rest of the culture should be taken to indicate a strongly developed food system or not. I suspect not. Experiments would be quite possible to see whether the more autonomous food system controlling its own sensory register is more open or more closed to experiment; I suspect that it would be more closed. Its autonomous register of food colours, food smells and food textures could only have become specialized as part of an effort towards creating a specially discriminated kind of 'good food'. The gastronomic community eating in this system would surely have finely developed palates for discriminating food sensations. The appearance of a half-banana stuck into a pineapple ring, simulating a candle, with a crystallized cherry on top for a flame, or a grapefruit with a cocktail stick and rice-paper sails looking like a boat, or even the yule-log chocolate cake with the marzipan robin perched on it would never be treated as serious food. It would be very difficult technically to research the register of food colours and textures just because no colour could be seen without being incorporated into a textured substance which affects the refraction of light. Texture alone would not present such difficulties: one could identify smooth, crumbly, straight-grained, fibrous, etc. But smells would present even more difficulty for testing. Here again, the question of the autonomy of the art form raises itself.

Social standards

In other parts of social life there is a common convention that rough texture is appropriate for more homely occasions, smoother for formality. I have heard hostesses apologize for not having sieved the spinach or the apple sauce, as if the smooth, silky flow of the food should match the smooth, silky clothes of formal dress. Perhaps texture of food is specially apt to feel pressures from the social system to express formality. If so, we have here another possible dimension of comparison between food systems, or between different parts of the same food system. It occurs to me that here is another matter capable of being systematically tested. I put forward the hypothesis that the pressure of the social system upon the food system will always tend to destroy the autonomy of the latter and when a social system is undergoing rapid social change, whilst harnessing the food system to its purposes, the possibility of developing an autonomous register of food sensations will be diminished. This has the reactionary implication that social stability is favourable to the development of food as an art form and social change inimical to it. Perhaps those countries which used to cast a stone at British culinary standards permitted a lower rate of social mobility. The recent raising of gastronomic standards in our own country could be less due to the new possibilities of travel than to the stagnation of our social system over the last twenty years – these are only suggestions that occur to me while following this line of thought. Michael Nicod's research on food habits in certain English families revealed a compact and highly organized set of rules. His focus on selected aspects of the food system seen as a system of rules making a formal pattern enables us to explain some characteristics of the nutritional part of the food system which otherwise remain mysterious. Nutritionists tend to deplore the preference of some parts of English society for carbohydrate and highly processed foods instead of more nutritious raw fruits and vegetables, but there is no explanation to my knowledge of how this kind of preference arises. In the food system in question there is obviously no place for raw fruit. Any housewife who puts money aside for buying raw fruit will still have to spend again on the main structure part of the food system. Fruit can only come into the system as a snack. She would be condemned by her family on all the criteria they use for judging what is a meal and what is a good meal if she were to try to serve them with raw fruit instead of pudding. Of course there is an important economic factor here. Carbohydrates and sugars are cheaper than meat and fruit. But what is interesting is the large amount of work the housewife is prepared to do herself in order to peel, cook and serve and wash up after her daily potato meal.

The combination of the food system as it has developed autonomously and the economic factors explains the extraordinary phenomenon of the British cheap biscuit. Here is an example of a national preference, the kind of taste-formation which the economists are only too glad to leave aside as not susceptible of economic analysis. The British like to have cheap biscuits and they do not mind whether they all taste much the same so long as they are very varied in their shapes and sizes, colours and geometrical decoration. The same designs of biscuits are found in other European nations but they are generally expensive and of good quality materials, with considerable difference between one biscuit and another as to its taste. The explanation that is offered here of the British demand for cheap biscuits is that the biscuit is a condensed symbol of all the food events and the social events of a day and a week and a lifetime. It has to be cheap because it has to be used so often to make the regular summation of the symbolic system which in the case of the food patterning that we have described occurs very frequently. It has to be cheap because it is an integral part of the working-class food system. From the perspective of this system the wedding cake can be presented plausibly as the most formal pile of biscuits offered in the course of a lifetime. As the ordinary biscuit sums up the daily and the weekly food system, so does the wedding cake sum up the high moment in the life-cycle. It is a sweet cereal confection on which a white liquid dressing has been poured, but the dressing has set into the hardest, shiniest and most improbably patterned crust. The icing of the wedding cake is able to express what it does because it is at the pinnacle of a very rigorously formalized set of rules which segregate liquid from solid with complete consistency right through all the constituent food occasions.

The Food Art Exhibition*

The teasing thing here is that food has come away from its context of the shared meal and stands in the context of the art gallery, as stuff to be set beside notable sculpture and painting. Separated from its normal context and away from the dietician's concern with ingestion, nourishment and excretion, it conveys a sense of surprise, even a hint of obscenity. If sex were the subject matter of the exhibition the effect would be the same. Even with very strong erotic implications, so long as the exhibition put sex in a context of love, potentially including every human emotion, so long as sex is shown ultimately as a social drive, the censor might not object to exclusively physical portrayals. But separate sex out from the social: on the one hand, there could be an exhibition devoted to the natural, historical, therapeutical, hygenic aspects, which would not parade as art, on the other, unsocialized, physical sex, sheer pornography.

This exhibition draws attention to parts of food, its colours and smells, its processes and materials, proposing them as objects aesthetically interesting in themselves. But one cannot see it as part of a long tradition of still-life food art in continuity with Chardin. Quite the contrary. The traditional still-life is a concentrate of the sociable. The

* The Food Art Exhibition, Catalogue Notes, Cambridge Festival, July 1977.

artist could be focusing on a domestic scene, but for a more quintessential depiction of domesticity he closes down upon the kitchen where the
media of domestic life are processed. Instead of a wedding feast, a
sacred supper or the scanty meal of tired potato pickers, the still-life
cues community life by the array of necessary things, the act of
preparation or even just the simple raw materials. The more that
sociability is explicit, the more the image is unchallenging and easily
acceptable. But here we are facing the other direction, away from its
social uses, to consider unsocialized food. So, perhaps, the exhibition
should be treated as a mild kind of food porn.

   It is topically well-tuned to sense the provocative effects and to know
the conceptual implications of presenting as art the evanescent materials
of food rituals. But why so much wit, ingenuity and energy? What are the
artists saying about food and art? Since their form of communication is
the exhibition itself, we have to fill in our own answers. They are
probably not meaning to glorify the industrial machinery that produces
food to ritualistically precise specifications. Very possibly, they are
mocking the rituals of eating. Perhaps this exuberance carries an austere
message of protest against ritualism as such. The exhibitors may be fired
with a yearning for a less mediated, less cost-constrained form of social
life, one in which persons may please one another with smiles and
speech and expressive bodily contacts. But this is a message they can
hardly pursue to its conclusion without putting themselves out of
business. For artists to argue for unmediated social experience, and so
against all media, would be to cut off the bough they are standing on, an
end to art.

   They are young: we can assume that in their generation the thought of
famine in the world is present to the mind. Food nourishes. For me, the
exhibition is an invitation to reflect on the essentially social and ritualistic nature of food, and the contrast between simple hunger and all the
elaborate paraphernalia of food presentation. A very extreme short-cut
to world hunger might seem to be to ban feasting and the squandering of
food in luxurious rituals. In Chinese culture, apparently, over-
indulgence in food and drink has always been 'a sin of such proportions
that dynasties could fall on its account' (Chang, 1977, p. 10). To forbid
feasting altogether sounds too radical, somewhat like vowing silence to
avoid speaking bad words. Supposing food were to be separated entirely
from its social communicative functions, so as to ensure its adequate
supply for nutritional purposes. Logically, in a society where food is only
to be used for strictly physical needs, it would be eaten privately, like

medicine, and it would be bad form to speak much about it, like harping continuously on one's digestion. I dread to think what would happen to food production and world markets in the short run if food were to be totally desocialized (but there would still be the demand for pet foods). However, even when the communist-led Peasants Association made detailed prescriptions for frugality in the 1920s their rules read reassuringly. There is scope for quite a lot of ritual in the following (Chang, 1977, p. 15):

> Sumptuous feasts are generally forbidden. In Shao-shan, Hsiang-t'an county, it has been decided that guests are to be served with only three kinds of animal food, namely, chicken, fish and pork. It is also forbidden to serve bamboo shoots, kep and lentil noodles. In Hengshan county it has been resolved that eight dishes and no more may be served at a banquet. Only five dishes are allowed in the East Three District in Li-ling county, and only meat and three vegetable dishes in the North Second District, while in the West Third District New Year feasts are forbidden entirely. In Hsiang-hsiang county, there is a ban on all 'egg-cake feasts,' which are by no means sumptuous. . . . In the town of Chia-mo, Hsiang-hsiang county, people have refrained from eating expensive foods and use only fruit when offering ancestral sacrifices (Mao Tse Tung, 1927, p. 50)

To treat food in its ritual aspect is to take account of its long spun out temporal processes. It is an evolving system that can be a metaphor for any other evolution, great or small, the evolution of just one marriage, and even of the whole human species. As Empson (1928) has it of the sea:

> Sand rope, the sodden goblet of the seas
> Holds, concentrate, her liquid pedigrees.
> We sum in port her banquet of degrees.

He explains 'Viewed as one cup of drink the sea is held in by the sands round it, from which one could make a glass goblet. The banquet (soup, fish, meat) follows the order of the evolution of species.'

'If music be the food of love. . . .' But the other way round makes sense too. Food, as the music of love, structures the days and the years with its rhythms. Leading up to great moments and down through diminishing cadences, its temporal framework plays the accompaniment to gifts and countergifts in other media. It can surely not be understood by being considered item by item ('piece-meal' is always a term of reproach). Its regular structure can stabilize shifting emotions and make promises of fidelity to be kept. Looking back on a marriage through a pergola of meals, small deviations from the main structure can be seen for what they were, nothing that disturbed the grand pattern. But one of the worst sins against food is offering it without love or friendship. In 'Counting the Ways', James Agee depicts the false mood of a marriage full of sly deceits and secret resentment, a life time together strung out on the reiterated question: 'What's for dinner?' and the fixed recital of an improbable favourite menu: 'meat marrow, chopped walnuts, parsley, and crême brulée'. Though complicated, it sounds a modest meal.

For ourselves, eventually we shall have to cut out eating meat. Taking food out of its social context forces us to consider what it is made of. In the end we shall not be able to stomach rearing animals to kill for foods. Once its ritual character is fully realized, we could aim to cut down the actual food content in the procession. After a whiff of one delicacy served on fine porcelain, a sip of that fragrant liqueur in rare crystal glasses, a dip of the fingers in perfumed water: a round of different food effects with their well judged appurtenances would constitute the ritual, supplemented with song and incense too. The guests would go home, health unimpaired, not seduced into eating and drinking beyond the call of appetite, not too soggy in mind and spirit to be capable of other forms of communion. There must be some vast misunderstanding of the place of food in human culture for this programme to sound as much like futurology as the total de-socializing of food. But some great revolution in our eating habits must surely be near at hand. Perhaps, it will be a shift from enjoyment of eating to enjoyment of smelling; perhaps it will be a shift to purely ritualistic enactments. In that event, the wholewheat, brown bread Eucharist of post-Vatican II would turn out to have been a move in the wrong direction, a misunderstanding and underrating of the meanings of food that were earlier conveyed by crisp white linen, gold plate, the wafer thin circle of bread that dissolved before it could be munched.

He is present in the breaking of the bread – not even in the eating of it.

By disengaging food rituals from bodily needs we can better observe the techniques of exclusion which separate rich from poor. How does one get the meal ticket? How do some peoples get excluded and cumulatively excluded until they are destitute of friends and then starving?

Some of the questions about poverty and so about famine are questions about rules of admission to rituals of intimacy and not directly about food at all.

Food is not feed*

These recipes will draw some wider attention to the anthropologist's interest in food. It was clever of the editor to choose this well-established form, the cookery book. Just as rightly, she has used the form in the free, inventive way of the great exemplars. From Culpeper to Beeton and Elizabeth David, from Brillat-Savarin to the *Larousse Gastronomique*, the recipe is seldom left to speak for itself. Her contributors have been asked to describe something about the ingredients and the context in which the food is prepared and eaten. Sometimes this means describing a hunt, a dance, a ceremony, even a swim. But it is not for the sake of nostalgic bedside reading. She has also asked contributors to deal with foods that can be procured in most Western capitals, so she clearly expects us to try them out at home, even if it means raiding the zoo or the tropical house at Kew. So far, a charming gesture to international gastronomy and help to the Royal Anthropological Institute which will benefit from any profits. But there is much more in this idea.

Perhaps Jessica Kuper's *Anthropologists' Cookbook* will be the first of a series, followed by one on beverages and then others homing in on herbs and flavourings, stimulants and sedatives. I hope that such a series might also expand in the other direction, with, say, a book on menus through the week, or something on people's ideas of how long they can go without food at all, their concepts of infant feeding and invalid cookery, of good cooking and bad, their general idea of the importance of the culinary arts among other cultural forms. Food-taking is often an occasion for prayer, not merely for grace, but a communion rite in itself. The idea of food underlies the idea of sacrifice. When the themes of blood-shed and life-giving are counterpointed in elaborate harmony at the high point of religion, the meanings of food could never be exhausted. In such cultures food would surely rank above music, above theatre, above dance and poetry. But the gastronomic arts are hardly likely to be developed there – perhaps rather the opposite. Perhaps gastronomy flourishes best where food carries the lightest load of spiritual meanings.

One reason why the anthropologists are interested in food is that it is such an apt medium for purely social symbolism, from private hospitality to great ceremonial dramas. This cook book, because of the structure

* In Jessica Kuper (ed.), *The Anthropologist's Cookbook*, New York, Universe Books, 1977, Introduction, pp. 1–7.

chosen for it, emphasizes the intimate end of the scale. Probably the other end, which sees stupendous waste and prodigal display, is much better known.

The peoples of the world are gradually becoming conscious in this era that the work of feeding their numbers is a common problem. Yet while millions starve, other millions waste food in sheer destructive splendour, while other millions quietly gorge on more than their physical capacity can stand. One would suppose that the twenty or so rich countries of the world, whose conscience is politically alert in this respect, would damp the home demand for food so that the impact of demand from the needy could be more effective. But no; in rich countries we find the paradox of general subsidizing of food. Subsidy going direct into the pockets and larders of those in want is obviously above reproach and not what I am referring to. But food is not necessarily what they want. The Director of the Wisconsin Institute of Research on Poverty arguing against the use of food stamps wrote:

> The first issue here is whether, aside from the public passion for feeding the poor, there is any lasting reason for dealing with food separately from the general and varied needs of people with low incomes. There is ample empirical evidence that people spend a substantial part of any increase in income on food. This is particularly true of the poor. . . . If . . . we try to make people spend substantially more on food (and correspondingly less on clothing, housing, transportation, education, etc.) than they would with an all cash benefit, we shall be facing a serious enforcement problem in preventing families from re-selling the stamps on food. (Watts, 1969)

A general all-round subsidy on food solves the administrative puzzle. But what a strange enactment it is, in a rich country, where slimming bread and slimming biscuits sell like hot cakes proverbially used to.

Some people would evidently like to eat less, but find it hard to do so. And yet deep emotions stir to a political outcry when the price of bread or meat or potatoes rises. Our elected representatives, when they think of hardship and poverty, jump to the idea of relieving it by handing out food. Historically poverty here meant hunger, as it does still in those starving places abroad. It seems that the charitable gift of food, once it has taken possession of the symbolic apparatus of our culture, has simply stayed on as top priority, the most self-evidently valuable form of alms. But this will not do. That argument would require us to adopt an unworkable model of human thought. The mind does not adopt an idea historically once and for all and remain subject to its dominion ever after. Such arguing is self-contradictory, for it cannot say how the first usurping thought got foothold in minds defined to be rather firmly closed to circumstances. The anthropological approach allows a more flexible view of the mind's activity. People would like to eat less, but they eat more: why? Because food is being forced upon them under pressure of social institutions which use food as a medium of relationship. To refuse the proferred relationship could be potentially a more harmful course than putting on weight. People think the poor are hungry: why? Giving food is the easiest and cheapest form of charity and it pleases the producers. But that would hardly explain its prestige as the noblest form of almsgiving. What about the undoubted fact that it is the least radical solution to problems of poverty: it is harder by far to reorganize society so that those who are excluded can be brought back into the system of reciprocal exchanges which is the basis of friendship and support. Voting to give food from public money is of its essence a non-reciprocal gesture. The recipient can only stay outside the mesh of personal transactions which would normally result in himself and his family getting social support and moving out of poverty. To translate a social loss into a physiological lack and then to remedy the latter is mere evasion. It ensures the poor will always be there, on the outside, a reproach to feasters and merry-makers, clearly left out, though not necessarily needing to be fed.

To explain how food draws such distracting, crooked, symbolic arguments to itself, one good illustration will make these uncomfortable thoughts clear.

The Gurage inhabit the fertile plateaux of south-west Ethiopia, west of the Rift Valley lake chain. (What follows is taken from the essay by William Shack, 1971.) They cultivate a hardy crop, ensete, the 'false banana plant', which provides a constant and abundant food supply; until the great Ethiopian drought of 1970, famine and starvation were unknown in Gurage history. Ensete is stored in deep earth pits. Most homesteads grow far more than year to year family requirements. Stored crops provide an almost inexhaustible food supply, with plenty for daily food, barter, ceremonial feastings and the occasional emergency when other crops have been damaged by weather.

Although supplied with plenty, the Gurage seem to be obsessed about food. They have two eating patterns, one public, when food is dispensed as a normal part of social intercourse; small, frequent meals, as suffused with etiquette and about as filling as our afternoon tea. The other is

private; after the daily round of visiting is over, late at night the family
starts to eat again in the secrecy of the dimly lit hut. This way the norms
of kinship and generosity to strangers and neighbours can be circum-
vented, without fear of gossip. The ridicule of neighbours could be
damaging, for dispensing food unsparingly is one of the few socially
acceptable ways of displaying power and prestige. The best food-
providers are the men who enjoy most prestige and authority in all
spheres of life. These successful men, and those who try to copy them
with more restricted means, both seem so anxious to keep enough to give
away later that they restrict the quantity taken in their three meals a day
to somewhere between handfuls and mere nibbles. But Shack also
mentions that some Gurage cannot afford to engage in hospitality, pared
down though it always is.

Here we have a well-described case of a people who grow enough
food for their year's needs and more, every year, but who are obsessed
with anxiety about it. They lavish far more labour and far more complex
methods of farming upon this easy crop than anyone else in the same
cultivating complex; they hoard supplies from year to year and they
hoard their cooked food in the day so as to eat it secretly at night. They
are understandably anxious about food, because it is the symbol of
success in a society that is strongly competitive but which does not allow
competition to be open. The only conspicuous display permitted to the
successful person is the gesture of lavish food-giving. Every other sign
has to be muted, secret influence in dim corners. When they eat,
personal restraint is the approved style. Overeating is regarded as coarse
and vulgar, and they always leave something on the dish (for 'Mr
Manners', as it were).

Dr Shack presents them as if suffering from a culturally induced
hunger. Everything they do focuses their anxieties onto food and
encourages them to worry, hoard and wait for it. They could easily be
more generous, give up secret feeding, make their public meals more
satisfying, have fewer of them, use up the year's harvest and wait
together for the next crop. But in context after context they clearly
choose to compete with one another, individually and secretly, and to
show off the results by these thin acts of visible hospitality. In such a
society, and in such a culture, what does it feel like to be unsuccessful? It
certainly must feel like not having enough food to dispense to all-
comers. And what comes to the mind of the fortunate when the miseries
of their less successful brethren are forced upon their attention? The
thought comes that hunger is the cause of their troubles (even if the

symptom is lack of appetite), and the further thought, that this can be cured by a dollop of food, is soon translated into action (1971, pp. 35–6).

Now, when a man complains of loss of appetite, nausea, and intermittent attacks of severe stomach pains, immediately suspicion is awakened that any of several potentially harmful spirits has 'touched' him. (Evil spirits are believed to dwell in the dense forests and alongside the streams which demarcate village settlements, forming spatial and social boundaries between areas of habitation.) Discomforts of this nature are culturally stereotyped 'signs' of super-natural affliction. If such nagging symptoms of illness persist and his condition deteriorates, the patient usually sinks into a semi-stupor, and although he may occasionally become conscious, is seldom able to take food or water. In this torpid or trance-like state the victim's breathing becomes difficult; the slow regular pace of breathing is interrupted momentarily by loud, hoarse, wheezing, not unlike an asthmatic patient, and those attending him respond by reciting a short word of prayer. Violent seizures of body trembling often overcome the patient, compelling his attendants to use force in holding him down on the sleeping mat; and in severe cases, partial paralysis of the extremities may set in. If there are no signs of a 'natural' recovery of health, as indicated by a recovery of appetite, a 'wizard' (*sägwära*) is summoned to divine the causes of the illness – that is, to ascertain the type of spirit believed to have taken temporary possession of the victim. After consulting oracles to reveal the spirit's name, in this case *awre*, the wizard prescribes a routine formula for exorcising the spirit, a conventional recipe which belongs to the common repertoire of adult Gurage knowledge about supernatural matters.

The rite of exorcism consists in feeding to the sick man an enormous dishful of ensete-food. Kinsmen and neighbours arrive at nightfall to take part in the ceremony, the hut is darkened, they chant to the hungry spirit which has seized their friend. The brimming dish is set before the patient, he lowers his head over it, a long shawl is draped to conceal him and the dish of food. Using both hands, he ravenously stuffs his mouth, eating as the company chants in time to his stertorous breathing. This goes on for twelve hours or more, till 'the spirit, speaking through the possessed person, utters with a sigh, several times – "*täfwahum*" – "I am satisfied".'

Anthropologists' interpretations of strange beliefs fall roughly into two kinds. One is the interest theory, the other the tangled web of culture. According to the interest theory, the explanation of an extra-ordinary belief depends on tracing the beneficiary. So the beliefs in the divinity of the king would be explained by the support they lend to the king's precarious authority. Spirit-possession likewise tends to be explained by showing what the possessed person gets in the way of moral support, sympathy, food and clothes (see I. M. Lewis, 1971, for a bird's-eye view of the subject). These approaches accord well with psychoanalytical theories of response to anxiety. But, like the latter, they tend to assume that the problems of credulousness and delusion arise most critically where the person who is possessed by an evil spirit is concerned. If this were all, the anthropologist merely interprets pos-session as a way of remedying a hard position. It suggests that the victim is rectifying his troubles by a confidence trick. However, the real problems of belief arise in the case of the person who is exploited by it, not the one who benefits. Here the second approach helps, the tangled web of culture. If we ask how the king's extravagant claims to obedience are made credible to the populace, the answer lies in the complex countering of one confidence trick by another, each with claims which only reflect the pattern of comparative advantage: the total belief system ends by representing the total of separate interests. In the case of invasive spirits demanding to be feasted, clothed and enriched, we ask why the husbands of possessed women give them any credence at all. Faced with speedy ruin, why do they not become violently sceptical of their wives' claims to be harbouring spendthrift covetous spirits? Why do they tamely fork out as required? The Gurage belief in seizure by a hungry spirit may be plausible to the victim who stands to gain a good meal. What makes it plausible to everyone else, especially to those who then have to give generously what they prefer to hoard?

The full explanation of the plausibility to the Gurage of the belief in affliction by hungry spirits is in the elaborately interwoven cultural themes of private competition, public restraint, fasts and tantalizing nibbles, and in the impossible reckoning of who is in control, except by assessing their capacity to distribute food. Dr Shack follows out the threads of culturally induced hunger and institutionalized deprivation of food to draw an extraordinary and convincing picture. But I am still more impressed by the solid reasons he gives for being anxious about food in a society in which a man's role can only be performed if he can distribute as well as receive it. He reports that all the cases of possessed victims were, by Gurage standards, poor men (1971):

[They] owned small plots of land with few ensete plants, and they were encumbered by long-standing debts arising out of borrowing cattle and money. I lack sufficient evidence to substantiate local hear-say that these victims of *awre*-possession had all recently undergone some personal crisis. Even so, in the strictest sense, such men of lowly means were not destitute, nor did they constitute a social category equivalent to the depressed occupational pariah groups and ritual outcasts found in Gurage society. But land, ensete and cattle are the principal economic resources that determine the extent to which Gurage men are able to achieve recognisable status and prestige by generously dispensing food. At the same time, prestigious men also enjoy the added nutritional rewards of participating in the monthly feast exchanges organised by members of the *mwakyarite* association.

The select list of members, who regale each other in turn in feasting-clubs where they gorge on raw meat, ensete and beer, includes all the important men in Gurage society. Questioned, no one could recall such a man ever being possessed by a hungry spirit. This is a society where the theory of equality is contradicted by big differences of wealth and where selection is made by secret paths of influence. Even the rule of primogeniture may not guarantee land to the eldest son if his father does not assess him as an 'ideal' son. Brother rivals brother. The lineage and community are strong, but within the corporate groupings each homestead is on its own. Not to be on the upward path is to be on the downward slope. Below the poor Gurage, however much encumbered by debt, are other lower levels of outcasts, landless and categories of ritually inferior status. The poor man loaded with debts has certainly got something to worry about. Nothing but a complete overhaul of Gurage political institutions would solve his problems. But those who have a good hand to play are not keen on stopping the game. Much easier for the rich Gurage to believe that loss of appetite, listlessness and nausea are symptoms that can be relieved by a ritual gift of food.

I tell this tale not to shock and discomfort, but because food is a blinding fetish in our culture, as among the Gurage. We cannot formulate a consistent policy about it, we cannot control our own uses of food, we tolerate cant and contradiction in respect of it. We simply do not know the uses of food, and our ignorance is explosively dangerous. It is more convenient for us to take a veterinary surgeon's view of food as animal feed, to think of it as mere bodily input, than to recognize its great symbolic force. Only reading casually through the pages that follow we feel a glow of enchantment that has little to do with physical needs. Food is not feed. Let this be a beginning to a systematic anthropology of food.

Notes

1   See M. Douglas, 'Self-Evidence', *Proceedings of the Royal Anthropological Institute*, 1972.
2   According to respondents to a survey organized by the Potato Marketing Board Survey, Research Bureau Limited, 'Potatoes: Qualitative Study', Job R.B.L. 10814.

References

Chang, K. C., ed. (1977), *Food in Chinese Culture: Anthropological and Historical Perspectives*, New Haven, Yale University Press.

Empson, W. (1928), *Sea Voyage*, London, Chatto & Windus.

Lewis, I. M. (1971), *Ecstatic Religion: an Anthropological Study of Spirit Possession and Shamamism*, Harmondsworth, Penguin.

Shack, William (1966), *The Gurage: a People of Ensete Culture*, Oxford University Press.

Shack, William (1971), 'Hunger, anxiety and ritual: deprivation and spirit possession among the Gurage of Ethiopia', *Man*, 6 (1), pp. 30–43.

Watts, Harold (1969), 'The Family Assistance Plan: an analysis and evaluation', *Public Policy*, 19 (2), pp. 323–53, quotes Watts's Testimony to the House Ways and Means Committee on the subject of Social Security and Welfare Proposals (91st Congress, 1st session, 15, 16 October 1969, pp. 2456–67), 1971.

5 Good taste: review of Pierre Bourdieu, *La Distinction**

When Nancy Mitford launched a general conversation about non-upper class speech, some rebuked her for raising a very non-U topic. It may be in bad taste to write a book on taste at all. However, a monumental study of modern French taste should earn a special success in England, where we are always fascinated by the strategies of social pretension. Pierre Bourdieu's *La Distinction* is no sudden excursus into the sociology of good taste. A distinguished anthropologist, he directs the Centre de Sociologie Européenne in Paris, edits and writes in *Actes de recherche en sciences sociales* and has published many important and profound studies in anthropology and sociology. With his colleagues, he has been study-ing the distribution of artistic judgment in France for nearly twenty years. Over time, several books and many articles on the subject have appeared. *La Réproduction* (1976) most directly prepares the ground for the present study. There he traced the way in which French education streams different categories of young people into socially appropriate parts of the established occupational structure. It manages to keep opening more and more educational opportunity without ever disturb-ing the old pattern of recruitment to social class. Though the system looks like a meritocracy, social background is still the strongest predictor of academic success and of entry to the liberal professions. From this well-established point the present work takes off.

The scope of the argument is very ambitious, being conducted at two levels simultaneously, philosophic and sociological. The book is also difficult to read, partly because of its style of writing and partly because of a distracting layout. For review it may help to interpret it as a dramatic work of which the general theme is an attack on doctrines of pure

* Review published in *The Times Literary Supplement*, 13 February 1981, pp. 163–9; Pierre Bourdieu, *La Distinction: Critique Sociale du Jugement*, Le Sens Commun, Paris, Les Editions de Minuit, 1979.

aesthetics. This means any philosophy which sets aesthetic judgment apart from other forms of discrimination and attributes to it a peculiar quality of purity or ultimate unanalysability. Doctrines of pure aesthetics or theories of pure art are as old as the beginning of professional art itself and very much alive today. Bourdieu's target includes both the philosophies which attribute to beautiful things a quality which is independent of any seductive or useful features and those which attribute to humans a faculty for recognizing beauty as such, independent of functional consideration. But the reader should take care not to be swept along too fast. A theory about the nature of aesthetic judgment is not the same as a teaching about what works of art should be like. To isolate a cognitive process as a distinctive form of artistic recognition is not to say that artistic expression is only found in rarefied detached and isolated pure forms. Bourdieu is content to characterize his chosen philosophical target by quoting from Plato, Schopenhauer and Kant. Without discussing it deeply, he mounts what he calls a vulgar critique of pure criticism, for which Kant is made a whipping boy. The objection is sociological, inspired by Ortega y Gasset's criticism that art, by being exclusive, is explicitly not popular and implicitly anti-popular. Such a tradition divides society into mutually antagonistic castes. Bourdieu joins the protest. He warns against philosophy that considers creativity to be tainted when it is involved in any political, commercial, pedogogic or decorative function and which only exalts pure art forms totally disengaged from other human concerns. His worry is with the divisive and exploitative potential of the pure art doctrine. The book is offered as a demonstration of how the legitimating of art as a set of professions and industries maintains a caste system in contemporary society.

This being the theme, the general setting of the play is how the legitimizing of high culture is done in contemporary France. The mood is Brechtian. It could have been tragic if the spirit of the little man who is the hero victim were crushed by what is done against him. If the working classes did not know that they are being excluded from high culture or if they did know and also cared, pathos and tragedy would dominate. But among all their other injuries, of which they are well aware, the working classes hardly feel scarred by this one. Making virtue of necessity, warm in their family life and convivial cafés, they can bear the hardship of being excluded from high culture. Bourdieu draws a convincing picture of the greatness of the divide between the judgment of the cultural dominators and culturally dominated. Each has a standard of basic humanity, decency and proper discrimination on which the other division of society fails. The dominating class cherishes a semi-bestial image of the *classes populaires* which are the working classes of British sociological analysis. Lusty and earthy, their untutored taste contrasts with legitimate taste and justifies it. In their turn, the working classes subscribe to a complementary image of upper class disorder and beastliness: they mock the mincing manners and sexual ambiguities of a social life not founded upon the sexual division of labour, dubbing men who are not manual workers as pederasts, one and all. They deplore modern painting as deforming of nature, experimental photography as a waste of film. They never go to *avant garde* theatre that treats of their plight. In this play the hero represents the ordinary people. However, their resentment and dislike of modern and classical art is actually good for the art legitimating industry since it thrives by keeping its treasures untainted by popular approval.

It suits the plot for the working-class hero to be drawn in a certain image. Attitudes we have seen elsewhere ascribed to dockers, lorry drivers, construction workers and other heavy manual workers are here idealized and attributed to all the masses of ordinary people with whom the privileged educated bourgeois contrasts itself. In this story the hero revels in his virility: eating and drinking heartily, laughing and blowing his nose noisily, he does everything manfully, with openhanded hospitality to family and friends. The character is somewhat overdrawn, perhaps necessarily for the size of the scene. But there is good reason why the hero only appears on stage for brief glimpses. He never gets to see legitimate art until it is out of vogue, he never goes to concerts or exhibitions. It is pointless for the sociologist to sound out his preferences between works of art he has never heard of. Though he would be surprised to have an aesthetic theory attributed to him, according to Bourdieu he takes an anti-Kantian position on matters of taste. The bourgeoisie puts more value on form than on substance or function. The working classes, reversing the judgment, value function and substance over form. A picture is beautiful to them if it recalls festive good things. A photograph is never for pure contemplation, but for showing to someone or memorializing something. These people are quite against the theory of pure art and have no sympathy with art for art's sake.

There are no real villains in the play. The rest of the cast is a variegated set of well-intentioned people, working at legitimating art objects and life-styles and subscribing implicitly to the theory of pure art. At the top, the dominant middle classes set the standards. They divide into two: the intellectuals and the rich bourgeois, who include industrialists and the liberal professions. Between them they control the process of legitimation. They oppose themselves to the petite bourgeoisie, but the attitude is not reciprocated. The petite bourgeoisie likes the upper classes and only wants to learn what is good; it does its best to copy within its limited means the standards it perceives as set by those above. But for its pains it is despised by the dominant classes as well as by the working classes (and one senses that the author does not sympathize with it either).

The background of the *dramatis personae* is very much part of the plot, which now must be unfolded. It starts with a questionnaire administered in 1963. After filling in the required demographic information, the respondent was asked about his furniture, leisure, favourite singers, books, films, painters, museums and galleries. He was asked to select which of the following opinions on music matched best to his own:
Great music is complicated.
Great music is not for us.
I like great music but I don't know it.
I like great music, for example Strauss's waltzes.
All good music interests me.
On the subject of painting likewise he had to select from:
Painting doesn't interest me.
Museums are not my strong point, I don't appreciate them.
Painting is difficult, to say anything about it you have to know.
I like the impressionists a lot.
Abstract painting interests me as much as the classical schools.

Once sorted into socio-economic categories, the answers focus a beam of enquiry into consumption patterns. Bourdieu's quarrel with pure aesthetics naturally allows him to include the purchase of ballet and concert tickets and the visits to museums along with other consumption. The same social pressures which legitimate high culture, legitimate also the life-style of its connoisseurs. Assortative processes work to bring harmony into the pattern of tastes in each home, so that life partners who feel they were made for each other because they like the same sports or music or literature, choose their friends for the same reasons; they are engaged in an enterprise which demands so much discrimination that even their furnishings and food will be chosen to match. This approach closely resembles the analysis of furnishings as an object code proposed earlier by Basil Bernstein and the principles of structural analysis applied to modern life go back to Roland Barthes. At every level above the level of the working classes, people are making distinctions in the name of beauty and using that title to separate themselves assiduously from the level below, though not from that above. The hard clear lines are drawn against what they do not like. Among the residual areas of what they may like without losing caste there is scope for choice.

Bourdieu only describes sketchily the principles by which he gets his picture of consumption classes. He apologizes for this; the work is still in progress, some of it is coming out in articles, the methodology will be the subject of a separate book. Much has been published already in *Actes de la recherche*. Meanwhile he explains as much as he considers necessary for the present study. The concept of human capital, used by educational sociologists and Chicago economists in a rather narrow way, is here expanded to include cultural capital, social capital, symbolic capital and honorific capital. Cultural capital is based upon educational qualifications but it includes subsequent self-education in various ways. Social capital is the advantage that comes to a child from a home well-endowed with cultural capital. Honorific capital means those forms of civic recognition that accrue to a successful life in the top echelons of industrial society. Symbolic capital is mostly available to writers and artists who can symbolize their virtuous commitment to social criticism without necessarily doing anything to disturb the balance of social forces. It is convenient to think of holdings in these four kinds of capital as spiritual resources; combined with economic resources they form a personal patrimony.

In all industrial countries a close correlation holds between three things, father's occupation, own education and own economic opportunities. Essentially Bourdieu's method is to split these components. He draws up a socio-gram of the dominant classes. On a horizontal axis, he starts from the patrimonial mix in which a lot of education goes with a little money; he then moves to those whose patrimony is made up equally of both education and money and ends with the last patrimonial mix which gives more money than education. He then draws a central vertical axis with social capital, which he playfully calls ancient lineage in the bourgeoisie but which is calculated on father's occupation. Those with a lot of money and a lot of education tend to belong to the established bourgeoisie which is marked at the top end of the social capital axis. The new arrivals at the bottom are a branch of the petite bourgeoisie, who are not so submissive to the canons of legitimate culture as the established members, especially if they are in the business of art production.

Now we have to translate the occupational grades into English grades that slot intelligibly into the general categories of *bourgeois*, petit bourgeois. Then we have to translate the tastes. A preference that the interior decoration of the home be *harmonieux* or *confortable*, or *intime* is no problem, but what does *composé* mean? Full marks to the 41 per cent of *services médico-sociaux*, *intermédiaires culturels*, and *artisans d'art* who at least knew that *composé* meant what they liked. But who are they?

The book includes a chapter on the sources of data which are many and therefore as difficult to reconcile with each other as to match to our Registrar General's categories. The tables for the popular classes name unskilled and industrial workers, agricultural workers, supervisors and workers in the service industries. Some tables for the petite bourgeoisie include craftsmen, small businesses, employees, middle administrative grades, technicians, teachers and new entrants to the petite bourgeoisie. Each of the major divisions is internally divided into a dominant and dominated section.

The intellectuals form one sector of the dominant elite, the higher grades of the civil service, engineers, academics and anyone who holds his position by accumulating capital. They honour an ascetic tradition. They define themselves by their austere intellectualism in contrast to the bourgeois taste for luxury. Their amusements are provincial museums rather than the great showy exhibitions. They favour *avant garde* theatre, which anyway happens to be cheaper. At the extreme, they include the left bank artists. Lacking the means for indulging a taste in rare antiques, they substitute a taste for the rustic, Roumanian carpets instead of Persian rugs, the restored farmhouse instead of the family manor, lithographs and reproductions in place of old paintings. They are critical of the existing moral order, according to Bourdieu, expressing a meritocratic revolt against a society founded on principles other than scholastic attainments. Always on the side of novelty, as leaders of taste, in the 1960s they liked Kandinsky, Picasso, Boulez. It turns out that these are the people who like their homes to look *composé* rather than *intime*. They have even turned against French traditional cooking in favour of foreign gourmet food or exotic eating places. According to Bourdieu, they are the dominated sector of the dominant class, but according to his description they do most of the legitimating and their judgment seems rather independent of the bourgeois taste.

The other sector of the dominant class (the bourgeois) comprises the liberal professions and the industrialists. They have plenty of money to indulge their tastes and so prefer luxury and comfort to austerity. They are the *rive droite*, patrons of boulevarde theatre and concerts. They like jewellery and ornate decoration, they buy foreign cars, books of art, illustrated magazines; they ski, water ski, go hunting, play tennis. As to legitimate art, they do not experiment; they prefer work which has been sacralized by time, the impressionists, Watteau. They subscribe to intellectualist values, but, unlike the intellectuals, their profession does not give scope for reinvesting any accumulation of cultural capital – so they enjoy cocktail parties and a heavy programme of social functions where they can publicly demonstrate conventional lavishness which will pay off professionally. In general they feel solidarity with the moral order and uphold it. They have the social optimism of people who are doing well while the intellectuals have the social pessimism of those who are having to strive.

To turn this into present English economic conditions presents formidable problems. At home, buying foreign cars is no longer a sign of affluence. Turning away from traditional English cooking is not yet a luxurious habit. By 1980 the same dominant sectors might feel the impressionists had received the popular accolade that shifts them from high-brow into middle-brow taste. That the actual results should be the same in France as in England or America is not to be expected – on the contrary, the interest lies in the differences. Presumably the same principles of analysis could be used anywhere to uncover the class structure that is held in place and legitimated by holdings in spiritual capital. Unfortunately, we must wait for the next book to get the principles. Unfortunately too, it is difficult to anchor the interpretation to the tables that are given. For example, take the hearty working-class family who are supposed in the text to sweep away petty distinctions of table service, to be lavishly hospitable and careless of form with their close friends and family. They are said not to submit eating to form – an instance of their anti-Kantian aesthetic. But when we look at the detailed answers we see that it is the working classes who prefer to offer their guests 'a real menu' rather than a buffet. What is that if not eating within forms? It is the working classes who say they like to end a festive meal with singing and to fill the evening with parlour games – distinctly formal to this reviewer's middle-class eye. One has the same uneasiness about the alleged difference with respect to using clothing to differ-entiate between indoors and outdoors, formal and informal. The working class seems no less concerned to make distinctions – witness the photographs of them in casual underwear in the kitchen – though not the same distinctions and marked within narrower economic limits. Their adherence to an anti-Kantian aesthetic is crucial to this story.

Suppose the statistics when analysed showed the *dramatis personae* differing from each other along a smooth and gentle gradient of education and social position? If the line is hard to discern at which good will for legitimate art stops and working class autonomy begins, the tale might not be one about exploitation, but about a country in which everyone was striving to exert that pure aesthetic judgment which Kant identified. The working classes in France have to be sharply differentiated from the petite bourgeoisie if Bourdieu's drama is to hold the stage. The same for the petite bourgeoisie itself. The story requires that their distinctive existence be established.

Dominant exploiters are often cast in a noble role: they attract admiration as well as hate. The exploited are also noble: they attract admiration, whether by stoically accepting their fate or by striving against it. But the conventional mythology depicts those in the middle as meanly colluding with the exploitative system, extracting their petty profits while mumbling fine phrases. Why do they attract only contempt? Why is the petite bourgeoisie not as trapped and exploited by the system as the other underclasses? Since they are so generally cast as absurd, we have to be careful of our own snobbish bias. Perhaps they are really silly. Perhaps we really have nothing at all in common with them. Perhaps their complicity with the exploiters should forfeit our sympathy. Whether the story has credibility depends very much on whether the author has drawn his petit bourgeois characters so convincingly that we can really believe in their existence as a distinctive class with distinctive problems and solutions.

If this method works, its application may turn up interesting variations of snobbery. It invites us to imagine the kinds of society that might totally subscribe to the pure aesthetic without any dividing line between dominator and dominated. But if all disagreement were strictly about technical competence, art would still be exclusive and divisive. Pure aesthetics in itself does not entail restless seeking after change. However, a society in which everyone conforms to the legitimated standards with no rebellion and no holier-than-thou rejection of vulgarity would be totally conservative. Is it the ideal that nothing new be legitimated? We can easily imagine the alternative, a society with no central legitimation of art, a nation of craftsmen, colorists, singers and folk musicians. Each little community and family would make its own aesthetic judgments unabashed by great precedents or new fashions – not difficult to imagine or recall from various historical periods or outback frontier communities.

If Bourdieu proposes that all challenges and competition be taken out of artistic work, he starts to sound like an old-time protestant denouncing the false pomps of the church. He is not against God, but against those who exploit their fellows by claiming the sole right to legitimate dealings in the sacred. He is not revealing the epistemological shakiness of a theory of aesthetic judgment, but attacking its exploitation for social purposes. He is showing the consequences of calling the changes in a particular way, so that the larger public has no sooner cottoned on to one idea of what art can be, than the whole direction is switched and what was legitimately beautiful becomes trash. As Michael Thompson expounded this theme, in his *Rubbish Theory*, the interesting questions are about kinds of legitimating, how soon the cycle changes, what scope an original artist may have in one society rather than another for challenging the legitimating process or escaping its adverse judgment. On Bourdieu's analysis the pace of fashion is slowed down by the bourgeois industrialists and liberal professions and would gallop out of control if artists filled the world. Whatever moral for society we should take from it, the great interest of Bourdieu's book will lie in the strength of his method and its reliability for asking comparative questions about fashions in contemporary society.

Clearly the scrutiny of reinforcing processes in the class system is important. One would like to know how much the control which the dominant class exerts through legitimating art is balanced by the opportunities for advancement on the ladder of a career in art. The records of French education suggest that it is not compensated. In that case we have a general model of European society which closely parallels the Indian caste system described by McKim Marriott. Both models start from identifying in the hierarchy of cultural values two distinct sources of advantage for anyone engaging in social interaction, one spiritual, one economic. Marriott identifies a Hindu substance code which classifies transactions in terms of subtle, spiritual elements, and gross material elements. The contrast of subtle and gross parallels Bourdieu's idea of a patrimony made up of spiritual and economic components. The top of the Indian system of castes, at least in theory, are the Brahmans who dominate the spiritual dealings, refuse to transact in any way that will weaken their position as legitimators and distributors of spiritual things. They seem to follow an austere rule, but epicurean delights are allowed within it – so like the austere intellectual tradition in France. Much more restricted, pinched, are the Indian silver workers and skilled craftsmen who only have their own trade to follow. They practise the rules of purity more assiduously and tend to be forced by other castes to keep to themselves – so like the self-imposed strictures and isolation of the petite bourgeoisie in France. The big landowners and princes tempt comparison with Bourdieu's liberal professions and big industrialists, distributing their social reciprocities over an enormous circle, luxury loving and highly sociable. At the bottom of the hierarchy the landless workers can only give gross substances and receive spiritual things from above. The Indian scheme does not pronounce on their docility or on their independence of judgment; indeed there are as few studies of Indian culture from their point of view as in Europe. But their weakness in a system in which spiritual capital is controlled at the top exactly corresponds to Bourdieu's description of the French worker dominated by the control of legitimate art. There is no doubt that the analysis is enormously enlightening, particularly in explaining why class segments who define their status in contrast with each other have so little mutual sympathy – why artists dislike teachers and teachers dislike the petit bourgeois. Let us hope that one day a solid book will pay honour to the petite bourgeoisie, either for its enslavement by others or for its spontaneous efforts to live within correct forms. For surely we do not wish to join the holiness rat-race by denying our petit bourgeois origins – that would be distinctly snobbish and even non-U.

References

Barthes, Roland (1967), *Système de la Mode*, Paris, Seuil.

Bernstein, Basil (1971), *Theoretical Studies Towards a Sociology of Language*, vol. I, *Class, Codes and Control*, ch. 8, 'A Sociolinguistic Approach to Socialization', London, Routledge & Kegan Paul.

Marriott, McKim (1976), 'Hindu Transactions: Diversity Without Dualism', in Bruce Kapferer (ed.), *Transaction and Meaning: Directions in the Anthropology of Exchange and Symbolic Behavior*, vol. 1, Institute for the Study of Human Issues, Philadelphia.

Thompson, Michael (1979), *Rubbish Theory*, Oxford University Press.

6 Population control in primitive groups*

This paper is about four human groups which attempt to control fertility. The first are the *Pelly Bay* Eskimos who regularly kill off a proportion of their female babies. The next are the *Rendille*, camel-herders in the Kenya highlands. They postpone the age of marriage of women, send numbers of their women to be married to polygamists in the next tribe, kill off boys born on Wednesdays or boys born after the next eldest son is old enough to have been circumcised. The third are the *Tikopia*, inhabitants of a small Pacific island measuring three miles across, isolated by 700 miles of sea. They used to use abortion, contraception, infanticide and suicide migration to keep their population down.

These are all groups who by their way of life would be counted as primitive peoples, within the usual range of an anthropologist's interest.

I will also mention a fourth group who restrict their numbers by only allowing the eldest son in each family to contract marriage and correspondingly maintain a large proportion of their female population in barren spinsterhood. These are the *Nambudiri Brahmins* of South India – by no means either poor, or illiterate, or primitive in any sense. I plan to use these examples as a basis for considering Wynne-Edwards's hypothesis that in primitive human groups social conventions operate homeostatic controls on population.

Wynne-Edwards's thesis is as follows. He asks how a balance is maintained between population density and available resources; what holds back the latent power of increase so that critical resources are not over-exploited? The problem stated thus includes an assumption that the normal distribution of a species is optimum. Wynne-Edwards

---

* Paper given to the Association of British Zoologists at the Annual Meeting of 8 January 1966.

actually goes so far as to say that normally the habitat provides what he calls, 'the best possible living' to species higher up the chain. I quote:

> Where we can still find nature undisturbed by human interference . . . there is generally no indication whatever that the habitat is run down or destructively over-taxed (each species affords) the best possible living to species higher up the chain that depend on it for food. (pp. 8–9)

His question is about restraint in the midst of plenty. What prevents predators at each point from so multiplying that they over-exploit their own resources?

His answer is inspired by the analogy with homeostasis in physiology. Physiological systems have controls which regulate the internal environment of the body and adapt it. If it can be established that population homeostasis parallels physiological homeostasis, then much behaviour that is apparently functionless can be explained by its contribution to population control. There appear to be density-dependent brakes which impose a ceiling on natural increase. It is important to the argument that the relevant ceiling is *not* imposed by starvation or by predators or natural hazards. Rather it is imposed by otherwise inexplicable aspects of social behaviour. For example:

(a) territorial behaviour limits the number of territories occupied in the food gathering area and deprives redundant males of feeding or breeding facilities;

(b) communal roosting has a function in providing a display of numbers;

(c) hierarchy is a way of cutting off the tail of the population 'at the right level', by excluding certain sections from feeding or breeding.

Finally, the analogy with physiology suggests that the higher species would exhibit more complex adaptations and that population homeostasis would tend to reach the greatest efficiency and perfection in human groups.

Wynne-Edwards extends his argument to human groups by citing enthusiastically a very early work of Professor Carr-Saunders (*The Population Problem*, 1922). There is indeed a remarkably close parallel between the approaches of the two authors. In so far as he discusses primitive human populations, Carr-Saunders's argument is as follows.

He starts with the premise that in any human society there will be a theoretical optimum size for the population (that will give the highest return of goods per head). If the density is greater or less than this desirable density, then the average income will be less than it might have been. He goes on to assume that this desirable optimum is actually attained in primitive populations, where it has been observed that the members live in evident enjoyment of satisfactory resources, relatively free from want and disease. To account for this achieved optimum, he looks for controls on population. He supposes that starvation is not an acceptable means of limiting numbers, because it makes social conditions unstable, and notes that anyway primitive people are better able to withstand hunger than we are (p. 231). The controls that interest him are imposed from within, social conventions which decrease fertility or increase elimination. Restricted territory, infanticide, head-hunting, such customs are in common use and the degree to which they are practised may be such as to approximate to the optimum number (p. 230). It is only fair to say that Carr-Saunders's book was written a long time ago. None of his other distinguished studies of world population repeats the argument. The anthropological reports which he quotes are out of date and the argument now sounds very naive. I started out with the intention of exposing its fallacies, presented anew by a zoologist. However, if one could adapt the argument to avoid certain inherent difficulties, I would find myself in some measure of agreement with the youthful Carr-Saunders.

The main difficulty with the Wynne-Edwards/Carr-Saunders thesis is that it is so protected from contradictory evidence as to be irrefutable. Wynne-Edwards only expects his thesis to apply where 'nature is kind and reliable'. The negative instances which he cites in chapter 20 are said to occur in highly variable environments and so to be compatible with the thesis which is framed for steady environments (p. 470). Carr-Saunders has the corresponding idea that savages are generally found to live in comfort and ease.

These assumptions make it difficult to select relevant data for testing the thesis in its extension to human groups. Are we expected to limit ourselves to savage communities which live in comfort and ease? This could be a very big restriction. What standards of comfort are we to apply, our own or theirs? Peoples whose population is obviously controlled by disease or starvation are to be excluded from the discussion. But there are degrees of starvation. Do we exclude the many peoples who face an annual hungry season between harvests or those who expect a famine every five years, or every ten or twenty years? In short, a principle of selection that conforms to these requirements eludes me. I therefore propose to include any primitive populations for whom good information exists.

The next difficulty with their approach is that under-population is not seriously considered. This omission enables them to take the actual given population at any time as the optimum.

If a zoologist tells me that the concept of under-population is not relevant to animal groups, I would accept it, but it is highly relevant to human demography because there are many classes of activity which require a minimum number of participants. Much anthropological evidence suggests that primitive populations are prone to *under*-population and that the latent power of increase, so far from being a threat to the resources, is not sufficient for the people to realize the full possibilities of their environment. If this were also true of animal populations, it would destroy the assumption on which Wynne-Edwards's problem and solution are based. There would be no problem to solve about internal social controls if in fact it could be shown that external controls, in the form of predators and external dangers, kept the populations at each point in the chain down well below the level at which it could threaten to over-exploit its food resources. But this is in fact frequently the case with human groups.

Now for a word about the danger of taking actual human populations at any given time as being at optimum size or density. It is about as defensible as if a town planner were to take the actual size of towns to be the optimum, without analysis or evidence. Thus Carr-Saunders infers from the immensely long pre-historic period through which mankind existed without attaining high densities that some kind of social controls must have operated to produce the optimum size (pp. 239–40). Again he argues that the existence of restrictive practices such as infanticide imply that the relevant populations are at an optimum size. It is as absurd as for the town planner to infer from the existence of parking meters that the traffic flow is optimal.

The idea of an optimum human population is too complicated to be inferred from such evidence. An optimum density or size can be defined in relation to the demands upon a particular resource. An optimum size in relation to land, for example, would be such that an additional unit of population would not proportionately increase the yield of the land per head, and a substracted unit of population would more than proportionately increase its yield per head. Such a concept is not always very relevant to actual densities. For example the Ndembu, a Lunda tribe in Zambia, living at a density varying from three to six per square mile, grow cassava as their stable crop. Cassava is very easy to grow. It does not require labour-intensive methods. The Ecological Survey of Northern Rhodesia calculated that, cultivating cassava with traditional Ndembu techniques, their tribal area would be capable of supporting a population of up to eighteen per square mile. Only near that point of density would the idea of the optimum for cassava cultivation become relevant. At the present density more or less units of human population would not affect the *per capita* yield. In actual fact the Ndembu are not likely to crowd together at the highest densities which their land permits for cassava-growing. Though cassava is their staple, their bread and butter as it were, they are not all that interested in cassava. They are passionately interested in hunting. Game is scarce in their region and the search for it causes them to move their villages when an area is hunted out. It would be nice to think that their actual low density represents the optimum for their hunting economy. But I see no reason for such optimism. They could as likely be *over*-populated from the hunting point of view – as to have struck a happy equilibrium between their demands on critical resources.

Here is another big difference between human and animal populations when we are thinking of optimum densities. For the animal population it makes sense to make the calculation in terms of critical resources and to recognize that the critical resource is not necessarily food; it may be nesting room or some other necessary amenity. But for human behaviour it can be more relevant to take into account the ceiling imposed by the demand for champagne or private education than the demand for bread and butter.

The shift that has to be made between the zoologist and the sociologist is a shift from the idea of a particular optimum (a size or density related to a particular resource) and a general optimum (a size or density related to the satisfaction of all kinds of demands – including demands for luxuries and leisure).

I give an example of a people who are under-populated from two angles, economic and social. They are the Western Shoshone, Indians native to Eastern California, who used to live by gathering grass-seeds and nuts. All the year they wandered from one floristic zone to the next as the seeds and berries ripened, but they wintered near the juniper pine nut crops, wherever they happened to be gathering these when the winter fell. Some of the Shoshone tribes lived at a density of *two to the square mile* in permanent villages. These are the lucky ones. They could sally out for short foraging trips and return to their fixed base. They could get to know each other, hold elections, have winter festivals and organize deer and rabbit drives. Others were much more sparsely scattered at *one person to two square miles*. Though they tried to come back to the same place each autumn it was not certain who would be spending the winter together. But at least they could have a festival and could organize a rabbit drive when the others arrived. The least fortunate in the most arid zones were living at a fantastic sparsity of *one person to thirty square miles*. They could never be sure of seeing the same party again from winter to winter, had few festivals and fewer rabbit or deer drives. According to the accepted standards of their own culture they were obviously *under*-populated. It is dubious whether these rabbit drives they had to forgo for lack of numbers are to be counted as a critical resource from a strictly economic or physiological point of view. The protein intake of rabbit meat would be very slight and, anyway, their staple was probably not deficient in vegetable protein. The needs which were not met because of low density were social and cultural. But once we admit such resources are relevant to the idea of optimum population we are a long way from both Wynne-Edwards and Carr-Saunders. I am going to argue that it is the demand for oysters and champagne not for the basic bread and butter that triggers off social conventions which hold human populations down.

In the absence of any reliable means of calculating a general optimum density, I shall take a position close to that implicitly adopted by Carr-Saunders. I shall try to assess what the people living in a particular culture would seem to regard as their optimum size, having regard not only to their demographic policy, but also to the pattern of goals which they appear to set themselves.

Now we come to the final and serious difficulty with the homeostasis theory of human population, which is that it visibly *does not* work. If it did we would not be worrying about a population explosion in India, Mauritius, Egypt, etc.

There are many examples of primitive peoples who hectically recruit newcomers when their basic resources are visibly running down. The Lele in the Congo were aware of deforestation and erosion, yet each village was more anxious to maintain or increase its *relative* size than to relate size to total resources. Other examples abound of political competition to increase numbers in face of economic pressures to reduce them. What is needed is an account of how population stability is achieved and under what conditions it breaks down. My argument is that human groups do make attempts to control their populations, often successful attempts. But they are more often inspired by concern for scarce social resources, for objects giving status and prestige, than by concern for dwindling basic resources.

Now I am ready to examine the four cases I started with.

First, the Netsilik Eskimos of Pelly Bay – in the 1920s they were an almost isolated group of 54 people. Though their area was rich in game their life was one of great hardship, endurance and hard-taxed ingenuity. Rasmussen said that there was scarcely any country on earth so severe and inclement for man. These Eskimo were at a special disadvantage because of their low mobility in winter. They had no drift wood. In the short time between thaw and freeze they travelled by kayak, but in winter their sledges made of old sealskin tents, folded and frozen stiff, or of blocks of ice, were heavy and difficult to move. They kept dogs, not for traction but for locating seals. They went sealing, caribou hunting and fishing in groups or singly, according to the seasonal cycle. Dr Asen Balikci, from whose researches I take this account, considers that in order to survive at all in their environment these people have to show great ingenuity and flexibility. In 1923 Rasmussen noted 38 cases of female infanticide out of 96 births for eighteen marriages. Their hunting and fishing economy places great emphasis on the division of labour between the sexes and a man without a woman is at a disadvantage.

Rasmussen was struck by the social difficulties and friction caused by competition for women, often resulting in fighting and killing. He was inclined to argue that the Pelly Bay Eskimo practised female infanticide to a pitch which endangered the survival of the group. However, the more recent anthropologist in the area, Dr Balikci, argues convincingly that the practice is a more flexible and sensitive instrument of demographic policy than was at first supposed. Decisions to kill a new-born infant were taken in the family. If the first-born were female it might possibly be saved, for fear of bringing bad luck on later births, but generally a family was reluctant to take on the charge of rearing a girl, especially if it had a daughter already. A man needed sons to hunt and fish for him when he was past his prime, but rearing a girl would benefit only her future husband. A girl child would not be killed if a future husband would betroth her, or if her grandmother were willing to adopt her as security for old age. So the supply of girls was not simply related to the pressures felt by their own parents. The young men who could not find a wife in their own group had another resource. They could marry girls from another Eskimo group living to the west who did not practise such a high degree of infanticide. Furthermore, although the disparity of the sexes was very marked in infancy, the balance was nearly even for the adult population. The mortality of adult men in hunting accidents, drowning, suicide and fighting, was much greater than for women. Thus, Balikci argues, this group driven to the edge of survival by harsh conditions, in practising female infanticide was contributing to its own survival and making a more or less successful attempt to control the balance of the sexes. Here we have an instance of infanticide genuinely used as an instrument of demographic policy.

According to my general thesis, this type of population control in the interests of bare survival is rare. More usually there is prestige rather than subsistence at stake.

The next human group I discuss are the Rendille, a tribe of 6,000 camel herders in Kenya (Spencer). The Rendille live on the meat and milk of herds of sheep, goats and camels. They cannot keep cattle because of the aridity and the rough terrain. Camels anyway give two to three times as much milk as a cow, in the wet season, and give adequate supplies in the dry season when a cow gives none. They can survive with water only once every ten days to two weeks, and in the wet season they need no water. They can travel forty miles a day and so can exploit vegetation in distant areas.

Rendille are aware that their population is limited to the size of herd that can feed it. Each herd requires a minimum number of people to manage it successfully. Smallpox in the 1890s reduced the human population to a too low level of manpower, so they lost stock. The great limitation of camels in these conditions is that the herds increase very slowly. Rendille believe their camels to be a fixed resource. A static stock population cannot support an increasing human population. Rendille are very different from their neighbours, the cattle-owning Samburu, who believe their herds can expand faster than human populations and that a poor man can grow rich in his own lifetime. Rendille have a problem of over-population in relation to camels. They deal with it by several measures:

By emigration: one third of the Samburu cattle herders are descended from emigrant Rendille, and Rendille still emigrate to this day.

By monogamy: a man is not obliged to help his sons to marry a second wife. A herd is not divided and goes only to the eldest son.

By late age of marriage for women: a slight excess of women is created by the Rendille custom of monogamy and met by allowing the neighbouring Samburu to marry their female surplus.

By killing off boys born on Wednesdays or after the circumcision of the eldest brother; ostensibly this avoids jealousy between brothers.

In this case a shortage of a critical resource, camels, is met with restraints on population. Again this is a fair case for Wynne-Edwards's general thesis.

If we go on like this, collecting positive instances of successful population control, we finally confront the main question – why do people *not always* practise population control? Why do populations explode? Why do some groups continue to welcome new recruits when crucial resources are visibly running down?

The answer lies in defining more precisely what are the conditions in which a resource is recognized as crucial and limited enough to provoke population policy.

We note that the Rendille camels are in the control of the elders. The whole society is under rigid social constraints, the elders have the whip hand against the juniors, their curse is feared, discipline is tight. In other words, the crucial scarce resource is the basis of all prestige in their society. It happens to be their bread and butter, but at the same time it represents caviar and champagne and all the symbols of status rolled into one.

The next example is the island of Tikopia. In 1929 there were 1,300 inhabitants. This group was fully conscious of pressure on resources, as well it might be, 700 miles from the nearest big island and needing to produce all its own food. Strong social disapproval was felt for couples who reared families of more than two, or at most three children. Their population policy was aimed at a steady replacement. It was exerted by contraception, abortion, infanticide and they talked of an ancient custom of pushing out to sea undesirables such as thieves. They lived on fish, root crops (taro and yams) and tree crops (breadfruit and coconuts). Even at the apparently dense population of 1929 they did not seem to feel pressure on land; particularly their rules about lending and borrowing garden land for root crops were very free and easy; they were much more strict about orchard land and particularly coconuts, which produced the cream which made all the other food palatable. Men would fight about orchard land, but not about garden land. In 1952 to 1953 two typhoons in succession produced a famine. Their villages and trees were wrecked and salt spray retarded the growth of their root crops. By this time the population (influenced by missionaries and administration) had relaxed its grip on itself and had increased to 1,750. During the famine there were 89 deaths, but only seventeen were attributed to starvation. There would have been a higher mortality if relief supplies had not been sent in from the government. The anthropologist, Raymond Firth, who was there in 1929 and also in 1952, gives a fascinating account of the Tikopian reaction to the famines. He considers whether it was famine or fear of famine, which seemed to have occurred every twenty years or so, which actually kept the population down to its size at any given point. But the number of deaths from the 1952 famine is so small, and even those from a 1955 epidemic (only 200) that he did not incline to this Malthusian interpretation. Instead, it seems that when they were sedulously restricting their population it was supplies of coconut cream that they had their eye on, not supplies of roots and cereals. Without food of good quality they did not like to hold feasts; without feasts they could not contemplate religious ceremonies; without ceremonies social life came to a standstill. They would exclaim, 'Tikopia does not exist without food. . . . It is nothing. . . . There is no life on the island without food.' The anthropologist remarks, 'These expressions alluded not so much to biological survival as to sociological survival' (p. 84). In making their estimate of how many months it would take to recover from the damage of the first typhoon, when they reckoned that it would be a year at least before the island was on its feet again, there was talk of people putting off to sea in despair. One very old man with experience of previous famines said, 'They say they will die, but they will not die. They will dig for wild yam roots which will not be exhausted and they will go and search for early yams and for wild legume' (p. 57). Summing up the native attitudes Firth concluded,

> Tikopia did not appear to be concerned with a balance between population and food supply in terms of mere subsistence. They would seem always to have been interested in quality as well as quantity of food, and indeed their estimate of the prosperity of the land is basically affected by this. (p. 54)

My last example illustrates the oysters and champagne factor in population control even more clearly. The Nambudiri Brahmins belong to one of the richest land-owning castes in Southern India. They are rich and very exclusive. To maintain their social and economic advantage they avoid dividing their estates, but allow only the eldest son to inherit and to administer it on behalf of his brothers (in the same way as the Rendille camel herders). The other sons are not allowed to marry at all. For each married couple only one son and one girl are likely to be allowed to marry.

The other sons console themselves with women of another caste, but the other daughters are kept all their lives in the strictest seclusion (Yalman). Only a very rich community could afford to seclude and condemn to sterility a large proportion of its women, and such a ruthless course must presumably be justified by the value of the prize, in this case maintaining a social and economic hegemony.

To conclude, it seems that population homeostasis does occur in human groups. The kind of relation to resources that is sought is more often a relation to limited social advantages than to resources crucial to survival. In the graded series which I have developed from the hard-pressed Pelly Bay Eskimos to the luxuriously settled Nambudiri Brahmins, the Rendille are important. Their camels are no luxury, but necessary for sheer survival, but I would suggest that the impetus for restrictive policies comes from the great social advantages which accrue to the older men who hold rights in camel herds.

This approach has the possibility of explaining the many cases in which population homeostasis does not appear to work. The argument is that policies of control develop when a smaller family appears to give a relative social advantage. The focus of demographic inquiry should therefore be shifted from subsistence to prestige, and to the relation between the prestige structure and the economic basis of prosperity. A small primitive population which is homogeneously committed to the same pattern of values and to which the ladders of social status offer a series of worthwhile goals which do not require large families for their attainment, is likely to apply restrictive demographic policies. Such a people would be the ritualistic and feast-loving inhabitants of Tikopia. In a stratified population it is in those sections which are most advantageously placed in relation to power and prestige in which policies of population control are spontaneously applied. Such a people would be the rich and exclusive caste of Nambudiri Brahmins.

When social change occurs so rapidly that the prestige structure is no longer consistent, we should expect population explosions to occur. Or if the whole traditional prestige structure is broken as a result of foreign oppression or economic disaster, again we would expect that the social controls on over-population would be relaxed. This happened in Ireland between 1780–1840. It is often said that the Irish population made such a remarkable increase in this period because of the adoption of the potato as a cheap form of food. But elsewhere in the eighteenth-century Europe the potato did not oust other staples (Salaman), and it is unfashionably Malthusian to argue that populations respond directly to increase in the means of subsistence. It is more plausible to adopt my general argument here and to suppose that the ruin of the native Irish society by the penal laws and the ruin of its foreign trade by English tariffs were the cause of the population increase. Similarly, to go further back into English history, the misery caused by the Enclosures and the Poor Laws would have a similar effect and help to produce the man-power for the Industrial Revolution.

It follows that there is a message here for the countries whose prosperity is threatened by uncontrolled population increase. In these countries we see the well-educated and well-to-do actively preaching family limitation and setting up birth-control clinics as a social service for the teeming poorer classes. They can counter resistance and apathy from the milling poor of the Caribbean, the outcastes of India, the landless labourers of Egypt and Mauritius. Their failure spurs them on to more enthusiastic propaganda. But if they would succeed, let them first look to their prestige structure. What hope of advance does their system of social rewards offer to those to whom they preach? Have the ladders of high prestige enough rungs to reach into the most populous sections of the community? If the prestige structure were adjusted, propaganda would be more effective or perhaps not be necessary. For given the right incentives, some kind of population control would be likely to develop among the poor as it apparently has amongst those who seek to administer the demographic policy.

References

Balicki, Asen (1960), 'Quelques cas de Suicide parmi les Esquimaux Netsilik', *Actes du VIe Congrès International des Sciences Anthropologiques et Ethnologiques*, vol. 2, Paris, pp. 511–16.

Balicki, Asen (1967), 'Female infanticide on the Arctic Coast', *Man*, vol. 2, no. 4, pp. 615–24.

Carr-Saunders, A. M. (1922), *The Population Problem: A Study in Human Evolution*, London, Arnold.

Firth, Raymond (1936), *We, The Tikopia: A Sociological Study of Kinship in Primitive Polynesia*, London, Allen & Unwin.

Firth, Raymond (1939), *Primitive Polynesian Economy*, London, Routledge.

Firth, Raymond (1959), *Social Change in Tikopia, Re-study of a Polynesian Community after a Generation*, London.

Friedman, Milton (1971) 'A Social and Ecologic Analysis of Systematic Female

Infanticide Among the Netsilik Eskimo', *American Anthropologist*, vol. 73, no. 5, pp. 1011–18.

Rasmussen, K. (1931), *The Netsilik Eskimos: Social and Spiritual Culture, Report of the Fifth Thule Expedition*, vol. 8, 1:1–542.

Salaman, S. (1949), *The History and Social Influence of the Potato*, Cambridge University Press.

Spencer, Paul (1965), *The Samburu*, London, Routledge & Kegan Paul.

Steward, J. (1938), *Paiute Indians*, American Indian Ethnohistory Series (California and Basin Plateau Indians), New York, Garland.

Turner, V. W. (1957), *Schism and Continuity in an African Society*, Manchester University Press.

Wynne-Edwards, V. C. (1962), *Animal Dispersion in Relation to Social Behaviour*, New York, Hafner.

Yalman, Yur (1963), 'On the Purity of Women in the Castes of Ceylon and Malabar', *Journal of the Royal Anthropological Institute*, vol. 93, no. 1, pp. 25–58.

7 Lele economy compared with the Bushong: a study of economic backwardness*

The Lele[1] and the Bushong[2] are separated only by the Kasai River. The two tribes recognize a common origin, their houses, clothes and crafts are similar in style, their languages are closely related.[3] Yet the Lele are poor, while the Bushong are rich. The Lele produce only for subsistence, sharing their goods, or distributing them among themselves as gifts and fees. The Bushong have long been used to producing for exchange, and their native economy was noted for its use of money and its specialists and markets. Everything that the Lele have or can do, the Bushong have more and can do better. They produce more, live better, and populate their region more densely.

The first question is whether there are significant differences in the physical environment of the two peoples. Both live in the latitude 5 degrees, in the area of forest park merging into savannah, which borders the south of the Congo rain forest. They both have a heavy annual rainfall of 1400 to 1600 mm. (40 to 60 inches) per annum. The mean annual temperature is about 78F(25C). As we should expect from their proximity, the climatic conditions are much the same for both tribes.

None the less, a curious discrepancy appears in their respective assessments of their climate. The Bushong, like the local Europeans, welcome the dry season of mid-May to mid-August as a cold season, whereas the Lele regard it as dangerously hot. The Bushong in the north tend to have a dry season ten days shorter (Bultot, 1954) than most of the Lele (see Figure 7.1), and the Lele soils retain less moisture, and the vegetation is thinner, so that the impression of drought is more severe, but otherwise there seems no objectively measurable difference in the climate to account for their attitudes.

* In Paul Bohannan and George Dalton (eds), *Markets in Africa*, Northwestern University Press, 1962, ch. 8, pp. 211–33.

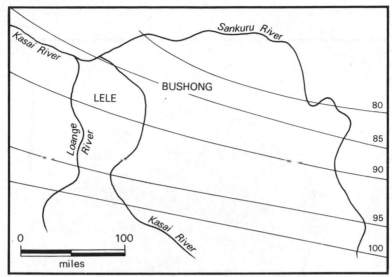

FIGURE 7.1 *Average length of dry season expressed in days*

There are certainly important differences in the soil, drainage and vegetation. The Lele are distinctly less fortunate. Their soils belong to the most easterly extension of the Kwango plateau system, and to some extent share in the sterility characteristic of that region. On that plateau, the soils are too poor to support anything but a steppe-like vegetation in spite of the ample rainfall. The soils consist of sands, poor in assimilable minerals of any kind, lacking altogether in ferromanganates or heavy minerals, and so permeable that they are incapable of benefiting from the heavy rainfall[4] (see Figure 7.2). On the Bushong side of the Kasai River the soil is altogether richer, and mineral deposits, particularly of iron ore, occur. Whereas Lele country is characterized by rolling grasslands with forest galleries along the river banks, Bushong country is relatively well-forested, although the sketch map tends to exaggerate the forested area on their side of the Kasai.

With such important differences in their basic natural resources, we are not surprised that Lele country is poorer and more sparsely populated. But how much poverty and how low a density can be attributed to the environmental factor? Can we leave the matter here?

There is no certain method of estimating the extent to which environment itself limits the development of an area. The Pende of Gungu, immediate neighbours of the Lele, inhabit an area even poorer

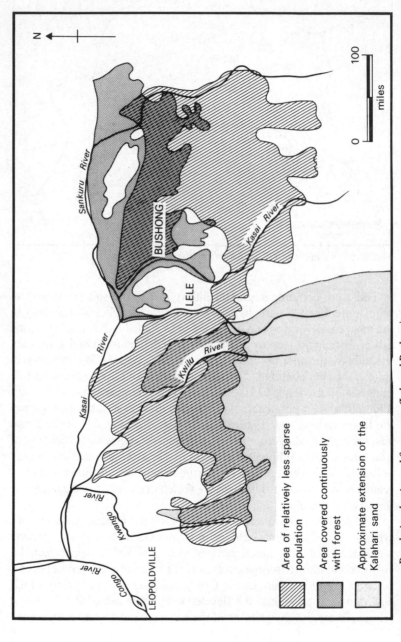

FIGURE 7.2 *Population density and forest cover (Lele and Bushong)*

in soils than the Lele area, and as poor as those worked by the notoriously wretched Suku of Kahemba and Feshi. The Lele are poor, but the Suku are known as a miserable, dispirited people, incapable of exploiting to the full such resources as their poor environment offers. The Pende are famous as energetic cultivators, well-nourished and industrious. All three peoples grow different staple crops; the Pende, millet; the Suku, manioc; the Lele, maize. There is obviously no end to the speculation one could indulge as to what the potentialities of the environment might be.

Congo geographers have been much occupied by the question of the relation between soil and population density. The whole Belgian Congo is an area of very low density. Fifty per cent of its surface has a population of less than 2.4 to the square kilometre (roughly 6 to square mile) (Gourou, 1955, p. 4). It is generally agreed (Gourou, 1955, cites Cohen; Nicolai, 1952, p. 247) that there is a rough correlation of poor sandy soils with low densities, insofar as the small stretch of relatively more populous country occurs in a favoured gap between the Kwango 'kalahari' plateau and sands to the north. However, it is also agreed that soil poverty in itself is not an adequate explanation of the pockets of extra low density which occur, especially on the second and fifth parallels of South latitude. Professor Gourou says emphatically and repeatedly that the sterility of the soils cannot be held to account for all the densities of less than two to the square kilometre (five to the square mile) in the Belgian Congo (Gourou, 1955, pp. 52, 57, 109; Nicolai, 1952). In Northern Rhodesia we have an illuminating case. The Ndembu live at an average density of six to the square mile, in many areas at a density of only three, but according to a careful calculation of the capacity of their land, worked according to their own methods, the area should be capable of supporting a population of from 17 to 38 to the square mile (6.8 to 15 per square kilometre) (Turner, 1957).

In short, we cannot assume, as some have done, that there is any universal tendency to maximize food production (Harris, 1959), or that the food resources of a region are the only factor limiting its population.

For the Lele and the Bushong the relative densities are as follows. The territory of Mweka, where the Bushong live, has an average density of 4–5 to the square kilometre (11 to the square mile). The BCK railway running through the area has attracted an immigrant population of Luba. If we abstract the railway zone from our figures, we find that the Bushong proper live at a density of (Gourou, 1955, p. 109) only 3 or 4 to the square kilometre, (7–10 to the square mile). The Lele[5] inhabit

Basongo territory, where the average density is from 2 to 4 to the square kilometre (5–7 to the square mile), but since the Lele account for only half the population (among recent immigrants of foreign tribesmen to work in the Brabanta oil concession, refinery and port, and among Cokwe hunters), we can suppose that until recently Lele themselves used to live at a mere 1.7 to the square kilometre (4 to the square mile).

When the geographers agree that poverty of soil is not a sufficient explanation for the degree of poverty prevailing in similar areas, we are justified in looking for a sociological explanation to supplement the effect of environmental factors. For one thing, it is obvious that the demographic factor works two ways. Low density is partly the result of inferior technology, applied to inferior resources, but it may also inhibit development by hampering enterprises which need large-scale collaboration.

If we now consider technology, we find many suggestive differences. In certain processes marked superiority would be likely to increase output. Others are proof of a higher standard of living. Surveying these, we find that in hunting, fishing and housebuilding, the Bushong worker uses more specialized materials and equipment than the Lele, and in cultivation he spends more energy and time.

Take hunting first, since the Lele are passionately interested in it and pride themselves on their skill (Douglas, 1954). In the eyes of their neighbours, it seems that they are notorious as inefficient hunters, particularly because they do not use nets, and only rarely make pit traps.

Hunting is the only occupation in which large numbers of Lele men regularly combine. They reckon that fifteen to twenty men and ten dogs are necessary for a good hunt. Using nets, the Bushong need a team of only ten men, and can hope to do well with five. In short, the Bushong hunter uses better capital equipment, and his hours of hunting are more productive.

Why should the Lele not have nets? The materials are present in the forest on both sides of the river, and the Lele know what nets are. Making a net is presumably a long task. In view of the local deforestation and the resulting paucity of game, it may be a case in which costly capital equipment is simply not worthwhile. Bushong nets are made by their women. Perhaps the rest of the answer lies in the different division of labour between men and women in each tribe, and the larger proportion of the total agricultural work which Lele leave to their women. Whatever the reason, we note that the absence of nets is consistent with a general Lele tendency not to invest time and labour in long-term equipment.

The same applies to pit-traps. Lele know how to make these, and frequently talk about them. The task requires a stay in the forest of several days and nights, or regular early dawn journeys and late returns. The traps are hard work to dig with only a blunt machete for spade, and once set, they need to be watched. In practice, few men ever trouble to make them. I suspect that the reason in this case is again that the amount of game caught by pit-traps tends to be disappointing in relation to the effort of making them, and that the Lele have felt discouraged when using a technique which is more productive in the thicker forests on the other side of the river.

Lest it be thought that the Lele neglect capital-intensive aids because hunting is a sport, a pleasure, and a religious activity, let me deny any parallel with English fox-hunting. The Lele would have applauded the French Brigadier of fiction who used his sabre to slay the fox. Their eager purchase of firearms whenever they can get the money and the licence shows that their culture does not restrict them to inferior techniques when these do not require long-term collaboration and effort.

In fishing the Lele are also inferior. Their country is well watered by streams and rivers, and bounded on two sides by the great Kasai, and on the west by the swift-flowing Loange. Along the banks of the Kasai are fishing villages, whose men dot the river with elaborate traps and fishing platforms. These fishermen are mostly Dinga, or Bushong, and not often Lele. In one northern village, near the Kasai, Lele women used to go every two days to the nearest Dinga village where, lacking claims of kinship, they obtained fish by bartering manioc. Compared with the Bushong, the Lele as a whole are not good at fishing, nor at canoe-making. There is no need to describe in detail the diversity and elaborate character of Bushong fishing equipment, but it is worth noting that in some types of fishing, using several canoes trailing nets, the team may consist of twenty men or more. These skills may be a legacy from their distant past, since the Bushong claim to have entered their territory in canoes along the Kasai river, while the Lele claim to have travelled overland (Vansina, 1956) and to have found the river banks already occupied by Dinga fishing villages.

If the Lele were originally landsmen, and the Bushong originally fishermen, this might account for more than the latter's present technical superiority in fishing. For primitive fishermen are necessarily more heavily equipped than are primitive hunters and cultivators. The need for fishing tackle, nets, lines, hooks, traps, curing platforms, and for watercraft as well as for weirs and dams makes quite a different balance in the allocation of time between consumer's and producers' goods. If they started in this area with the typical balance of a fishing economy, this may have meant an initial advantage for the Bushong in the form of a habit of working for postponed consumption.

Be that as it may, Lele mostly leave fishing to their women. Their simple method is to block a slow-moving stream, so as to turn the nearest valley into a marsh. In this they make mud banks and ponds, where they set traps for fish scarcely bigger than minnows. A morning's work draining out such a pond and catching the fish floundering in the mud yields a bare pint or so of fish. In the dry season they make a two-day expedition to the Lumbundji, where they spread a saponaceous vegetable poison over the low waters, and pull out the suffocated fish by hand, or in baskets.

As to housing, Lele and Bushong huts look much alike. They are low rectangular huts, roofed with palm thatch. The walls are covered with rows of split bamboos or palm ribs, lashed on to layers of palmleaf, on a frame of strong saplings. Deceptive in appearance, Lele huts when new look much sturdier than those of the Bushong, but in practice they last less well: the Lele hut is more roughly and quickly made. A well-built one will last about six years without repair, and, as they are capable of being renewed piecemeal, by the substitution of new walls or roof thatch, they are not replaced until the whole village is moved to a new site, and the owner decides that he has neglected his hut so long that it will not stand removal. A hut in good condition is transported to a new site, with from six to eight men carrying the roof, and four at a time carrying the walls.

Bushong huts are also transportable. They are made with slightly different materials. For the roof thatch, they use the leaves of the raffia palm, as do the Lele. For the walls, they use the reputedly more waterproof leaves of a dwarf palm growing in the marshes. Over this, instead of palm ribs split in half, they sew narrow strips of bamboo, where available. Lele consider bamboo to be a tougher wood than palm, but it is rare in their region. The narrow strips are held in place by stitching in pleasing geometric patterns (Nicolai and Jacques, 1954, pp. 272 ff.). A rich Bushong man, who can command labour, can build a hut that will last much longer than the ordinary man's hut, up to fifteen years without major repairs. The palace of the Nyimi at Mushenge, which was still in good condition in 1956, had been originally built in 1920.

The Bushong use an ingenious technique of ventilation, a movable flap between the roof and the walls, which lets out smoke. It is impossible to say whether they do this because their building is too solid to let the smoke filter through the walls, or whether they are more fastidious and painstaking about their comfort than the Lele, whose huts do certainly retain some of the smoke of their fires.

Within the hut, the furnishings illustrate the difference in material wealth, for the Bushong have a much greater refinement of domestic goods. They sit on stools, lay their heads on carved neck-rests (often necessary to accommodate an elaborate hair style). They eat from basketry plates, with iron or wooden spoons. They have a bigger range of specialized basketry or wooden containers for food, clothing, cosmetics. A man who has more than one hat needs a hat box and a place for his metal hat pins. Lele do not make fibre hats, and only a few men in a village may possess a skin hat. The beautiful Bushong caskets for cosmetics are prized objects in many European museums. When a Lele woman has prepared some cosmetic from camwood, she uses it at once, and there is rarely enough left over for it to be worth storing in a special container. Only a young mother who, being cared for by her own mother after her delivery, has nothing else to do but grind camwood for herself and the baby, stores the prepared ointment in a little hanging basket hooked into the wall, enough for a few days.

Dr Vansina was impressed with the high protein content of the Bushong diet, with the large quantities of fish and meat they ate, and the variety in their food. The Lele give an impression of always being hungry, always dreaming of meat, often going to bed fasting because their stomach revolts at the idea of a vegetable supper. They talk a lot about hunger, and *ihiobe*, an untranslatable word for meatlessness and fishlessness. The Bushong cultivate a wider range of crops and also grow citrus fruits, pineapples, pawpaws, mangoes, sugar cane and bananas, which are either rare or completely absent in the Lele economy.

In short, the Bushong seem to be better sheltered, better fed, better supplied with goods, and with containers for storing what they do not immediately need. This is what we mean by saying that the Bushong are richer than the Lele. As to village-crafts, such as carving and smithing, the best of the Lele products can compete in quality with Bushong manufacture, but they are much scarcer. The Lele are more used to eating and drinking out of folded green leaves than from the basket plates and carved beakers common among the Bushong. Their medical instruments, too, are simpler. If, instead of cutting down a gourd top, they carve a wooden enema funnel for a baby, they make it as fine and thin as they can, but do not adorn it with the elaborate pattern found on some Bushong examples.

Before considering agriculture, we should mention the method of storing grain, for this is a rough index of output. Both Lele and Bushong houses are built with an internal grain store, suspended from the roof or supported on posts over the hearth. Here grain and even fish and meat can be preserved from the ravages of damp and of insects by the smoke of the fire. Most Lele women have no other grain store. Bushong women find this too small and use external granaries, built like little huts, raised a few feet above ground. These granaries, of which there may be one or two in a Lele village, are particularly characteristic of the southern Bushong villages, while in the north the huts which are built in the fields for a man to sleep in during the period of heaviest agricultural work are used as temporary granaries. The Lele are not in the habit of sleeping in their fields, except to shoot wild pig while the grain is ripening. This may be another indication that they do less agricultural work than the Bushong.

When we examine the techniques of cultivation, we find many contrasts. The Bushong plant five crops in succession in a system of rotation that covers two years. They grow yams, sweet potatoes, manioc, beans, and gather two and sometimes three maize harvests a year. The Lele practise no rotation and reap only one annual maize harvest. If we examine the two agricultural cycles, we see that the Bushong work continuously all the year, and that the Lele have one burst of activity, lasting about six weeks, in the height of the dry season.

Here is the probable explanation of their dread of the dry season. There is, in fact, surprisingly little range in the average monthly temperatures through the year. For the coldest month, July, it is only 2C less than the hottest month, January (Van den Plas, 1947, pp. 33–8). None the less, the Europeans and the Bushong welcome the period from mid-May to mid-August as the 'cold season', probably because they enjoy the cooler nights and the freedom from humidity. But the Lele, enduring the sun beating on them from a cloudless sky while they are trying to do enough agricultural work for the whole year, suffer more from the dust and impurities in the atmosphere and from the greatly increased insolation. The relatively cooler nights may make them feel the day's heat even more intensely.

Apart from the differences in crops cultivated, we may note some differences in emphasis. Lele give hunting and weaving a high priority throughout the year, while the Bushong think of them as primarily dry-season activities. Traditionally, the Lele used to burn the grassland for big hunts (in which five or six villages combined for the day) at the end of the dry season, when the bulk of their agricultural work was done. If the first rains had already broken, so much the better for the prospects of the hunt, they said, as the animals would leave their forest watering places to eat the new shoots. As the end of the dry season is the time in which the firing could do the maximum damage to the vegetation, it has been forbidden by the administration, and if permission is given at all, the firing must be over by the beginning of July. The Bushong used to burn the grassland in mid-May or early June, at the beginning of the dry season, when the sap had not altogether died down in the grass.

The cycle of work described for the Lele is largely what the old men describe as their traditional practice. It was modified by the agricultural officers of the Belgian Congo. Lele are encouraged to sow maize twice, for harvesting in November, and in April. Manioc is now mainly grown in the grassland, instead of in the forest clearings. There are some changes in the plants cultivated. Voandzeia has been replaced by groundnuts, some hill rice is sown, and beans in some parts. These are largely treated as cash crops by the Lele, who sell them to the Europeans to earn money for tax. The other occupation which competes for their time is cutting oil-palm fruits to sell to the Huileries du Congo Belge, whose lorries collect weekly from the villages. Lele complain that they are now made to work harder than before, to clear more land, keep it hoed, grow more crops. They never complain that cutting oil-palm fruits interferes with their agricultural programme, only that the total of extra work interferes with their hunting.

This is not the place for a detailed study of Bushong agriculture. It is enough to have shown that it is more energetically pursued and is more productive. One or two details of women's work are useful indications of a different attitude to time, work and food. Lele like to eat twice a day: in the morning at about 11 o'clock or midday, and in the evening. They complain that their wives are lazy, and only too often the morning meal consists of cold scraps from the previous night; they compare themselves unfavourably with Cokwe, who are reputed to have more industrious wives. In practice, the Lele women seem to be very hard-working, but it is possible that the absence of labour-saving devices may make their timetable more arduous.

For example, one of their daily chores is to fetch water from the stream. At the same time, they carry down a heavy pile of manioc roots to

TABLE 7.1   Annual cycle of work

	Bushong		Lele
Dry Season			
Mid-May	Harvest beans, maize II, yams. Clear forest Burn grassland for hunt	Hunt, weave draw wine	Clear forest for maize
June	Hunt, fish, weave, repair	" "	
Mid-July to 15 August	Burn forest clearings, gather bananas and pineapple. Plant hemp	" " " "	Women fish in low waters
	Hunt, fish, plant sugar cane and bananas Send tribute to capital period of plenty	" "	Burn forest clearings Sow maize
Wet Season			
Mid-August	Lift ground nuts	" "	Fire grassland for hunting
September	Sow ground nut. Sow Maize I. Collect termites	" "	Sow voandzeia, plant manioc, bananas,
October		" "	peppers; sugar cane, pineapples
November		" "	(occasional) and raffia palms in
Mid-December		" "	forest clearings, with maize
Little Dry Season			
Mid-December	Sow maize II; sow voandzeia	" " " "	Green maize can be plucked
January	Sow tobacco, sow maize II	" "	Maize harvest
Wet Season			
February	Lift ground nuts, sow beans, collect termites and grubs Reap maize I (Main crop)	" "	Lift voandzeia
March	Reap maize I. Sow tobacco, beans, yams, manioc	" "	
April to Mid-May	Gather beans, sow voandzeia and tobacco	" "	

soak for a few days before carrying them back to the village. Bushong women, on the other hand, are equipped with wooden troughs, filled with rain water from the roofs, so that they can soak their manioc in the village, without the labour of transporting it back and forth. Bushong women also cultivate mushrooms indoors for occasional relish, while Lele women rely on chance gathering.

Bushong women find time to do the famous raffia embroidery, perhaps because their menfolk help them more in the fields. Lele men admiring the Bushong *Velours*, were amazed to learn that women could ever be clever enough to use needle and thread, still less make this elaborate stitching. The Bushong culinary tradition is more varied than that of the Lele. This rough comparison suggests that Lele women are less skilled and industrious than Bushong women, but it is probable that a time-and-motion study of women's and men's work in the two economies would show that Lele men leave a relatively heavier burden of agricultural work to their women, for reasons which we shall show later.

Another difference between Bushong and Lele techniques is in the exploitation of palms for wine. Lele use only the raffia palm for wine. Their method of drawing it kills the tree; in the process of tapping, they cut out the whole of the crown of the palm just at the time of its first flowering. During the few years before the palm has matured to this point, they take the young yellow fronds for weaving, and after drawing the sap for wine, the stump is stripped and left to rot down. Lele have no use for a tree which has once been allowed to flower, except for fuel and building purposes. The life of a palm, used in this way, is rarely more than five years, although there seems to be some range in the different times at which individual palms mature.

The Bushong also use this method on raffia palms, but they have learnt to tap oil palms by making an incision at the base of the large inflorescene, a technique which does not kill the tree. Presumably this technique could be adapted to raffia palms, since the Yakö of Cross River, Nigeria use it (Forde, 1937). But neither Lele nor Bushong attempt to preserve the raffia palm in this way, and Lele do not draw any wine from oil palms, although these grow plentifully in the north of their territory. According to Lele traditions oil palms were very scarce in their country until relatively recently, and this may account for their not exploiting it for wine. But here again, consistently with other tendencies in their economy, their techniques are directed to short-term results, and do not fully use their resources.

To balance this picture of Lele inefficiency, we should mention the weaving of raffia, for here, at least, they are recognized as the better craftsmen. Their raffia cloth is of closer texture than Bushong cloth because they use finer strands of raffia, produced by combing in three stages, whereas the Bushong only comb once. Incidentally, the fine Lele cloth is not suitable for velours embroidery.

Lele take pride in producing cloth of a regular and fine weave, and they refuse inferior cloth if it is proffered for payment. A length of woven raffia is their normal standard of value for counting debts and dues of all kinds. How little it has even now become a medium of exchange has been described elsewhere (Douglas, 1958). Raffia cloth is not the medium of exchange for the Bushong, who freely used cowries, copper units, and beads before they adopted Congolese francs as an additional currency. Raffia cloth is the principal export for the Lele, whereby they obtain knives, arrowheads and camwood. This may explain why un-adorned raffia cloth holds a more important place in the admittedly simpler economy of the Lele than its equivalent in the diversified economy of the Bushong.

If we ask now why one tribe is rich and the other poor, the review of technology would seem to suggest that the Lele are poorer not only because their soil is less fertile, but because they work less at the production of goods. They do not build up producer's capital, such as nets, canoes, traps and granaries. Nor do they work so long at culti-vation, and their houses wear out quicker. Their reduced effort is itself partly a consequence of their poorer environment. It is probable that their soil could not be worked by the intensive methods of Bushong agriculture without starting a degenerate cycle. Hunting nets and pit-traps are less worthwhile in an area poor in forest and game. But certain other features of their economy cannot be fully explained as adaptations to the environment.

When Lele timetables of work are compared with those of the Bushong, we see no heavy schedules which suggest that there would be any shortage of labour. Yet, their economy is characterized paradoxi-cally by an apparent shortage of hands, which confronts anyone who seeks collaborators. When a sick man wants to send a message, or needs help to clear his fields, or to repair his hut, or to draw palm wine for him, he will often be hard put to find anyone whose services he can command. '*Kwa itangu bo – No time*', is a common reply to requests for help. His fields may lie uncleared, or his palm trees run to seed for lack of hands. This reflects the weakness of the authority structure in Lele society, and does not imply that every able-bodied man is fully employed from dawn to dusk.

Some anthropologists write as if the poorer the environment and the less efficient the techniques for exploiting it, the more the population is forced to work hard to maintain itself in existence; more productive techniques produce a surplus which enables a part of the population to be supported as a 'leisure class'.[6] It is not necessary to expose the fallacies of this approach, but it is worth pointing out that, poor as they are, the Lele are less fully employed than the Bushong. They do less work.

'Work', of course, is here used in a narrow sense, relevant to a comparison of material wealth. Warfare, raiding, ambushing, all planning of offensive and defensive actions, as also abductions, seductions, and reclaiming of women, making and rebutting of sorcery charges, negotiations for fines and compensations and for credit – all these absorbingly interesting and doubtless satisfying activities of Lele social life must, for this purpose of measuring comparative prosperity, be counted as alternatives to productive work. Whether we call them forms of preferred idleness, or leisure activities, or 'non-productive work', no hidden judgment of value is implied. The distinction between productive work and other activities is merely used here as rough index of material output.

If we wish to understand why the Lele work less, we need to consider whether any social factors inhibit them from exploiting their resources to the utmost. We should be prepared to find in a backward economy (no less than in our own economy) instances of decisions influenced by short-term desires which, once taken, may block the realization of long-term interests.

First, we must assess in a very general way, the attitudes shown by the Lele towards the inconveniences and rewards of work.

For the Bushong, work is the means to wealth, and wealth the means to status. They strongly emphasize the value of individual effort and achievement, and they are also prepared to collaborate in numbers over a sustained period when this is necessary to raise output. Nothing in Lele culture corresponds to the Bushong striving for riches. The Bushong talk constantly and dream about wealth, while proverbs about it being the stepping stone to high status are often on their lips. Riches, prestige, and influence at court are explicitly associated together (Vansina, 1954).

On the other hand, Lele behave as if they expect the most satisfying roles of middle and old age to fall into the individual's lap in the ripeness of time, only provided that he is a real man – that is, normally virile. He will eventually marry several wives, beget children, and so enter the Begetter's cult. His infant daughters will be asked in marriage by suitors bearing gifts and ready to work for him. Later, when his cult membership is bringing in a revenue of raffia cloth from fees of new initiates, his newborn daughter's daughters can be promised in marriage to junior clansmen, who will strengthen his following in the village. His wives will look after him in his declining years. He will have stores of raffia cloths to lend or give, but he will possess this wealth because, in the natural course of events, he reached the proper status for his age. He would not be able to achieve this status through wealth.

The emphasis on seniority means that, among the Lele, work and competitiveness are not geared to their longings for prestige. Among the Bushong, largely through the mechanism of markets, through money, and through elective political office, the reverse is true. It also means that Lele society holds out its best rewards in middle life and after. Those who have reached this period of privilege have an interest in maintaining the *status quo*.

All over the world it is common for the privileged sections of a community to adopt protective policies, even against their own more long-term interests. We find traces of this attitude among old Lele men. They tend to speak and behave as if they held, collectively, a position to be defended against the encroachments of the young men. Examples of this attitude have been published elsewhere. Briefly, secrets of ritual and healing are jealously guarded, and even knowledge of the debts and marriage negotiations of their own clans are deliberately withheld from the young men, as a technique for retarding their adulthood. The old are realistic enough to know that they are dependent ultimately on the brawn and muscle of the young men, and this thought is regularly brought up in disputes, when they are pressing defence of their privileges too far: 'What would happen to us, if we chased away the young men? Who would hunt with us, and carry home the game? Who would carry the Europeans' luggage?' The young men play on this, and threaten to leave the village until eventually the dispute is settled. Although it does not directly affect the levels of production that we have been discussing, this atmosphere of jealousy between men's age-groups certainly inhibits collaboration and should probably not be underestimated in its long-term effects.

Lele also believe in restricting competition. At the beginning of the century, the Lele chief NgomaNvula tried to protect the native textile industry by threatening death for anyone who wore European cloth. If a Lele man is asked why women do not weave or sew, he instantly replies: 'If a woman could sew her own clothes, she might refuse to cook for the men. What could we give them instead of clothes to keep them happy?' This gives a false picture of the male contribution to the domestic economy, but it is reminiscent of some modern arguments against 'equal pay' for both sexes.

Within the local section of a clan, restrictions on entry into the skilled professions are deliberately enforced. A young boy is not allowed to take up a craft practised by a senior clansman, unless the latter agrees to retire. In the same clan, in the same village, two men rarely specialize in the same skill. If a man is a good drummer, or carver, or smith, and he sees an aptitude for the same craft in his son or nephew, he may teach the boy all he knows and work with him until he thinks the apprenticeship complete. Then, ceremonially, he hands over his own position, with his tools, and retires in favour of the younger man. This ideal is frequently practised. The accompanying convention, that a boy must not compete with his elder kinsman, is also strong enough to stop many a would-be specialist from developing his skill. Lele openly prefer reduced output. Their specialist craftsmen are few and far between because they are expected to make matters unpleasant for rivals competing for their business. Consequently, the Lele as a whole are poorer in metal or wooden objects for their own use, or for export.

Lastly, it seems that Lele old men have never been able to rely on their junior clansmen for regular assistance in the fields. As a junior work-mate, a son-in-law is more reliable than a fellow-clansman. This is so for reasons connected with the pattern of residence and the weak definition of authority within the clan. An unmarried youth has no granary of his own to fill. Work which he does to help his maternal uncles, father, or father's brothers, is counted in his favour, but he can easily use the claims of one to refuse those of another, and escape with a minimum of toil. Boys would be boys, until their middle thirties. They led the good life, of weaving, drinking, and following the manly sports of hunting and warfare, without continuous agricultural responsibilities.

The key institution in which the old men see their interests as divorced from those of the young men is polygyny. Under the old system, since the young girls were pre-empted by the older men, the age of marriage was early for girls (eleven or twelve), and late for men (in their thirties). It would be superficial to suppose that these arrangements were solely for the sexual gratification of the old men. One should see them as part of the whole economic system, and particularly as one of the parts which provide social security for the old.

The division of labour between the sexes leaves the very old men with little they can do. An old woman, by contrast, can earn her keep with many useful services. But old men use their rights over women to secure necessary services, both from women and from men. Through polygyny, the principles of male dominance and of seniority are maintained to the end. To borrow an analogy from another sphere, we could almost say that the Lele have opted for an ambitious old-age pensions scheme at the price of their general standards of living. We shall see that the whole community pays for the security in old age which polygyny represents.

In the kingdom of ends peculiar to the Lele, various institutions seem to receive their justification because they are consistent with polygyny of the old men and delayed marriage of the young. The latter were reconciled to their bachelorhood, partly by the life of sport and ease, and partly by the institution of wife-sharing by age-sets. They were encouraged to turn their attention away from the young wives in their own villages by the related custom of abducting girls from rival villages (Douglas, 1951). Inter-village feuding therefore appears to be an essential part of the total scheme, which furthermore commits the Lele to small-scale political life. The diversion of young men's energies to raiding and abducting from rival villages was a major cause of the low levels of production, for its effects were cumulative. The raiding gave rise to such insecurity that at some times half the able-bodied males were engaged in giving armed escort to the others. Men said that in the old days a man did not go to the forest to draw palm wine alone, but his age-mate escorted him and stood with his back to the tree, bowstring taut, watching for ambush.

Coming from Bushong country in 1907, Torday was amazed at the fortified condition of Lele villages:

> Here, too, we found enclosures, but instead of the leaf walls which are considered sufficient among the Bushongo, the separations were palisades formed by solid stakes driven into the ground. Such a wall surrounded the whole village, and the single entrance was so arranged that no more than one person was able to enter at one time. (Torday, 1925, p. 231)

Simpson also remarked that Lele men, asked to carry his baggage from their own village to the next, armed as if going into strange country. Such insecurity is obviously inimical to trade.

We have started with polygyny as the primary value to which other habits have been adjusted, because the Lele themselves talk as if all relations between men are defined by rights to women.

The point is the more effective since the Bushong are monogamous. We know well that polygyny elsewhere does not give rise to this particular accumulation of effects. Are there any features peculiar to Lele polygyny? One is the proportion of polygynous old men, indicated by the high rate of bachelorhood. Another is in the solutions they have adopted for the problems of late marriage. In some societies with extensive polygyny, the institutions which exist for the sexual satisfaction of the young men are either wholly peaceful, or directed to warfare with other tribes and not to hostilities between villages. Thirdly, where the chain of command is more sharply defined (as in patrilineal systems, or in matrilineal societies in which offices are elective or carry recognizable political responsibilities, as among the Bushong), then polygyny of older men is less likely to be accompanied by attitudes of suspicion and hostility between men's age-groups.

Having started our analysis with polygyny and the high rate of bachelorhood, tracing the various interactions, we find the Lele economy constantly pegged down to the same level of production. Something like a negative feedback appears in the relations of old to young men: the more the old men reserve the girls for themselves, the more the young men are resentful and evasive; the more the young men are refractory, the more the old men insist on their prerogatives. They pick on the most unsatisfactory of the young men, refuse to allot him a wife, refuse him cult membership; the others note his punishment, and either come to heel or move off to another village. There cannot be an indefinite worsening in their relations because, inevitably, the old men die. Then the young men inherit their widows, and, now not so young, see themselves in sight of polygynous status, to be defended by solidarity of the old.

So we find the Lele, as a result of innumerable personal choices about matters of immediate concern, committed to all the insecurity of feuding villages, and to the frustrations of small-scale political life and ineffective economy.

If we prefer to start our analysis at the other end, not with polygyny but with scale of political organization, we come to the same results. For whatever reason, the Bushong developed a well-organized political system (Vansina, 1957), embracing 70,000 people. Authority is decentralized from the Nyimi, or paramount chief, to minor chiefs, and from these to canton heads, and from these to village heads. Judicial, legislative, and administrative powers are delegated down these channels, with decisions concerning war and peace held at the centre by the Nyimi. Political office is elective or by appointment. Appropriate policing powers are attached to leaders at each point in the hierarchy. Leaders are checked by variously constituted councils, whom they must consult. The Nyimi maintains his own army to quell rebellions. Tribute of grain, salt, dried foods, and money is brought into the capitals, and redistributed to loyal subjects and officials. The chiefly courts provide well-rewarded markets for craftsmen's wares so that regional specialities are saleable far from their sources. Even before the advent of Europeans there was a food-market at Musenge, the Nyimi's capital. No doubt the Kasai River, protecting them from the long arm of the Bushong Empire, is partly responsible for the Lele's never having been drawn, willy-nilly, into its orbit, and accepting its values.

The Lele village, which is their largest autonomous unit, is not so big as the smallest political unit in the Bushong system. (The Lele villages average a population of 190, and the Bushong villages 210.) True, there are Lele chiefs, who claim relationship with Bushong chiefs. Each village is, indeed, found within a chiefdom – that is, an area over which a member of the chiefly clan claims suzerainty. But in practice his rights are found to be ritual and social. Each village is completely independent. The chief has no judicial or military authority. He claims tribute, but here we have no busy palace scene in which tribute payers flock in and are lavishly fed by the special catering system which chiefly polygyny so often represents.

When a chief visited a village, he was given raffia cloths, as many as could be spared. Then the villagers asked what woman he would give them in return. He named one of his daughters, and they settled a day to fetch her. The girl became the communal wife of one of the age-sets, the whole village regarding itself as her legal husband and as son-in-law to the chief. Son-in-lawship, expressed their relation to him until the day that he claimed the girl's first daughter in marriage. Then the relation became reversed, the chief being son-in-law to the village. The raffia gifts and women which went back and forth between the chief and village were not essentially different from those which linked independent villages to one another in peaceful exchange. None of this interfered with the autonomy of the village.

The simple factor of scale alone has various repercussions. There is no ladder of status up which a man may honourably climb to satisfy his competitive ambitions. There is no series of offices for which age and experience qualify a man, so that in his physical decline he can enjoy respect and influence and material rewards. The Bushong lay great emphasis on individual effort and achievement, but the Lele try to damp it down. They avoid overt roles of leadership and fear the jealousy which individual success arouses. Their truncated status system turns the Lele village in on itself, to brood on quarrels and sorcery accusations, or turns it, in hostility, against other villages, so promoting the general feeling of insecurity. The latter makes markets impossible, and renders pointless ambition to produce above home needs. The old, in such an economy, unable to save, or to acquire dignity in their declining years by occupying high, political office, bolster their position by claiming the marriageable women, and building up a system of rewards reserved for those who begat in wedlock. And so we are back again to polygyny and prolonged bachelorhood.

This picture has been partly based on deductions about what Lele society must have been like twenty years before fieldwork was begun. Before 1930 they could still resort to ordeals, enslave, raid, and counter-raid, abduct women, and pursue blood-vengeance with barbed arrows. They still needed to fortify their villages against attacks. By 1949 the scene had changed. The young men had broken out of their restraining social environment – by becoming Christians. They enjoyed protection, from mission and government, from reprisals by pagans. They could marry young Christian girls who, similarly, were able to escape their expected lot as junior wives of elderly polygynists. Raiding was ended, age-sets were nearly finished. Old men had less authority even than before. The young Christians tended to seek employment with Europeans to escape the reproaches and suspicions which their abstention from pagan rituals engendered.[7]

It would be interesting to compare their performance as workers in the new and freer context. One might expect that, away from the influence of their old culture, Lele performance might equal or surpass that of Bushong. Unfortunately, the framework for such a comparison is lacking. Neither tribe has a high reputation for industry with its respective employers, compared with immigrant Cokwe, Luba and Pende workers. This may simply be because the best reputations are earned by tribes which have longest been accustomed to wage-labour.

One is tempted to predict that, in so far as it is due to social factors, Lele are likely to change their name for idleness and lack of stamina before long. In 1949–50 they were not forthcoming in numbers for plantation labour or for cutting oil-palm nuts. By 1954, when a scattering of small shops through the territory had put trade goods within their reach, they had become eager to earn money. The restrictive influence of the old social system was already weaker.

We may now look again at the demographic factor, and distinguish some effects on it of the economy and the political system. It is obvious that in different types of economy, the active male contribution may have different time-spans according to the nature of the work. If there were a modern community whose bread-winners were international skating champions, footballers, or miners at the coal-face, their period of active work would be briefer than in economies based on less physically exacting tasks. A primitive economy is, by definition, one based on a rudimentary technology, and the more rudimentary, the more the work consists of purely individual physical effort. Moreover, the simpler the economy, the smaller the scope for managerial roles and ancillary sedentary work. The result, then, is that the period of full, active contribution to the economy is shorter.[8]

If we compare Lele and Bushong economies on these lines, we see that the 'age of retirement' is likely to be earlier for the Lele. The typical Bushong man is able, long after he has passed his physical prime, to make a useful contribution to production, either by using his experience to direct the collaboration of others or in various administrative roles which are important in maintaining the security and order necessary for prosperity. The Lele economy, on the other hand, with its emphasis on individual work, gives less weight to experience and finds less productive work for the older man to do. We can only guess at the differences, but it is worth presenting the idea visually, as in Figure 7.3.

Furthermore, at the other end of the life span, the same trend is increased because of the late entry into agricultural work of Lele men. The young Lele is not fully employed in agriculture until he is at least thirty and married, the Bushong man when he is twenty.

Figure 7.4 illustrates the idea that the active labour force in the Lele economy, as a proportion of the total population, is on both scores smaller than it is with the Bushong. The total output of the economy has to be shared among a larger population of dependants.

The comparison of the two economies has shown up something like the effects of 'backwash' described by Professor Myrdal (1957). First we

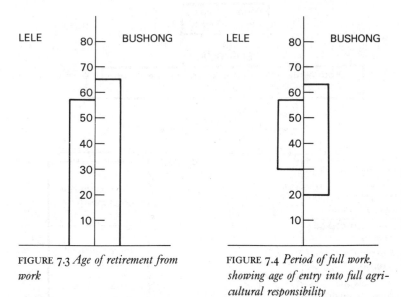

FIGURE 7.3 *Age of retirement from work*

FIGURE 7.4 *Period of full work, showing age of entry into full agricultural responsibility*

see that in the environments there are initial disadvantages which limit development. Secondly, we find that in the social organization itself there are further inhibiting effects which are cumulative, and which work one on another and back again on the economy, technology and population, to intensify the initial disadvantages. We have tried to present the interaction of these tendencies in a simplified form in Figure 7.5.

'Nothing succeeds like success.' Somehow, sometime, the Bushong took decisions which produced a favourable turn in their fortunes and set off interactions which resulted in their political hegemony and their wealth. The Lele missed the benefits of this civilization because of their location on the other side of the Kasai River, their poorer soils, their history. The decisions they took amounted to an accommodation of their life to a lower political and economic level. Their technology was inferior, so their efforts were backed with less efficient equipment, and their economy was less productive. Their old social system barred many of the chances which might have favoured economic growth.

Anthropologists sometimes tend to discuss the adoption or rejection of new techniques in terms of a cultural mystique, as if dealing with irreducible principles, of which no analysis is feasible.[9] The Lele may be taken as a case in point. Their preference for their own inferior techniques, in spite of awareness of better methods used across the

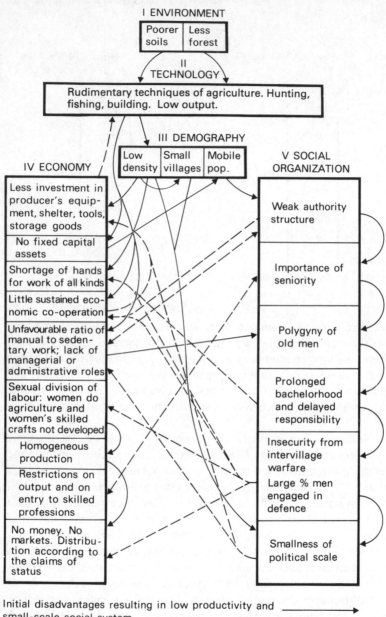

FIGURE 7.5 *Lele Economy and Social Organization*

river, depend on certain institutions, and these again on their history and environment. Through economic analysis we can break down the effect of choices, each made reasonably enough in its own restricted context. By following up the interactions of these choices, one upon another, we can see how the highly idiosyncratic mould of Lele culture is related to a certain low level of production.

Notes

1   The Lele are a tribe, inhabiting the west border of the Bakuba Empire. They are divided into three chiefdoms, of which only the most westerly has been studied. The Chief of the eastern Lele, at Perominenge, apes Kuba fashions in his little capital; the men wear basketry hats held on with metal pins, the chief has some of the dress and paraphernalia of the Nyimi. How much deeper this resemblance goes, it is impossible to say, since conditions at the time of fieldwork were not favourable for study of this chiefdom. Everything that is said here concerning the Lele refers to the western Lele, whose chief, when visits were made in 1949–50 and 1953, was Norbert Pero Mihondo. The field work was carried out under the generous auspices of the International African Institute, and of the Institut de Recherche Scientifique en Afrique Centrale.

2   The Bushong are the ruling tribe of the Kuba Kingdom. They were studied in 1953–6 by Dr Vansina, to whom I am deeply indebted for his collaboration and for supplying unpublished information for this paper.

3   According to the Lexico-statistical survey conducted by Dr Vansina, there is an 80 per cent similarity between the two languages.

4   We are very grateful to M. L. Cahen, Director of the Musée du Congo Belge, Tervuren, for guidance on the physical environment of the two tribes.

5   According to P. Gourou (1951), the average density of the population of all tribes for the Basongo-Port Francqui region, in which the Lele now account for only half, is 3 to 4 to the square kilometre. This agrees with calculations based on the total number of Lele in that area, about 26,000, and the extent of their territory, about 63 by 110 miles, which give a Lele density of roughly 4 to the square mile, or 1.7 to the sq. km.

6   For the most widely read statement of this view, see Herskovits, 1952 (Part V, 'The Economic Surplus') and for a list of reputed subscribers to this view, see Harris, 1959.

7   This process has been described in Douglas 1959b.

8   This approach was suggested by Linton, 1940.

9   See Benedict (1956, p. 187): 'Among primitive peoples, this lack of interest in "progress" has been proverbial . . . Every primitive tribe has its own cultural arrangements which ensure its survival . . . They may be culturally unin-

terested in labor-saving devices. Often the value they put on time is extremely low, and "wisdom" is far more valued than efficiency. Our cultural system and theirs are oriented around different ideals.'

References

Benedict, Ruth (1956), 'The Growth of Culture', in *Man, Culture and Society*, ed. H. Shapiro, New York, Oxford University Press.

Bultot, F. (1954), *Saisons et Périodes Sèches et Pluvieuses au Congo Belge et au Ruanda-Urundi*, Brussels, Publications de l'Institut National pour l'étude agronomique du Congo Belge.

Douglas, Mary (1951), 'A Form of Polyandry among the Lele', *Afrique*, vol. 21, pp. 1–12.

Douglas, Mary (1954), 'The Lele of the Kasai', in *African Worlds*, ed. D. Forde, London, Oxford University Press.

Douglas, Mary (1957), 'The Pattern of Residence among the Lele', *Zaïre*, vol. 11, pp. 818–43.

Douglas, Mary (1958), 'Raffia Distribution in the Lele Economy', *Africa*, vol. 28, pp. 2 ff.

Douglas, Mary (1959a), 'Age-Status among the Lele', *Zaïre*, vol. 13, pp. 386–413.

Douglas, Mary (1959b), 'The Lele of the Kasai', in *The Church and the Nations*, ed. A. Hastings, London, Sheed & Ward.

Douglas, Mary (1960), 'Blood-debts among the Lele', *Journal of the Royal Anthropological Institute*, vol. 90, no. 1, pp. 1–28.

Forde, D. (1937), 'Land and Labour in a Cross River Village', *Geographical Journal*, vol. 40, no. 1.

Gourou, P. (1951), *Notice de la carte de la densité de la population au Congo Belge et au Ruanda-Urundi*, Brussels, Institute Royal Colonial Belge.

Gourou, P. (1955), *La Densité de la population rurale au Congo Belge, etc.*, Brussels, Acad. Roy. Sci. Col. Mem. 8, 1, 2.

Harris, M. (1959), 'The Economy Has No Surplus?' *American Anthropologist*, vol. 61, no. 2, pp. 185–200.

Herskovits, Melville J. (1952), *Economic Anthropology*, New York, Knopf.

Linton, Ralph (1940), 'A Neglected Aspect of Social Organization', *American Journal of Sociology*, vol. 45.

Myrdal, Gunnar (1957), *Economic Theory and Underdeveloped Regions*, London, Duckworth.

Nicolai, H. (1952), 'Problèmes du Kwango', *Bulletin de la Société Belge d'Études Géographiques*, vol. 25, no. 2.

Nicolai, H. and Jacques, J. (1954), *La Transformation du paysage Congolais par le Chemin de Fer, L'Exemple du B.C.K.*, Acad. Roy. Sci. Col. Brussels, Sect. des Sci. Natu. et Med. Mem. in 8, XXIV, L.

Torday, E. (1925), *On the Trail of the Bushongo*, London, Seeley, Service & Co.

Turner, V. W. (1957), *Schism and Continuity in an African Society*, Manchester University Press.

Van den Plas, A. (1947), *La Température au Congo Belge*, Pub. Minis, Colon., pp. 33–8.

Vansina, Jan (1954), 'Les Valeurs Culturelles des Bushong', *Zaïre*, no. 9. pp. 900–10, November.

Vansina, Jan (1955), 'Initiation Rituals of the Bushong', *Africa*, vol. 25, pp. 138–52.

Vansina, Jan (1956), 'Migration dans le Province du Kasai', *Zaïre*, pp. 69–85.

Vansina, Jan (1957), 'L'État Kuba dans le cadre des institutions politiques Africaines', *Zaïre*, vol. 11, pt 1, pp. 485–92.

8 The exclusion of economics*

Not for a long time, perhaps not since the seventeenth century, has there been such a widespread disposition in Europe to question the fundamental assumptions on which our society rests. The questioning is of the helpless, discontinuous, kind, shooting out challenges from one base and then from another, but never able to assemble a critical synthesis. In this urgent and disorganized debate about the nature of society, a lively economic anthropology would make some useful remarks. But no such engagement with contemporary problems is to be seen. Surveying anthropology in Britain today, the eye uses the current pattern of esteem as a selector for seeing what is happening and how it came to be. As with all other subjects, what is not happening is not noteworthy. Yet it is worth reversing the normal trend of the history of science and noticing this particular gap, if only because the case history is illuminating.

Although it got off to a brilliant start with Mauss's *Essay on the Gift* in 1925, fifty years later economic anthropology is very much on the fringe of the subject. It should have been a thriving interdisciplinary enterprise, but therein lay its weakness. All subjects grow strongest where they are most autonomous. The centre of an intellectual discipline is defined by its capacity to settle its own theoretical problems on its own terms. Around this centre the most forceful exponents find it most worthwhile to cluster. The fringes are for the fringy. Thus a centripetal force in the institutional framework of knowledge exerts a magnetism for talent, time and funds. This magnetism of the centre needs a little time to get established. Continual turbulence at the boundaries of a subject interferes with its influence. In the physical sciences, industrial and government investment in research exerts strong countervailing power, so that the boundaries are constantly being redefined to incorporate interdisciplinary finds.

*From *The Times Literary Supplement*, 6 July, 1973, pp. 781–2.

But anthropology has not been heavily subsidized for its applied research. As an academic subject it is unlike physical sciences and unlike law and economics in that its findings involve no big financial interests nor do its trainees look outwards to well-rewarded professional careers beyond the cadres of the university. Nor is it like the arts subjects, which have a symbiotic relationship with literature and philosophy, carried on outside the seminar room. Able to insulate itself as much as it likes from countervailing powers of all these kinds, and therefore all the more susceptible to the magnetism of the centre, anthropology has peacefully developed over the past fifty years its most nearly autonomous fields, kinship and symbolism, with informal political structures also running, and of course, its own methodology. These subjects have in turn succeeded in developing an autonomy of their own, so that though they are rooted in a sociological perspective they take conspicuously little account of the economic foundations of social life.

It should be impossible to propose a typology of kinship, or politics, or religion that has nothing to do with economics. But it is the case that an adequate theoretical base for economic anthropology which could be relevant to thinking in these branches does not exist. The definition of centre and fringe is the best explanation I can proffer for the absence of the vigorous economic anthropology able to subtend theories of kinship or symbolism and ready to tangle with current criticisms of economic organization. Economic anthropology had to be on the fringe because it needed the collaboration of economics. Because it takes a great deal of effort and determination to go out and get cross-disciplinary collaboration at the necessary theoretical level, and because this main effort is inevitably drawn to the centre, this branch has languished.

Its history in England is roughly as follows. From the outset anthropology has always had a streak of knight-errantry. Whatever additional theoretical concerns it adopts, there is the recurrent wish to prove that primitives are rational beings like ourselves. This perspective generally has a harmful influence. For one thing, it is too limited; for another, it is too easy. The antique weapons which can tilt that windmill are too clumsy for more challenging tasks. The theme that primitives are rational like us was very insistent in the economic anthropology of the 1930s. Its main effort was bent to proving that economic analysis could be applied where no markets existed. The currency won for the term 'non-market economy' shows that the effort was successful. It would be nice to be able to say that anthropologists of those days, seeing the need for a cost-benefit analysis that would apply across the board to both monetary and non-monetary transactions, started to develop exchange theory. Though that did eventually arrive, economic anthropology of this early period displayed a more submissive posture towards classical economic theory. It was satisfied at that time to demonstrate that with a little ingenuity the concepts of capital, labour, wages and entrepreneurship could be applied absolutely anywhere.

The two most elaborate monuments to that approach came out in 1939. Raymond Firth's *Primitive Polynesian Economy* and Goodfellow's *Principles of Economic Sociology*. Their theoretical apparatus made no pretence of any practical use. It lay as a decoration upon the contemporary theme of showing that anthropology was a repository of insight concerning natives' thriftlessness and reluctance to do wage labour. By the sheer weight of their armoury these two books must have delivered the *coup de grâce* to the infant subject struggling to survive. For after that date the war intervened, and when anthropology started again this particular approach was dead. Firth himself turned away from non-market economies and concentrated on peasant markets. Anyone who was still interested in the economic foundations of social life tended to incorporate something about the mode of production in a chapter in the beginning of a general monograph along with geography and climate and in a chapter at the end something on monetization as a factor of social change. A few interesting articles in regional journals recorded curious quirks of money and markets in exotic places. In future, if anthropologists were interested in economic analysis they directed themselves to peasant societies. There was no attempt to synthesize an approach to non-market economies, no attempt to create an all-over theoretical partnership with economics, no attempt at a general theory or even a typology.

From this decade's record, we might merely conclude now that the beginnings of this as well as of other social sciences were confused and murky and be content to recall how very recently the argument that primitives are also rational came to be widely agreed. But in the 1930s other significant work in economics was being pursued in a rather different spirit. Audrey Richards described a distributive system so loaded with disincentives that productive capacity every year fell short of subsistence needs (*Land, Labour and Diet in Northern Rhodesia, 1939*). This was a successful linking of home economics and agricultural economics with the analysis of a political system where free competition was entirely suppressed. By contrast, Cora Dubois wrote an insightful account of how unbridled economic competition fulfilled a political function among North Californian Indians ('The Wealth concept as an Integrative Factor in Tolowa-Tututni culture', in *Essays presented to Kroeber*, 1936).

The next stage should have been to pave the way for development economics by establishing a comparative approach to non-market economies. This Margaret Mead had attempted in a small symposium entitled *Co-operation and Competition among Primitive Peoples* (1937). However, none of these three anthropologists pursued their early line of work. One can suppose that they were not well-enough placed in the institutional structure of their discipline to influence its trends. One can suppose also that they would have needed help from economists. The pressure of the centre against the fringe was being felt.

So economic anthropology lay quiet until Karl Polanyi's *Trade and Market in Early Empires* (1957) sounded a clarion call of enthusiasm. This time anthropology was going to make sense of the economic behaviour, not of colonial subjects, but of the ancient civilizations of Europe, Africa and America. But no servile application of economic concepts was advocated. A Marxist training encouraged Polanyi to throw overboard the theoretical apparatus designed for capitalist controllers of industrial markets. The new economic anthropology would start afresh, reject the so-called formalism of the 1930s and develop its own theoretical tools for getting at the real substance of economic relations. With such high hopes and so little technical skill anthropology reached descriptive levels it had rarely plumbed before. Like idealistic *communards* turning their back upon Western technology, the self-styled substantivists divided their time between polemics against the rejected doctrines and trying to invent wheels and clocks from scratch. While one classified means of payment into special purpose and general purpose money, and another distinguished between peripheral and central markets, a third got interested in the rate of time-cost discounting. Soon they would surely have discovered the rate of interest, but for the fact that substantivism in its turn is now being overtaken by Marxist anthropology. This last has a better chance of survival since at least it is fringy in two camps instead of one.

Though economists admit the limitations of their subject, they also know that for interpreting market trends, it works. At various practical levels, whether for the *Investors' Chronicle* or for Inland Revenue calculations, economics as a set of analytic techniques satisfies some strong demand. Hence, its vigour. The edifice of economic theory continually sustains attacks from critics who denounce its unrealistic assumptions and over-axiomatized procedures. It generally survives unimpaired. Ironically, just when the substantivist attack on formal economic analysis was being prepared, within the citadel of economics a parallel attack inspired by the very same reasons, was already launched. The substantivists were to argue that economic behaviour in non-market societies was too deeply embedded in institutional life to be analysed according to price or utility theory; embeddedness required a more sociological approach. But J. S. Duesenberry had already argued that consumer behaviour in the market economy was so deeply embedded in social institutions that utility theory could not account for it (*Income Saving and the Theory of Consumer Behaviour*, 1949).

This little book drew on anthropology for its insights. It should have been a landmark for economic anthropology since it implicitly invited anthropologists to join a cross-disciplinary exercise, not on the fringe but at the very heart of economics. For Duesenberry was out to challenge nothing less than Keynes's fundamental psychological law that men are disposed to increase their consumption as their income increases, but not by as much as by the increase in their income. These considerations will lead as a rule to a greater proportion of income being saved as real income rises. 'We take it as a fundamental psychological rule of any modern community that when income rises it will not increase its consumption by an equal absolute amount, so that a greater amount must be saved.' That law was a ripe plum for economic anthropology to take. But the anthropologists happened to be facing the other way at the historical moment when co-operation was called for.

The weakness of economics for analysing consumer behaviour is still unchanged. Whenever there is a question about the effect of consumer behaviour on prices, existing economic theory can deliver a good working answer. For in such cases, the theory is asked only to explain the interface between the consuming public and any particular set of markets. It can take one commodity at a time, or several, to work out the consumer's response to market changes. But whenever the consumer's multiple objectives have to be considered in terms of their hierarchical relation to one another, economics is at a loss. It cannot say anything for sure about savings, yet the choice between consuming now, or consuming later is of central interest to economics since the level of future income depends on their saving. Duesenberry contributed to economic theory something approximating to the advertiser's stock picture of how the consumer behaves. It is worth seeing how much this exercise drew upon the anthropologist's traditional field in order to underline the point that an entry cue was muffed.

Rejecting the economist's atomistic model which assumed that every individual's consumption behaviour is independent of all other individuals, Duesenberry tried to account systematically for envy and competitive display. He started by recognizing that all goods tend to be ranked on a culturally agreed scale. An individual does not freely choose his consumption, but operates within his culture. *The People of Alor* provided the anthropological model for understanding how standards of consumption enter into the competition for differentiated social status. For this kind of society, there is continual pressure on the consumer to spend more. Each consumer can satisfy these social pressures well or less well according to his position in the income distribution of his population. One whose income is high in the distribution will be able to satisfy all the requirements socially imposed upon him and still have a residue for saving. One whose relative income position is low will always be shelling out and so will never be able to save.

Duesenberry's relative income theory rests on four principles, the culturally derived pressure to consume, the cultural boundary of a population, the principle of social emulation within a given culture, the residual character of saving as 'feasible non-consumption' after the cultural demands have been met. With this kit he is able to treat the long historical movement of real income as irrelevant. Over a period, continuous cultural change makes rising demands for increased consumption. In each period we are dealing, as it were, with a different culture with its own distinctive standards of consumption.

The tidiest example with which he proved his point was the comparison of Negroes and Whites at the same income level. In New York and Columbus the standardized savings of Negroes and Whites are compared with their average incomes. At each income level the Negroes saved more. How to account for the difference in the marginal propensity to save? Duesenberry takes each as a separate community. The Negro group as a whole is poorer than the White group. Therefore, the percentile position of any Negro's income in his own group is higher than the percentile position of any White with the same income. Therefore, he will expect that the Negro, being relatively better off in his own community than his White counterpart, would save more. Similarly, with professionals versus other social categories in the total population, he quotes a survey in which 11 per cent of professional people identify themselves with the upper class socially and only 5 per cent consider themselves as economically upper-class. So this would account for their recorded tendency to be dissatisfied with their income at each level since it would seem relatively low in the population in which they class themselves.

Duesenberry's approach suggests a programme for social anthropologists to go forth and identify the cultural boundaries of various populations and to discover the ratio of consumption to saving at the different points in the income distribution. The anthropologist contributing to such a programme would point out that the people of Alor are not the only ethnographic case in the world. He would suggest distinguishing the people of Alor from, say, the people of Tikopia. A typology of culturally derived consumption pressures would develop. In some cultures, where emulation and display prevail, party finery and the wassail bowl might indeed drain all but the longest purses. In others, a prudent investment in consumer durables such as rope mats and canoes could figure in a spending pattern which might also require some form of personal saving from all. From here the anthropologist would challenge Duesenberry's assumption that individual saving is necessarily left to private judgment and thus forced into a vulnerable residual category. Individual savings are not necessarily less visible or less subject to public pressures than consumption. For once commodities have been conceived as the expression of sub-cultures it is clear that the culture is just as likely to impose a careful allocation of consumption behaviour between the present and the future as to require emulative display.

Communal pressures to provide for the future can be strong. In a small-scale community the penury of old age may be just as glaring and rebukable by public disdain as a failure to give a bigger and better feast than the Joneses. Max Weber argued that thrift took first place in the cultural values of early Protestant Europe. Duesenberry's model has no room for a cultural bias towards thrift. Supplementing his limited ethnographic range, it would have been possible to anticipate his broad gist of Milton Friedman's actuarial theory of consumption developed a decade later. Here again, with his *The Theory of the Consumption Function* (1957), we have work in economics which is of paramount interest to anthropology. But the anthropologists were going to be too deeply enshrouded in their substantivist home-spun to notice it.

From the foregoing it is clear what the preconditions of interdisciplinary collaboration should be. First, economic analysis must be established at the centre of anthropology itself. In order to do this it must focus critically upon those autonomous areas of the subject which so far manage to make do without it, kinship and symbolism. Marshall Sahlins has recently made a good start on the first by a wide-ranging attempt at synthesis around the theme of the domestic mode of production. At first sight, the second seems more intractable until we recall that fetishism is a part of the study of symbolism. Marxists and psychoanalysts have joined in a negative attack on the fetishism of commodities. Anthropology would be more positive. It would focus attention not on the commodities, not on the physical or the psychological needs they supply but on the pattern of relationships they subserve.

Whenever consumption goods change hands, someone is communicating with someone else. Commodities define social categories: exactly as Nuer define kinsmen as those with whom sexual relations are prohibited and identify categories of kin according to whether or not they are entitled to receive cattle at the marriage of a daughter, so we define inclusive and exclusive categories by rules about degrees of sharing and giving of commodities.

No amount of welfare grants calculated on basic needs will cancel the meanings which the language of commodities declares. Poverty is not a lack of goods but exclusion from social esteem and power. Alms will never change that meaning. A vitalized economic anthropology would make alms-givers dissatisfied with their material gifts. It would apply its radical criticism to every branch of knowledge in which foreshortened perspectives close on the physical properties of goods instead of revealing the pattern of social relations which they create.

Each branch of the social sciences has been bogged down until it learns to draw a distinctive line between the level of human behaviour its techniques are adapted to analyse and all other levels. Long before Durkheim had required the isolation of 'social facts' in his rules of method, economics had carved out a sphere of economic facts by disregarding the ends of human activity and concentrating on scarcity. In anthropology this process has required a continuing effort to disengage one theoretical field after another from intrusive assumptions from common sense. In each case, enlightenment has come from deciding to disregard the physiological levels of existence which underpin the behaviour in question. For interpreting bizarre kinship terminologies, we at first assumed that the clue to the use of Father or Mother was some early system of marriage and procreation. Advance required kinship terms to be cut free from their obvious biological meanings and treated as a metaphorical system based upon engendering and rearing but applied to the organizing of social relations. More recently, Lévi-Strauss has justly ridiculed the idea that a gastronomic criterion reserved the most delicious foods as totems. Animals are chosen to be tabooed because they are good to think, not because they are good to eat. Thus he revealed a systematic interrelation between natural and cultural species in some fields of primitive thought.

In the nineteenth century medical materialism blocked ideas in comparative religion about the contagiousness of magic. Scholars were side-tracked by occasional signs of medical justification for rites of purification. But these rites are better understood as means of affirming boundaries between cognitive categories than as dealing with pathogenes in the bacteriological sense. In the same direction, Chomsky has insisted on the theoretical advance to be gained by cutting the study of language free from assumptions about its practical uses. He approvingly quotes Humboldt, who

> regards it as a mistake to attribute language primarily to the need for mutual assistance; the purely practical use of language is characteristic of no real human language, but only of inventing parasitic systems . . . the form of language is a generative principle fixed and unchanging, determining the scope and providing the means for the unbounded set of individual creative acts that constitute normal language use. (*Cartesian Linguistics*)

In the same direction lies a contemporary programme for economic anthropology exacting in its scope and power. But only stone age tools are ready for it because the unguided and unconscious interaction between centre and fringe in the institutional arrangements of the subject have left this one social science which claims to see mankind as a whole without an adequately developed theory of economics.

9 Cultural bias*

1 Culture

1 Problems of comparison

By establishing expertise on culture, Frazer created a great forum for our subject. If anthropologists neglect culture, we could well dwindle to a sub-section of sociology or even of geography in European thought. Culture is a blank space, a highly respected, empty pigeonhole. Economists call it 'tastes' and leave it severely alone. Most philosophers ignore it – to their own loss. Marxists treat it obliquely as ideology or superstructure. Psychologists avoid it, by concentrating on child subjects. Historians bend it any way they like. Most believe it matters, especially travel agents. The intellectual gap that yawns is a reproach to anthropology, for ours is the only discipline that has any pretensions to be dealing with culture systematically.

By popular enquiry an anthropologist is often asked to explain behaviour for which no ready-made explanations lie handy. The questions often concern the relation between culture and personality. 'Why are the Latin cultures hot-blooded?' 'What makes some peoples ritualistic?' 'Why have the Dutch always been so clean?' 'How do you explain national character?' The questions float up from a deep conviction that people do what they do because they are what they are. So refuge in ignorance is not acceptable. There is an expected range of answers which ought to rest on some theory about inherited character, whether inherited by genetic or cultural processes.

A distinguished list of American anthropologists from Boas and Kroeber have reflected upon culture and its patterning. I hope it is not

*Originally Royal Anthropological Institute, Occasional Paper, 35, 1978.

too summary to divide their work according to the point on which they sought to pin explanation. One strong tradition has treated culture as autonomous. Culture itself was its own explanation and explained what else could happen by the otherwise arbitrary restrictions and permissions arising from within its patterns. Opler's concept of cultural themes,[1] because of its explicit affinity to Kluckhohn's 'cultural configurations' and Talcott Parsons's 'value attitudes' can be used to illustrate this style of argument.

> It is the thesis of this paper that a limited number of dynamic affirmations, which I shall call *themes*, can be identified in every culture and that the key to the character, structure and direction of the specific culture is to be sought in the nature, expression, and interrelationship of these themes.... The term theme is used here in a technical sense to denote a postulate or position, declared or implied, and usually controlling behaviour or stimulating activity, which is tacitly approved or openly promoted in a society.

The gauntlet thus thrown down seems to put the weight of explanation upon the logical interconnections of the various themes in a culture. But, in practice, when it comes to explaining the shift from one set of themes to another, Opler takes account of external social influences, though his theoretical position does not lead him to systematize the latter along with the themes which are supposedly dominating behaviour. In my opinion, to separate culture from other social influences is a disastrous way to open the enquiry, for it blocks curiosity at the outset. Taken to be *sui generis*, culture needs no explanation, only analysis. The whole subject is put into a glass case, protected from the rude probings of the public. Social pressures to exploit, to dominate or to be liberated are treated as if they were as irrelevant as events going on at a different level of existence.

The second group of cultural anthropologists have sought to trace a connection between child-rearing customs and cultural patterns.[2] At least they tried to link the manifestation of cultural distinctiveness to some kind of human action, even if it was only a feedback between the weaning and bodily training of babies, their subsequent personality development and cultural forms. This self-explaining circle bridged the gap from babyhood to adult behaviour in one leap. It implied a gloomy view of human adaptability. According to their kind of delayed Calvinist predeterminism, the human personality is adaptive in infancy, but soon sets into a hard mould. After an early age there is nothing much that can be done to break out. In consequence this theoretical stance is helpless in face of change. Individuals so manifestly do overcome and transform their cultural origins. No wonder that culture-change became almost a catchword summarizing the crucial problems of anthropology in the late 1930s and 1940s.[3] This work allowed no place for the social dimension as such and developed no analytical tools for thinking about how sociology and culturology could be grafted together.

However, the unfashionable path I wish to tread was charted most famously by Ruth Benedict in *Patterns of Culture*[4]. In this influential book she holistically insisted upon the internal consistency of a culture and identified three types: Appollonian (the equilibrium-loving, moderate Zuni), Dionysiac (the ecstatic, immoderate, sensationalist Kwakiutl), and the anxiety-ridden, secretive, paranoiac Dobuans. Why she had only three, whether she should have had four, or five or fifty cannot be answered since she gave no rules for deriving them in the first place, except a general interest in the matching of culture and personality. Another group of theories makes a more serious attempt to derive culture and social forms together from ecological factors likely to shape them both. Hoebel convincingly explains Eskimo culture as rewarding the behaviour which is best adapted to help the community to wreak a livelihood out of their hard natural surroundings.[5]

The criticism from this side of the Atlantic is that this whole corpus of professional studies either chooses arbitrarily a focus for straight deterministic theories (the child-rearing or the environmental basis) or it makes culture into something independent on which the rest depends. Its independence is mysterious, unexplained and unchallengeable. It occupies in the theory of culture the place of the elephant standing on the tortoise standing on the elephant in oriental cosmology. Moreover, the cultural typologies float in the dusty air of seminars and museums, only becoming real as blackboard tabulations or labels on display cases. Those who first concentrated on the internal consistency of culture seemed to be bringing in some richer account of behavioural constraints. But modern exponents of the logic of cultural categories now take care to detach culture from any living human beings, focusing upon linguistic phenomena as the guide to hidden thought processes.[6] They then proceed to inspect its logical structure microscopically. Refining their techniques they gradually introduce very limited laboratory-like social situations.[7] The individual and his social concerns are gradually being reintroduced, but in micro-analysis only. Before that, it is fair to say that in cultural theory the individual himself was very much downgraded. The human person was made into an automaton whose choices are controlled, whose thoughts and values are passively received from the ambient culture.

Who are we to criticize this long, scholarly effort? Standing on the side-lines, often jeering, we English anthropologists have paid little attention to culture. We have given little help to understanding how it interacts with the social dimension. In the outcome we too are the poorer for there being no general theory of how culture and society are related, no special theory of cultural change, still less one about cultural stability.

Here to Cambridge many researchers come whose work in New Guinea suffers from this lack. For years they have been rumbling in complaint about the inadequacy of existing theoretical frameworks for interpreting this cultural region.[8] Rebuking each other for taking over African models of society, they are clearly casting around for an interpretative scheme that will fit better to the Melanesian ethnography. But are the disconcerting forms of behaviour specific to Melanesia? It could be that a general theory is needed that will explain both the favoured African model and a Melanesian one, as well as some examples from Africa, North America and the Mediterranean, Asia and even from industrial society.

It is not difficult to summarize some of the salient features of the cultural complex in Melanesia that seem to fit so badly to the preconceptions of anthropologists trained on African research. Melanesian society seems to be typically organized by individual competitive exchanges, with varying degrees of incorporation, while the dominant principle in African ethnography is incorporation with more limited scope for individual transactions. From this the rest seems to flow. From African studies, ethnographers reported a philosophy of formal hierarchy, often in societies with little real disparity of status,[9] and even in the great kingdoms constitutional checks and balances are built in to control the mighty individual.[10] In New Guinea the very opposite: no philosophy of hierarchy, rather an ethic of equality, contradicted by real disparity of status. Between the Big Man at the top and the Rubbish Man at the bottom of the pile, no philosophy of distributive justice explains the difference, except the *de facto* power of might.[11] Their institutions organize equality of opportunity, generally dispersing a rich man's heritage and setting his sons to start from scratch. But disparity emerges in each generation in unpredicted peaks and troughs.[12] This unpredictability of status is another feature contrasting with the 'office' described by Meyer Fortes.[13] The Tallensi society he knows so well allots to every person, man, woman and child, a precisely defined place, with such clear rights and duties to be performed in each that the whole society can be described as a structure of co-ordinated offices. Another is in the institution for sponsoring, selecting and promoting able leaders, usually oblique and inconspicuous procedures supported by a generally high judgment placed upon ambition in a young person.[14] Most famous is the ostentatious affirmation of rank in squanderous feasting. Underlying these cultural effects, from tribe to tribe are seen variants of transactional freedom. In some tribes there are restrictions on market behaviour: some things are reserved from buying and selling. In others practically no advantage is not purchasable one way or another. It would be impossible to explain to such people the fuss that was made about the Watergate scandals. In such cultures they expect their secrets to be stolen or bought and they take precautions. A gradient from the imperfect to the most perfect competition reaches in Kapauku the most perfect competition that any free-trading economist could ever conceive of: complete mobility of all resources, most allegiances buyable and sellable. The Big Man is the banker; in his strong box everyone else is prudent to deposit his valuables, because only he can muster the biggest defence against thieves.[15]

To press the contrast, notice three values which are frequently cited as characteristics of New Guinea cultures. First, their opportunism and eclecticism: contrast their enslavement to changing fashion with the alleged conservatism of primitive cultures. Second, their individualism which – combined with their opportunism – makes it difficult to build up a reserve of social capital. For example, Pospisil noted that when a bridge collapses, instead of repairing it, all those who had contributed a part at the behest of some once-current leader, now carry off their own logs to put to some new need.[16] Third, their secularity: ethnographers do not usually spend ink on reporting absent forms of behaviour, but in New Guinea they record their surprise at finding that the great rituals are often secular, and that instead of shared piety to communal gods, each man has his own spiritual power working for him, a private source of strength and inspiration, and not a focus of public morality. Or else the emphasis is placed upon private manipulation of religious symbols, on contractual rather than on communal regulative powers in religion, or upon the individual's freedom to select at will from a wide range of fragmentary cosmological notions instead of upon a coherent, collective religious consciousness.[17] It is always possible to argue that the appreciation of religious ideas grows with improvements in the quality of research. Certainly there are now some modern ethnographies of New Guinea that could be used to undermine the stereotype of religious forms that I am seeking to identify. But improvement in ethnographic understanding in Africa has worked the other way to break down the contrasted stereotype of African religion and introduce cases of more pragmatic, contractual kinds of dealings with spirits and ghosts. More likely, both stereotypes are wrong and each region has a rich variety of cultures.

Taking individualism, eclecticism and pragmatism as summarizing the contrast with African ethnography, we begin to see that New Guinea type cultures have been in Africa all the time. Daryll Forde pointed out that a highly commercial, competitive, eclectic Big Man type of culture had long existed in West Africa, especially in the pre-colonial period,[18] and had been ignored by scholars devoting attention to corporatist functionalism. His studies of the Yakö show his own shift from describing lineage formation and integrative rituals[19] to observing a secular, calculating attitude to spiritual remedies,[20] and competitive forms of conspicuous display and feasting between ranked clubs.[21] In another ethnographic region they could have been called Feasts of Merit and the cross-regional parallels would have been easier to see.

2 The negotiating individual

The first source of our troubles as cultural anthropologists is that we have no adequate conception of the individual. Necessarily somewhat parasitic upon sociology, we share its strengths and weaknesses; and this particular failing is one we all have in common. Aaron Cicourel attacks sociology for setting in the middle of role theory a mindless robot in place of an intelligent being.[22] Any account of roles and statuses, he says, ultimately presupposes an active perceiving person, able to read cues and size up situations. The theory always pays lip-service to intellectual activity going on inside the head of the performers, but it is a mere token salute, recognizing rewards and penalties, judging what amount of deviant behaviour will be tolerated, punishing the deviance of others. A formidable list of textbook quotations shows that our students are given a stereotype of society consisting of well-trained sheep-dogs picking their way through institutional mazes. Whereas we know that many social situations are fraught with ambiguity: each individual has latitude to misroute, redirect and even reconstrue. If their actual procedures of interpretation were taken seriously, claims Cicourel, sociology would install something more like real live human beings at the centre of its theory, instead of automatons. It follows that instead of a fixed institutional structure, it would be faced with an infinite vista of social transformations. The theory would not be static, but perhaps too uncontrollably dynamic.

Not surprisingly, sociology finds even Cicourel's cogent form of ethnomethodology difficult to accept, wilder ones more so. Something vital is still missing from the picture of the real live individual; that something is culture. After doing a good hatchet-job on role theory's short-comings, Cicourel has turned round and done the same to the new cultural anthropology which claims to study the rules which govern the structure of meaning. But Cicourel pours scorn on the academic effort to draw cognitive maps. Each minutest experience, as it is interpreted by real live individuals, is deeply embedded in the past, while in the present it ripples in ever-widening contexts. He ridicules the ethno-scientists' pretensions to skim off a little surface meaning and analyse it. Everything he writes about our colleagues strikes this anthropologist as good, clean fun, but it is a pity that he never writes anything about English social anthropology at all. For we are his natural allies. We also believe that our work is to understand how meanings are generated, caught and transformed. We also assume that meanings are deeply embedded and context-bound. We are also stuck at the same fence that he balked. Like him, we cannot proceed very far without incorporating real live cultures into our analysis. For the cognitive activity of the real live individual is largely devoted to building the culture, patching it here and trimming it there, according to the exigencies of the day. In his very negotiating activity, each is forcing culture down the throats of his fellow-men. When individuals transact, their medium of exchange is in units of culture. Their disputes are about standards and values, how town-life should be lived and justified, how country life should be supported, by this list of urban values and that list of rural ones.[23] But it is important to know whether culture is infinitely transactable. How plastic is it?

Among all living beings, humans are the only ones who actively make their own environment, the only ones whose environment is a cultural construct. Culture is no passive object of negotiation; it is not a solid deep-storage system, nor a fixed set of logical pigeonholes for retrieving embedded memories. With some pliability and some toughness of its own, there are yet limits to the negotiability of culture. To discover these limits is the problem I discern as common now to sociology and anthropology.

I have sketched some weaknesses in conceiving of the social individual and some weaknesses in dealing with culture. My remedy is to think out a better account of the social context. I mean by this a context conceived in strictly social terms, selected for its permitting and constraining effects upon the individual's choices. It consists of social action, a deposit from myriads of individual decisions made in the past, creating the cost-structure and the distribution of advantages which are the context of present-day decisions. We will pick from the coral-reef accumulation of past decisions only those which landscape the individual's new choices: the action is this afternoon, the context was made afresh this morning, but some of its effects are long, slow fibres reaching from years back. With such a view of the social environment we can try to make allowance for the individual's part in transforming it, minute to minute. Here I am assuming a collective consciousness, in Durkheim's sense,[24] that manifests itself in these two ways, by making penalty-carrying rules and justifying them. Paradoxically, the task of bestowing life upon the individual in sociological theory is to ignore what is peculiar to individuals and attend to what is publicly shared and therefore accessible to sociological methods.

The reason for focusing upon the social context defined in this way is that each pattern of rewards and punishments moulds the individual's behaviour. He will fail to make any sense of his surroundings unless he can find some principles to guide him to behave in the sanctioned ways and be used for judging others and justifying himself to others. This is a social-accounting[25] approach to culture; it selects out of the total cultural field those beliefs and values which are derivable as justifications for action and which I regard as constituting an implicit cosmology.

Having divided experience into social context and cosmology, the next step is to get a full array of possible social structures. A start for this will be to construct (yes, I mean construct, fabricate, think up, invent) two dimensions. One clue to finding a relevant pair of dimensions is to follow the polarizing of sociological thought between individualism and group behaviour. Instead of plumping for one or the other, as has been the usual form, the procedure I am advocating is to show both, always present as possibilities. I use 'grid' for a dimension of individuation, and 'group' for a dimension of social incorporation.[26]

Thrown across the social environment, these co-ordinates should measure effects that are not always triggered by closure or expansion in

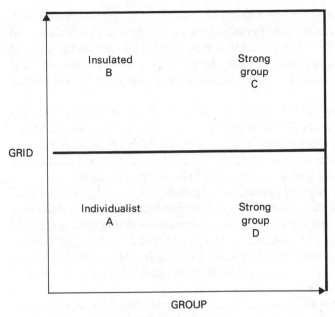

FIGURE 9.1 *Four types of social environment*

the wider economic-political domain, but sometimes by individuals who choose to interpret a situation as if its possibilities were closed or not, by individuals who, in their negotiation with others, can open a scene that was shut or slam doors that were ajar. How to set the individual in a social context is the first problem I hope to solve by this method. One of its strengths is to separate out the environing factors which are usually treated as flowing from a breakdown in group norms. Following Maine,[27] most anthropologists (and others) have assumed that the shift from status to contract goes in step with the breakdown of corporate groups, as if the increase of individual freedom could only be traded against decrease in group strength. I am trying to present a less impoverished view of social change.

Because of this strong tradition, when we try to think of the individual in a social context, we normally think of the corporate group or groups to which he belongs. The group itself is defined in terms of the claims it makes over its constituent members, the boundary it draws around them, the rights it confers on them to use its name and other protections, and the levies and constraints it applies. Group is one obvious environmental setting, but we seem unable to conceive of the individual's environment if it is not a group of some kind. We can conceive clearly enough of individuals transacting, as such, with other individuals, but their behaviour is then set in a vacuum. To illuminate this invisible background, we have to catch the external side-effects of individual interaction, to note those which create most constraint upon individual behaviour.

The term grid suggests the cross-hatch of rules to which individuals are subject in the course of their interaction. As a dimension, it shows a progressive change in the mode of control. At the strong end there are visible rules about space and time related to social roles; at the other end, near zero, the formal classifications fade, and finally vanish.

At the strong end of grid, individuals do not, as such, freely transact with one another. An explicit set of institutionalized classifications keeps them apart and regulates their interactions, restricting their options. At this point for grid, male does not compete in female spheres, sons do not define their relations with fathers. The grid is visible in the segregated places and times and physical signs of discriminated rank, such as clothing and food.

Moving slowly down grid, the boundaries begin to be arbitraged. Individuals, deciding to transact across them, weaken the classifications. The mode of control changes its nature. It sinks below the surface. The substantive signs of ascribed status are scrapped, one by one, and supplanted by abstract principles. Of these, one is sacred still, that is the holiness of contract itself. As individuals are supposed to transact more and more freely, the rules governing transactions may even multiply. Society turns into a veritable market, and for every new kind of deal, further external effects transform the social structure.

For thinking about this structure at low grid, transactional models which would seem to be ideal are, paradoxically, of no use. Clearly one would expect transactional analysis to get in the way of constructing the group dimension. But for grid it is equally cumbersome. It can use the insights afterwards, but generates none. What is needed is a net to catch the side-effects, the 'externalities' of individual transactions. For these, I draw heavily on Basil Bernstein's ideas on visible and invisible pedagogies.[28] As he shows for teaching institutions, strong insulation holds so long as power is securely monopolized. Insulations are the result of effective power. They are also a means of making it effective all the way down from its source to the boundaries of control. Classifications are enforced in an effort to stabilize power, to filter information, ration it, limit access. According to the locus and energy of change, the system of classifications weakens; control moves down grid. A more open, competitive environment gives individuals more options, to deal or not to deal, to choose their own partners. But one result is that selectivity is the dominant feature of the new environment; everyone knows that they are choosing and being chosen. Every Yes to an invitation to join something new is a No to the old classification of individuals in society. The new down-grid rules which emerge are designed not to segregate, but to give each individual a fair turn. These fair-comparison rules, as distinct from insulations, render their own segregating effects invisible. The definition of 'amateur' in the Rules of the Amateur Rowing Association is an example of both. Clearly those who drafted it wanted to protect sport from professionalism, at first sight an intention to make the competition a fair one. But a quite explicit insulating intention is avowed as well.

Encycl. Britt: 1911

Committee of the Amateur Rowing Association –
No person shall be considered an amateur oarsman, sculler or coxswain

1. Who has ever rowed or steered in any race for a stake, money or entrance fee.
2. Who has ever knowingly rowed or steered with or against a professional for any prize.
3. Who has ever taught, pursued or assisted in the practice of athletic exercises of any kind for profit.
4. Who has ever been employed in boats or in manual labour for money or wages.
5. Who is or has been by trade or employment for wages a mechanic, artisan or labourer, engaged in any menial duty.
6. Who is disqualified as an amateur in any other branch of sport.

As we read on, we notice that the exclusion of menial workers carries a socially insulating purpose. Since 1911 the definition of amateur, still important, has lost this excluded class because the very concept of menial workers has lost its meaning. This is a good example of how the shift down of grid changes the character of rules from insulating to fair-comparison, the latter being the rule that makes the market workable.

Low grid without group is the place on the chart which generates internal pressures for change. It has no control on information. Any forces making for equilibrium are continually subject to disturbance.

Better than a static scene, think of people here as milling around, occasionally emerging for a time into a society that seems very like the ideal of the free market, but always under threat of developing towards monopoly (up-grid) or moving into protective cartels and price rings (up to and to the right). Whatever they do, they subscribe to a basic justifying principle which is in harmony with the anchorite's view of personal liberty – and always perplexed at the difficulty of putting it into practice outside the anchorite's cell. We can call this basic principle 'frontier individualism' of which I shall have more to say later. It is invoked at the frontiers of knowledge and experiment, as well as at territorial and political frontiers.

'. . . These were frontier, pioneer times, when personal liberty and freedom were almost a physical condition like fire or flood, and no community was going to interfere with anyone's morals so long as the amoralist practised somewhere else . . .' – so Faulkner describes the attitude of people who eventually decided to form the town of Jefferson.[29] He was describing in this book the shift from zero up and across the diagram, from free independent individuals to a society where an explicit set of institutional classifications keeps individuals apart, regulates their interactions, restricts their options. At such a point, female does not compete in male spheres, nor blacks with whites. Moving the other way, down-grid, we can trace out systematically the consequences of reduced insulation. Logically first comes weaker definition of roles and greater ambiguity in relationships. The people trying to operate in this world find their actions judged by multiple criteria, less explicit sequencing and rules for promotion. The resulting problems about evaluation together with the whole set of consequences of invisible controls has been analysed fully by Basil Bernstein, as already acknowledged.

Though education is, of course, the very sifting process itself, we can expect to find parallel behaviour and moral judgments in any sector of the class structure.

I will follow out the trend under two heads, increasing uncertainty and increased emphasis on individual achievement. First, for uncertainty: as insulation decreases, the organizing principles of society become increasingly obscure. As statuses themselves become challenged, each world view that partly reinforces a status pattern becomes challengeable. So as grid weakens, there will be increasing scope for scepticism about metaphysical principles and their fit to experience. There will be pressure to doubt any mutual support between theories about God, nature and morality. The way is open for scientific enquiry, of which more below. The same atmosphere of intellectual openness will foster tolerance, for the grounds for intolerance are eroded and the power to suppress contrary views is weakened. To tolerate disagreement, it will be necessary to separate politics from religion. The microcosm-to-macrocosm unity of knowledge will fall apart; structuralism will have to be rediscovered. Individual variation will be tolerated, no longer a symbol of threatened classification. Eccentricity may flourish. Moral and social deviance can barely be defined. In the end it will be very difficult to get consensus on what is indecent, pornographic or un-natural, for every such definition impinges on the cardinal principle of individual freedom to transact. If there were any poignant thing which individuals would have shared in common, it could be a sense of being fringy. Since in this cultural type there is no centre, each individual centre to his own world, each knows what it is to be peripheral to whatever else is going on. The Rosencrantz-and-Guildenstern feeling fosters reluctance to define norms sharply, even if the intellectual tools for doing so were at hand.

Here we have the social pre-requisites for the cultural mood which Professor Trevor-Roper has called Erasmianism. He argues that it was not Calvinism which had nurtured the capitalist spirit, but the persecu-tion in certain Catholic states of this long-established attitude repre-sented by the enquiring and tolerant mind of Erasmus. The exile to Protestant courts of these technically skilled and educated Erasmians would explain how capitalism became associated with the protestant ethic. The princedoms which had ejected the scholars and financial experts employed a mode of control which Erasmianism threatened. Rigid dogma, control of curiosity, doctrines of centrally instituted channels of salvation, holiness located, this became the Tridentine Catholicism which rose in arms against Erasmian tolerance and scep-ticism.

All these effects can be inferred as flowing from increasing uncer-tainty. Familiar though it sounds it still has a pleasing air. But later the story is less comforting. One notices that whatever part of this two-dimensional field is under scrutiny, there is always some trouble lurking there. This approach is never a judgment upon individuals. On the contrary, it exculpates them and claims compassion, not blame. No part of the map is good in itself. Each has its own torments and temptations. The task of anthropology is to recognize them.

Consider what it would be like to live in an environment where progressive transformations through the years have led, through low grid-favouring choices and low grid-favouring justifications, to the stage at which the only achievement is individual. Then reflect on the consequences. New Guinea ethnographers have recorded so many examples. The individual who would not seek status is the only deviant. He who seeks it needs to engage a team of supporters, each contracting with him separately for what their allegiance is worth. Anthony Forge describes how a Big Man in Abelam gains control of his own villagers, files a secret dossier of magic on them, one by one, and then uses their work in exponentially prestigious exchanges with an opposite number in another district. Each leader is out for himself. Their respective followings gain by each success. But no Big Man is secure. His rival and supplanter lurks, who will one day oust him and take his place.[30]

The fall-out from any system which pitches individuals against each other, contract by contract, man by man, is that in the end the only reckoning of achievement depends on size of support. This is a fearsome condition of society because it tempts individuals to get benefits of scale.

When competing to get the largest following, market principles apply. Competitors must sense intuitively the marginal costs of personal input, especially their time. At low grid, time becomes immensely precious. This leads to a screening of people they can afford to spend it on: other leaders with large followings are worth more valuable time than smaller fry. But how to know who is who? Information costs soar. Oh! the name-dropping and false claims to be well-connected which have to be sifted, the genealogical reference books, consultancies, brokerage and marketing of secret skills. Claims to know psychological magic is a special effect of the pressure to get benefits of scale. But the excluding procedures must be discreet. They must not offend the basic doctrine of the unique value of each individual human person, because this doctrine justifies the enlarged scope for negotiation. The screening goes politely underground. At the surface the Big Man with a big smile and a big handshake, seems to be entirely accessible. Of one chairman of the UN it was said that nothing was more surprising than the warmth of his greeting as you stepped inside his office, except the amazing speed with which you found yourself outside the door again.

Access to the Big Man is a taxing problem for everyone, but it is also a problem for himself. A high value on personal privacy helps the screening process. This accords with the cardinal ethic of individual value. But the private bathroom, like the ex-directory telephone, also protects from unwanted solicitations in a society where other insulating barriers have gone down. The large-scale feast is a way of maximizing the use of time in personal contacts. Ostentatious hospitality is a feature of Papuan, Kwakiutl, West African, modern industrial and any other low-grid ethnography.

There is an economic consequence of the great value of time: the economy with low grid tends to be impatient or near-sighted. Work is directed to quick gains. Resources are exploited for the short-term. Marx believed 'over-consumption' to be a feature of modern capitalist society. Without contradicting him, there is a wider context still in which modern industrial society can be set. A serious cause of the short-time perspective is the very uncertainty we signalled earlier.

Economists frequently say that they are perplexed by the different value set upon leisure time in different social classes. Their explanations tend to be based upon the local peculiarities of western industrial society. It is argued that the upper classes have more education and so more ideas about what to do with their time, or the upper classes, having more sense of social responsibility, engage their spare time in more good works, or that the increase in consumption goods has far surpassed the increase in leisure time, so the rich are harried by terrible problems of squashing more consumption into the same time-slots. But since the rate of time-cost discounting must always go up with the lower grid, it seems that the same explanation that does for non-industrial societies should do for ours.[31] I would ask ethnographers to look for grid variables and check out this correlation about the value of time in tribal society.

It would seem to follow that the competitive, weak grid society tends to exploit fully its physical resources and cannot control the ruthless squandering of large-scale entertainment. Very different are the economic possibilities of economizing in strong group systems. The group can command a power of belt-tightening from its members and it has other ways of solacing them for loss of their material comforts. When the Franciscans first arrived in England in the thirteenth century they were a small group, very poor. Here is an example of how their very poverty enhanced the value of the group.[32]

The novice Fitzjoice who returning from a begging tour, to carry flour and salt and a handful of figs for a sick brother in his cape and a bundle of wood under his arm, . . . never accepted anything unless it was of rigid necessity. His self-denial was such 'that it happened to him once to suffer such extremity of cold as to believe that he was then and there about to die. As the brethren had not the wherewithal to make him warm, their brotherly love taught them a remedy; they all gathered round him and pressing close to him, like a litter of pigs, they made him warm.'

The full moral of this case is that the Franciscan Order went straight for group advantages and soon made its singleness of purpose effective in its control of English cultural life.

3 Method

Grid-group analysis treats the experiencing subject as a subject choosing. It does not suppose that the choices are predetermined, though costs may be high and some of the parameters may be fixed. The method allows for the cumulative effect of individual choices on the social situation itself: both can interact, the individual and the environment, and either can move, because the environment is defined to consist of all the other interacting individuals and their choices.

The method starts by identifying choices which lead to further social transformations in a given direction. A group is not taken to be formed, solid, existing independently of the volition of its constituent members. Their investment of time and energy quickens its life and marks its boundaries. Once they withdraw their own commitment, it dissolves away. Every time a member appeals successfully to the paramount need to ensure the survival of the group, its being in existence can be used as a more powerful justification for controlling individuals. Likewise in the case of the grid dimension. The one single cultural value that justifies the movement towards low grid is the unique value of the individual person. Calling on an ethic of individual value, each person can be justified for breaching constraints upon his freedom. This principle is basic to low grid because it extends the individual's scope for negotiating. Each basic principle, the value of the group, the value of the individual, is the point of reference that justifies action of a potentially generative kind. When one wins heavily against the other, the slide starts towards strong group or towards low grid. When each pulls against the other the tension is a dialogue within society.

In any particular case the slide in question may not affect the whole community but rather shift one individual into another part of it. For example, when a turkey farmer in 1957, having paid off his overdraft of

£3,000, approached the bank again in 1958 to ask for a loan of £8,000 he was refused. Then asking for the £3,000 overdraft facility to be restored, he was again refused on the grounds that if he really needed £8,000 the sum of £3,000 would clearly not be enough to carry him through the year. 'This information was given me by the bank manager of Barclays, and I asked at this stage to see the local director who had taken the decision.' Evidently the debt-encumbered farmer soon moved into circles where such meetings were everyday matters. However, at this first meeting he was referred to an accountant who seemed to act as a receiver for the bank.

> I quickly made my position clear to the new accountant that I did not
> have any intention to go into liquidation, and that if that was the plan
> between the bank and the new accountant, they had better think
> again. I informed him that if necessary I would call a meeting of the
> creditors. This point was taken and gradually there was a return of
> confidence between myself and the bank.

The season went well and only six months later the farmer had paid back all the creditors. A paragraph later in this biography, he writes 'In the autumn of 1959 I purchased my first aerodrome from the Air Ministry at an auction.'[33] He had changed his chances when he refused to accept the relevance of restricting up-grid rules and the pressure to go into liquidation. He forced on his sources of credit his vision of what should be done and proposed a different calculus of risk. Disregarding the visible controls and definitions, he got past the counter, through the sprung doors, into the carpet-covered rooms where directors chat each other up in a world of invisible controls.

But this biographical example should not give the impression that down-grid is always towards promotion and managerial control. Before decasualization measures changed the Manchester dock-side scene, a typical piece of low-grid cosmology could be heard: 'Dockers are not really solid – it's each man for himself and the devil take the hindermost.'[34] On the other hand, in dockland the social world of checkers is up-grid of that of dock hands, more secure, more clean and comfortable and with higher status. Royal families may well be higher grid than their equerries who can with less ado drop out of their roles and change their whole life-style. One of the special merits claimed for this whole approach is that it cuts across the class structure.

It is a method of identifying cultural bias, of finding an array of beliefs locked together into relational patterns. The beliefs must be treated as part of the action, and not separated from it as in so many theories of social action.[35] The action or social context, is placed on a two-dimensional map with moral judgments, excuses, complaints and shifts of interest reckoned as the spoken justifications by individuals of the action they feel required to take. As their subjective perception of the scene and its moral implications emanates from each of them individually, it constitutes a collective moral consciousness about man and his place in the universe. The interaction of individual subjects produces a public cosmology capable of being internalized in the consciouness of individuals, if they decide to accept and stay with it. This particular approach does not assume that they must. It is not an exercise to demonstrate the sociological determination of thought. If I were tempted in that direction I would have to face an insoluble problem in accounting for social change. As Durkheim saw, once he had explicitly developed the analysis of how social categories are internalized in the individual mind, he had no way of understanding private dissent.[36] Consequently, he proposed a static analysis of the relation between beliefs and behaviour. But this present argument allows plenty of scope for individual disagreement, rebellion, mustering of support to change the whole context, or of emigration from one place on the map to another more congenial. This argument closes no doors upon psychological theories of personality. It presupposes that some mixture of self-selection and of adaptation accounts for a fit between personality measurements and grid-group social position. It is essentially compatible with a psychology of the will. When asked by philosophical friends what epistemological base I choose to anchor this approach to social reality, I answer certainly not upon economics, nor upon technology, nor upon psychology. It is, in fact, not anchored at all, but floats upon the shifting interaction of intelligent subjects. What I claim to be stable and determined is not their individual positions but the range of cosmological possibilities in which they can possibly land themselves by choosing to deal with their social problems in one way or another.

For many years I have been struggling to make comparisons within anthropology. I have tried to compare the conditions for different kinds of witchcraft beliefs, or for matrilineal or pawnship institutions.[37] Always the thing I have sought to understand has slid through my fingers like a hairy rope, each twist and pull bringing up a new segment to challenge the bases of classification. Without typologizing there can be no generalizing. With grateful acknowledgment to Rodney Needham,[38] I realize that I have finally hit upon a polythetic method. Polythetic classification identifies classes by a combination of characteristics, not requiring any one of the defining features to be present in all members of a class. Each included member only needs to show a majority of the features in the class. An advantage of this method is that it does away with sharp dichotomies. Checking along its scale ordering, it is possible to say whether one set of associated features are more typical than others. So instead of worrying about definitions of witchcraft or ancestor cults, I am now looking for combinations of beliefs in all the possible social contexts in which the individual has to operate – all the possible social contexts here being limited and clarified by the grid group axes. Instead of isolated bits of behaviour, I have now got structures of behaviour, structures whose parts, *ceteris paribus*, hold together in the ways described below. But before launching into the analysis, I must first indicate the level at which I assume that these structures can be found. Necessarily, because of the ethnomethodological assumptions which I have taken aboard, the operative level is that at which excuses are required from individuals and made by them and where moral judgments materialize into pressures from other persons to act in certain ways. If I speak of group, then, though the group may be ever so big, so that all the members cannot possibly know each other well, there would have to be in all parts of it a pressure from face-to-face situations to draw the same boundaries and accept the alignment of insiders and outsiders. A unit such as 'England' or 'the Catholic Church' would not qualify as 'group' in this sense. Likewise for grid, however widespread its manifestation over thousands of people, the relevant level of analysis is that at which people find it necessary to explain to each other why they behave as they do.

This level may be conceived as the social accounting level, the level of justification and explanation. The two dimensions have to be drawn up in such a way that, with other things being equal and the ethnographic context being properly understood, they can be taken and applied to any social accounting context. I have, therefore, tried to define group in a technical sense appropriate to this exercise, so that it captures those personal pressures and excludes other kinds of larger, looser, more nominal and impersonal group formations. The scale for group starts from an environment in which a person finds himself the centre of a network of his own making which has no recognizable boundaries. He knows people, they know people, and the social horizon is entirely indefinite. Moving away from this zero group position, he may belong to several associations which, themselves, are clearly bounded so that they can say who is and who is not a member. But since he belongs to several, their membership can be overlapping; not necessarily. Then, for scoring the array of environments for group strength, the investigator needs to consider how much of the individual's life is absorbed in and sustained by group membership. If he spends the morning in one, the evening in another, appears on Sundays in a third, gets his livelihood in a fourth, his group score is not going to be high. The strongest effects of group are to be found where it incorporates a person with the rest by implicating them together in common residence, shared work, shared resources and recreation, and by exerting control over marriage and kinship. A ghetto or commune or small sect such as those referred to in Chapter 7 of *Natural Symbols* will serve as examples of extreme strong group. There seems to be little difficulty in developing a set of criteria that will give a scale for comparison of group strength defined in these ways.

Grid is much more difficult. Some of the decisions taken for developing a grid scale may seem arbitrary and they are open to improvement once the problems have been seized. The intention is to establish a dimension on which the social environment can be rated according to how much it classifies the individual person, leaving minimum scope for personal choice, providing instead a set of railway lines with remote-control of points for interaction. Strong grid, defined in this way, is in itself not difficult to assess. The problems arise in assessing how the move down towards zero takes place, and where to place zero. With the help of Dr James Hampton, the grid dimension has been constructed with four components.

The first is insulation, as just described, which corresponds to strong social classification in *Natural Symbols*.[39] With reduced insulation, three other possibilities are likely to open up, representing different kinds of individual freedom in society: autonomy, control and competition. I give them in a list, but no ordering in the scale is implied in the order of listing. Any environment which scores high marks for all three is correspondingly low in the grid dimension; medium scores for these three give a medium position; likewise, high scores for any one and low for the other two may cancel out and give a medium position. The reasoning is as follows. A person who is not in a strongly classifying, insulating environment, will be moving down towards zero if he can enjoy a good degree of independence in his decisions. So autonomy contributes a component in measuring the downward shift towards an individualist environment. To estimate it, one could ask how freely a person disposes of his own time, of his own goods, chooses his collaborators, chooses his clothes and food. This component is the reverse side of the next one, since it stands for negative freedom from control by others. But such personal autonomy may become a very different social experience if it is added to positive control over other people. Not only may they not say nay, but the individual in control is actually limiting their autonomy by his power of command. Together, these two components, if they characterize the social environment, would stand for a universe of independent autocrats each controlling a servile population further up-grid. But a third component has to be added to take account of the interaction of these independent beings with each other. Since by definition, there are fewer society-wide rules to govern their interaction the further down-grid we move, each individualist must be expected to negotiate his relationships with the others. They will be organizing themselves, as a result of the inter-actions, into big leagues and small leagues and eventually squeezing some of their number out of the ranks altogether. This is because control over persons is at issue, a sign for power. We can move this scale down to the point where all rules are negotiable, fair comparison rules. This is a competitive individualist environment where invisible controls keep a man slaving at his farm or desk, for his own rewards. We could stop and put zero here. Or we could go on and add a measure for the possibility of individualism having run so wild that everyone makes their own rules and breaks them whenever it pays to do so, a further extension of autonomy.

But fairly enough, this could be regarded as an experience that goes beyond society, a period or place of rulelessness that could be seen as transitional between stabler periods or places of ordered social life. No matter, for our purpose this can be included as nearest to zero point of low grid; and the whole component which takes account of the inter-action of autonomous beings with each other can be called competition. Even a Shaka, a Stalin or Talleyrand, or Genghis Khan or Alexander the Great, however much at the top of the universe they appear, regard themselves as insecurely poised. They believe in the existence of their rivals and in the competitiveness of their environment.

So when insulation is scored negatively there are three other compo-nents able to be combined differently with each other and producing different environmental effects. The diagram is only intended to show modes of social control. It does not trace or measure the distribution of power except indirectly, and says nothing about the amount of power in the system being studied. The people allocated to the top left-hand corner are being controlled from somewhere else, since they belong to no group. But the amount of control they endure depends on the application of the *ceteris paribus* rule through the whole population studied. And the source of control could be from groups on the right side from which they are excluded, or from the blind forces generated by competition in the bottom left.

Apart from not dealing with power, and not dealing with many other things, this diagram does not deal with the possibility of voluntary withdrawal from society. In another study I put this possibility of withdrawal at zero on a slightly different diagram,[40] for it seemed one sensible place from which to build up the scheme. However, withdrawal creates several difficulties for this exercise. There are at least three possible ways in which it could be reasonably represented in the two dimensions. One could conceive of a family unit as the smallest possible group and since small groups are generally defined by their boundary against the rest of society, this smallest withdrawn group could appear as a minimum commune at the extreme right on the horizontal axis. Again, anyone who is strongly insulated by rules and regulations not of their own making (top left vertical axis) can, nevertheless, embrace them willingly and make a subjectively defined autonomous place where he has been forcibly consigned. This brings the subjective status of the whole scheme into sharp relief before I am ready to deal with it. However much I am trying to show how subjective perceptions of the environment influence decisions and validate themselves so that there will ultimately be a match between subjective and objective criteria, at this stage of developing a tool of analysis I have to be careful to demonstrate the match, not take it in circular fashion for an assumption. Then there is the question of putting total withdrawal at the zero point of grid where each individual decides that there are no rules, hence no social constraints. These various forms of withdrawal each interfere too much with the uses to which the tool can be put. I, therefore, decide to take total withdrawal, however defined, right off the map. Anyone who succeeds in living without yielding to the pressures of high grid, without being tempted into the transactions of low grid, without being immersed in any group, however feeble, such a one deserves to escape this categorization of mundane social processes. However, the withdrawn individual is not necessarily silent. Immune as far as possible from the pressures of other people, the hermit none the less speaks to the wider society. Though he is off our map of social control, in the very act of evasion he presents a view of what human nature might be like. What he says on this subject is powerfully interesting to others caught in the toils he has escaped. To this I must return, for he tends to preach and to be heard.[41]

II Cosmology

1 Constraints from the social context

There is no reason to expect sudden breaks in continuity from one context (and its supporting cosmology) to another. But for purposes of demonstrating the present argument, it will be clearest if only extreme cases are considered. I will, therefore, take four cosmological types and show how they are linked to four extreme types of social context. The exercise consists first in drawing out the implications for social life of the four corner positions on the chart (Figure 9.1). These have been numbered for easy reference when the cosmological bias is being explained, so that inferences from social context to cosmology can be scrutinized. It is convenient to start with bottom right D, (strong group, weak grid), and to move around the chart anti-clockwise. This is because so many contemporaries, themselves being located in the bottom left A square of the diagram, find it difficult to recognize that their own judgments predictably correspond to any social contexts. If they were to read about themselves first they might be tempted to declare the inference from a pattern of social constraints to an integrally related pattern of values to be an outrageous parody, whereas if they patiently follow the argument through its less familiar sitings, the method will have been grasped and the case for the low group cosmologies on the left may earn a fairer hearing.

Square D (bottom right of diagram)

Strong group, weak grid
  1   The social experience of the individual is first and foremost constrained by the external boundary maintained by the group against outsiders.
  2   The extreme case of strong group will be one in which the members gain their whole life-support from the group as such. The more unregulated commerce a member may have with other groups or individual outsiders, the weaker the controls exerted at 3 below.

3   Individual behaviour is subject to controls exercised in the name of the group.

4   Following from the low-grid condition, formal internal divisions, segregating, delegating and specializing roles will be absent.

5   Consequent on 4, relationships between individuals will be ambiguous, and there will always be difficulties about adjudicating rights which remain implicit.

6   Consequent on 4 and 5, the instruments for resolving internal conflict are inadequate; only the sanction of withdrawal of the privileges of membership and resulting expulsion from or fission of the group can be effectively applied.

7   Consequent on 4 and on 2, the drastic character of the only definitive solutions to personal conflict will produce a tendency to drive disagreement underground. Ill-will and frustration are likely to flourish below the surface and provide fuel for attempts to muster support to expel awkward personalities.

8   Consequent on 7, there will be covert factions in the group.

9   Consequent on 6 and 7, a need to control admission and to strengthen the boundaries against outsiders will be apparent to members of the group wishing to avoid its disintegration.

10   Consequent on the weaknesses of organization and control indicated at 4 to 8, the group will tend to be small and hopes for its long persistence disappointed; it will be subject to fission.

Square C (top right diagram)

Strong group, strong grid

1 as for 1 at D, a constraining group boundary.

2 as for 2 at D, life support from the group.

3 as for 3 at D, control of individual behaviour.

4   Following from the strong grid condition, C is organized internally into separate graded compartments, has scope for internal specialization of roles and may accordingly distribute its resources unequally between members.

5   Consequent on 4, it has an armoury of different solutions to internal conflicts, upgrading, shifting sideways, downgrading, resegregating, redefining.

6   Consequent on 4 and 5, the group can be bigger than groups at D since it can devolve, federate, become tributary to another etc. in the various ways that entitle any given case to be located at C.

7   Consequent also on 4 and 5, the C group can expect to persist longer without fission.

8   Consequent on the evident feasibility (7) of persisting as a group into the future, it can make levies on its individual members to ensure capital investment to endow its posterity.

9   Consequent on 8, the feasibility of persisting as a group being made realizable through the capital investments undertaken for the group, it does persist in fact longer than groups at D.

Square B (top left of diagram)

High grid
The social context dominated by insulation.

1   In the extreme case, by definition the individual has no scope for personal transactions.

2   In the extreme case the sphere of individual autonomy is minimal.

3   The individual's behaviour is ordained by the classifications of the social system, fully defined and without ambiguity.

4   There are no rewards to which he can aspire, other than those for fulfilling his allotted station.

5   By definition, since there is no group boundary enclosing him he is excluded from such groups as there may be.

6   The power which maintains the constraining insulations upon him is remote, impersonal, either the group's powers of exclusion 5, or the competitive energies in A alone, or a mixture of both.

7   Though peripheral to all decision-making, by definition, the individual may yet belong to the largest category of the population in a given society.

Square A (bottom left of diagram)

Low grid
A social context dominated by strongly competitive conditions, control over other people, and individual autonomy.

1   By definition the social experience of the individual is not constrained by any external boundary.

2   And by definition is not constrained by substantive signs of ascribed status: all the existing classifications are only provisional negotiable boundaries.

3   Following 2, relations between individuals will be ambiguous, obligations implicit.

4   Individuals can transact freely. In so far as they find the terms of trade, as it were turned against them, they will press for rules governing transactions, to enforce the honouring of contract or to make restrictive agreements. Both such outcomes will shift the environment away from full zero; the public control of contracts represents a small shift up grid for everyone involved, the price rings a small shift right towards group. The extreme case of free individual transaction is the environment described as the free market for which complete mobility of resources and complete knowledge of prices are the main conditions enabling individual firms of roughly the same size and power to compete.

5   In the extreme case at 4, the big rewards go to the innovating individual who can spring a surprise on his competitors.

6   Consequent on 4, economies of scale are to be reckoned worth making, hence a pressure to expand the sphere of operations and to specialize.

7   Consequent on 4, any possibility of controlling the market depends on having allies who will enforce something equivalent to company law or engage together in restrictive practices.

8   Consequent on 6 and 7, individuals will be engaged in selectively screening their potential acquaintances for useful services and rejecting potential passengers who can do nothing to increase their range of activities.

9   No one in this social environment can expect anyone else to support him if he fails to deliver or sets the wrong price on his own services; the failures produce the casualties of the system.

10   Consequent upon 1, 2 and 3, there is no way of reckoning success in this environment except by size of following. 10 exacerbates the pressures implicit in 4, 6, 7, 8 and 9.

2   *Cosmological derivatives*

Given these four distinctive contexts which can be located on a grid and group chart, the next stage is to elucidate elements of cosmology which are not circularly implied in the definition of social context and to show that a distinctive cosmological bias is generated by the character of explanations and justifications that are plausible in each social context. The four heads which I have chosen to illustrate these derived cosmological schemes are: (1) views on nature; (2) views on time; (3) views on human nature; (4) views on social behaviour. What follows should be in a conditional, provisional tense, dependent on empirical testing which is not yet done. I write it in the present to bring out the inferential character of the argument.

2.1 Nature in general

Nature is a concept normally contrasted with nurture or culture. How this contrast is made depends on the experience of society. Roughly: if society is seen as potentially good, the contrast with nature may lose sharp definition. But if society is seen as evil, then the contrast with nature will draw the latter as good. But the matter becomes more complicated. Let us get a closer focus by considering the contrast with nature as a general source of models for good behaviour. Then, assuming that foreigners and foreign parts by their strangeness do not come into the ordinary definition of culture which is used as a basis for proper conduct, let us consider attitudes to going abroad to see if they vary according to grid and group. Following that, considering that the contrast of nature and culture comes up particularly clearly with the training of children or animals for social life, let us set up a section for attitudes to 'pre-nature'. Finally, let us consider those attitudes to nature which are derived at second remove from these cosmological biases, and which are seen in the cultural processes of organizing space, garden, cookery and medicine.

2.1.1 Contrasted with 'culture'

Taking D, strong group, first, the dominant social condition in this section is that all human beings are divided into insiders and outsiders (D1), the latter hostile and the former continually disappointing expectations. Given the ambiguity of all internal relationships and the difficulty of adjudicating disputes (D5) and given the life-commitment to the group (D2) which suppresses conflicts since they cannot be openly resolved except by expulsion (D6) – given all the resultant worries about social life, the dampening of competition, the fear of jealousy and factionalism (D8), the attitude to nature will be very distinctive. No elaborate theorizing or pressure for intellectual coherence, since an anti-intellectual bias towards 'small is beautiful' will best support a small group's decision to opt out of wider social interactions. A typically homespun philosophy corresponding to the same decision reveals an implicit division in nature which is put to use whenever social action resolves practical dilemmas by dividing 'us' from 'them'. Even within the protective walls of the sect or commune a danger is recognized of infiltration from outside (D9). Apart from papering over the cracks with rites of formal conciliation, action to solve disputes takes the form of unmasking wolves in sheep's clothing and expelling spies from the ranks of the faithful. So we should expect to find 'nature' outside society divided as is society itself into lambs and wolves, along with other favourite metaphors of vulnerable 'us' and predatory 'them'. The image of nature includes that which is not social but can be incorporated into society; vulnerable, lovable, natural victims, and, on the other hand, menacing, predatory, ineducable nature. Even human 'culture' is not always what it seems. So 'nature' has its two aspects. This is not merely an extension of metaphors, but derives from the use made of nature in moral justifications. A recognized class of de-natured human beings provides a way of resolving moral and political dilemmas. Scapegoating and expelling will be justified by discovering the enemy in the camp and denouncing his actions with favourite metaphors of poison, contamination and the need to purge. Along these lines of analysis the rich work on witchcraft in central African village politics can be used to exemplify and support the argument.[42]

Turning now to C, the group here survives not only by justifying its boundary against outsiders (C1) but also by justifying its separate graded compartments (C4) and their relations as part of a whole (C6). So here one should expect an intellectual effort to elaborate a transcendental metaphysics which seeks to make an explicit match between civilization and the purposes of God and nature. Synecdoche in metaphors of society and nature shows their isomorphic structure and expounds their reciprocal support. Nature, especially in its symmetries and regularities is conceived to be on the side of the good society. It is possible to conceive of unnatural behaviour in animals and it is reprobated just as much as in humans. Whereas in D, both nature and culture have their rotten core, in C an ideal undivided nature is part of the encircling ambience of culture, with God sustaining both.[35]

> Nor think in Nature's state they blindly trod;
> The state of Nature was the reign of God.

(Alexander Pope)

The experience of organizing and reorganizing social relations and affirming them by means of ritual dispensations and consecrations encourages a theory of an active ritual process for maintaining proper harmony between nature and culture, so this is the place on the chart where the practice and theory of divine sacrifice is found most highly developed. The uses of nature in moral justification are all-pervasive in the C group. Going against nature means a threat of failure, unnatural vice is condemned. This is the social context in which theories of Natural Law flourish and the analysis of cosmology by grid and group is intended as a further carpet-pulling-from-under-the-feet for that theory, if it were still needed. I also risk the suggestion that this is the kind of social environment in which doctrines of atonement flourish and which can make sense of a full once-and-for-all historical incarnational theology.

The grid dimension starts with the individual transacting as an individual with others and ends with the individual strongly insulated from others. The rights of the individual to transcend boundaries of all kinds are the grounds of arguments to brush aside social conventions. So all along the grid dimension (with low group), the individual is being placed in contrast to society, the concepts of nature and of the human person are likely to be assimilated together, so that the individual cries out against his fetters in the name of nature. Society is defined as not-nature.

On the top left side, dominated by insulation (B1, 2 and 3) and consequent enforced withdrawal from free social activity, people cannot be expected to show theoretical elaborations of the concept of nature in the cosmos. The intelligibility of an individual's experience here is very slight. Intellectually as well as socially reflexiveness is limited. Bernstein says:[43]

> Reflexiveness refers to the degree to which an individual is able to make explicit verbally the principles underlying object and person relationships . . . Roles may be more or less insulated from each other and so may the meanings to which the roles give access. Where the meanings made available through different roles are highly insulated, we could say that there is low reflexiveness; where the meanings made available through different roles *reverberate* against each other (low insulation) we could say there is high reflexiveness.

Because of his peripheral situation (B7) the cosmology he can create is likely to be a 'things of shreds and patches' picked up eclectically from other sectors. The most adaptive response will be a great passivity since there are no rewards and no escapes (see high grid (B4)).

Lastly, the low-grid cosmology A is an accommodation to the harsh experience of competitive society (A4–8). The individual experiences other humans as anonymous, merciless, putting him under continual threat of withdrawal of support, under pressure to deliver, to make promises or lose credit. Society is an unremitting source of worry as well as of rich prizes. Corruption, self-seeking and aggression (A8 and 9) will tend to be seen as the characteristic features of human social life; in contrast nature is idealized as good and simple: 'Every prospect pleases and only man is vile.' But a wistful sense of alienation from nature never wins against the excitement and rewards of competition (A5).

Because of the continual selectivity in the social environment (A7 and 8) low grid is intellectually vigorous, enquiring and demanding the highest standards. If he is not allowed to get by with sloppy performance, why should musicians, cooks, waiters, builders and the rest? In any field of competence, low grid demands high levels of performance, in craftsmanship, style and syllogistic argument. It is conscious of another special sense of culture to contrast with Nature, that is Culture with a capital letter. It indicates an aspect of social life separated from the dirty compromises of commerce, politics and economics, an innocent, pure condition of high Culture. The value of Culture tends to be used as a justificatory weapon in moral arguments in the same way as group traditions in C, and as nature everywhere.

For any position with extremely low group, nature represents all that is innocent and despoiled by civilization, the obvious victim with whom the individual identifies himself. The dangers to nature will reliably muster support and sympathy, as nature pleads mutely for protection against the blind, anonymous social forces which threaten every individual. The paradox for low grid is that while subscribing to this pervasive view, it has to be engaged in exploiting resources for the quick and big results required for approval at low grid (A10).

2.1.2 Abroad

The small sequestered community at D will see no need or reason to travel to strange places: abroad may be interesting because of the group's historical origins there, and travel for the sake of conducting missions or visiting shrines. C has the same view on travel. But at D the outside is inimical and predatory, its evil character one of the initial grounds for seclusion of the group. C gives a different nuance to its xenophobia; the exotic and foreign is opposed to nature as understood at home, so it is unnatural and its unnaturalness a support to boundary-maintenance. Turning to the low group side, B can entertain the wildest most erratic notions about abroad, as it rarely goes there except in a strictly controlled situation, such as military service, and any real encounter with foreigners is unlikely. A yearns for foreign travel; it feels the attraction of the safari holiday, the wilderness-escape-adventure holiday, to relax momentarily the special pressures of low grid (A4–10). Anyway, its search for novelty (A5 and 6) and for new areas of expansion (A6) ensure that low grid loves foreigners and foreign ways.

2.1.3 Pre-culture

For small strong group D and larger group C, animals and children if they are to be domesticated have to be disciplined, and so neither area has inhibitions about using exemplary and deterrent arguments to justify inflicting physical pain on them in their own interest. Likewise plants must be trained to fulfil nature and fit society. 'Spare the rod and spoil the child' and 'Cruel to be kind' are maxims which can be heard, though more confidently in the less ambiguous context of society at C, where a more consistent training programme is likely to be developed. With low group, high grid has a continual social experience of punishment and so has no special theoretical problem about training the young, any more than it has with anything else. But A clearly prefers the theory of education that does most justice to the concepts of natural goodness and the evils of civilization, that is, self-expressing and self-teaching. However, inhibitions prevent this doctrine from being espoused wholeheartedly. For in the low-grid environment there is much to teach which cannot be imparted to little ones without contriving hidden controls and disciplines that contradict the overt theory of education. More of this when we come to theories of society in these cosmologies (see 'Gardening' and 'Cookery' below).

2.1.4 Cultural processes

The first three aspects of attitudes to nature have been strictly derived from their uses as weapons of argument in the different social contexts. They are not proposed as metaphors, mirrors or reflections, but as the very stuff of social interaction. However, once 'nature' is seen to take on certain features in this way, the people living in that environment and fabricating by their strategies with each other certain views of nature, have created for themselves a distinctive pool of metaphors. These metaphors lie more handily to them in the further work of developing their own identity as part of the social environment to which they are committed. So we can turn out attitudes to nature which are not derived directly from the social action, but at second remove are derived from the cosmological bias which can be more directly stitched back into the social action.

Relations between people require mediating materials, and these are processed. The quality of the social relations and the character of the cosmological bias suggest that in all spheres the nature-culture contrast will affect aesthetic judgments.

Space

All social relationships take place in a spatial dimension. The organization of space lends itself to microcosm/macrocosm effects. In the society at D we would expect the small closed group to use a recursive patterning of external boundaries at all levels; village boundaries will be clearly demarcated, compound and house boundaries likewise (D1). Within the house, bed, lavatories, kitchens are likely to be segregated by rules which protect individual privacy. This is contrary to what we might expect if we were looking for a simple reflection of the rules of the society. For ambiguity and openness (D4 and 5) are the prevailing conditions of social life, but the individual still has to be defined as the unit of social intercourse, and since nothing else defines him, the model of the village, fenced around, copied and recopied from larger to smaller contexts is an easy one on which to establish a generalized individualism. Group C will go much further in developing complex metaphors of symmetry, inequality and hierarchical relationships in its use of space. For B the compartmentalism enforced by the larger society will be passively used and reproduced without special meanings accruing. But A in its competitive environment, competitively adopts high standards of spit and polish, tidiness, style in decoration and elegance, so it will make a distinction between public space, strongly classified, and private space, untidy and mixed, hence some of its inhibitions about free expression principles of education.

Gardening

C and D will both evidently seek to hedge around the different areas, vegetables, flowers, front and back, etc. But D will not be specially interested in gardening as a cultural activity, whereas C is likely to use this medium to justify and expand its view of society as hierarchized, trained and compartmentalized. So with topiary, clipped borders, trees trained to weep or lopped to give light, formal gardens present ingenious arrangements dominated by design. I cannot predict or generalize about gardening activity at B. At A if gardening is a medium of social relations it is at once a medium for competition. So look for subtle contrived

effects, plants brought from afar, cherished skilfully to thrive in un-
wonted climate and soil and made to look natural there. The seasons are
defied and colour glows all the year round, elaborate landscaping
enlarges the sense of space and gives a 'natural' effect.

Cookery

In D the classification of edible foods is likely to assert the prohibition
against eating carnivores. Lambs and wolves have their different claims
to be classed inedible.[44] For those parts of nature which are *prima facie*
edible, expect long and complex boundary-passing processes for transforming the raw into the cooked and little possibility of recognizing the
original object once it has passed through the process. Danger being
more in focus than enjoyment, one would expect restrictive attitudes to
drink, drugs and smoking. For the larger more complex group at C the
criterion of edibility will depend on the synecdochical pattern which
projects social structure and moral values onto nature.[45] The passive,
insulated high grid cosmology at B should be like D in having no
objections or predilections about packaged and highly processed foods,
but its restricted experience makes it conservative in its tastes. But A
treats food as one more medium for competition. So it prefers imaginative, innovative processes and rare products (not necessarily new, for
antique skills can be rare too). Its eclectic openness to fashion, its
readiness to lose boundaries, brings zest to the search for culinary
novelty. Cooking time is shortened[46] for here there is not the special
value set in B and D on denaturing natural products to render them
edible (and see also below).

Medicine

D, small group, has an ideal of possibly good and effective therapy which
it finds regularly frustrated by the wrong moral attitudes of doctor and
patient. It places special emphasis in its therapy on the strength of bodily
boundaries, and on purging out evil that may have intruded. In C
however (the larger and more complex group) since nature is held to be
on the side of God and the good society, therapy will show more trust in
it. Nature will cure on its own, given half a chance; rest, sleep and the
proper nourishment for signalling invalid status will achieve and cure,
without leaching, bleeding, purgations or other violent interventions. A
lock and key theory of science credits the right formula with power to
work of itself, *ex opere operato*. Time is on the side of the doctor (see
below 2.2.1). At B pills and pink medicine are seized upon like any occult
remedies, without more reason or theory than consulting the horoscope.
At A medicine belongs to Culture with a capital letter. The latest

development of science is the only good enough medicine. It is chic to know the names of new diseases and treatments and to be identified by association with them.

2.2.1 Time as a resource

In the small group at D time is not a resource in short supply. The boundaries of the group set limits to its uses (D1). The low grid means that time will not be compartmentalized (D4), so it will be used very flexibly with no rules against using office time or drinking time for promoting group concerns, or separating work from play, or free conversation time from politics, 'shop' or religion. As with the larger group C, time is a community resource, and as Weber noted (in *The Protestant Ethic*) the group imposes on its members required participation in leisure and group celebrations. On the low group side at B, time is not a personal resource since by definition it is all plotted out. A treats time as an individual resource, always in short supply, on which much more must be said, below.

2.2.2 The attitude to old age

This varies in each case. In D old age is a convenient principle for settling dilemmas (D4 and 5) about precedence, and becomes a source of status in itself. Hence there is no incentive to disguise the changes of age in personal appearance or to stay looking young. However, since this is a frustrating social life (D7), old age is likely to be disappointed and the old should take care not to draw to themselves the scapegoating energies of the rest of the community (D6). However, since everyone in the group is there for life (D2) there will be a full demographic range of social representation, as also in C (C2). Time and death are part of the closed cycle of life which the group encompasses and transcends by its own persistence. Turning to the low group side, at the top left, a normal population of B may often consist of an above average proportion of the aged. But being insulated they do not see other generations in their day to day affairs. At A, age in itself is not a criterion for deference, nor an overt principle of segregation by seniority. So here, without group, there is no way of conceptualizing what being aged means, or of showing any recognition. Anniversary celebrations of individuals will avoid numbering the years. Time's passage is not a criterion for intimacy, distinguishing between old and new friends. But in A there are some special problems. In this competitive cosmology the harsh principles of selection (A8) may eliminate the aged and less competent from the lives of the prime (who have driven them up-grid) so the individual will tend not to meet people outside his own generation. Personal appearances in low grid should be young and active, tensions and disappointments should be concealed, the style should be one of apparent relaxation and readiness to take anything on. Older men here will be quicker to adopt cosmetic aids, hair dyes, youthful looking cuts, their walk will seem springy. In contrast, the people who grow old in D and C not only know how to look, they have no reason to hide the physical marks of aging – (recall the Breton village described by Edgar Morin where a woman had no claim to beauty until her face was wrinkled!). So in D and C there will be distinctive styles of communication for each generation, in speech, dress etc. and each cohort will be ready to claim the rights appropriate to itself. Unlike the group at D, fewer disappointments lie in wait for the old in C; they know how to behave, they represent the successful continuity of the group, they are needed at the numerous group-celebrating rituals. C is a better place to grow old in.

2.2.3 Attitudes to youth
In D, youth not being insulated or set apart (D4) the young are likely to be so assimilated that any disagreements between young and old are treated as conflict between insiders and outsiders. So no specific youth-age conflict would be likely to be recognized. For C, however, its attitude to youth depends on a major factor that lies outside of grid and group analysis. If the group is successful in attracting and holding resources (C8) and in closing the channels of information from outside so that its theory of distributive justice (2.4.1) is credible and seen to be equitable, there may be no generation gap, the youth may be loyal and assimilable to the task of reproducing the society. But this depends entirely on how well the group manages its heritage. People at B may be afraid of youth, seeing so little of them (2.2 above). A has tolerance for its hallmark; it does not close options, being so socially and intellectually open. It tolerates the rising generation very well and takes its part. Sometimes the competitive cosmology endures the paradox of sympathizing with rebellions disastrous to its interests.[47] But it can tolerate a lot of mixture and confusion.

2.2.4 Time past
On memorialism first: though it has nothing much to raise public monuments to, B respects the burial places of its private dead. But in A the famous dead are part of Culture with a capital letter as well as being

now a harmless uncompetitive part of nature. There is much scope for valuing their memory. Apart from centenaries of every imaginable kind, wall plaques, park benches, dog drinking troughs, even ashtrays proliferate to record the individual dead, whose memory also gives scope for entrepreneurial energies in fund-raising for good causes to set up bigger monuments to them. C and D, on the side of strong group, will obviously set up memorials to important group events.

Attitudes to history vary, but a close relation holds between the sense of time past, the expectation of the future and the response to millenial prophecies in all cosmologies. In the small group D, liable to frequent fission, the record of its history from its foundation is briefer than that of the larger and more complex group, C, because the points of differentiation are fewer. From the very beginning of the world, to the founding ancestor, to the recent breakaways that led to the immediate present, is but a few short steps. Correspondingly, the perception of the future is also less discriminated. This means that the sudden arrival of the millennium is more credible here than at C which exists in a longer time-span both as to the past and future (C7, 8, 9). Plans have been laid for many tomorrows so it is contradictory to expect the end of the world tomorrow. But both C and D have a strong historical sense: they select from the past a loyal justificatory charter for their present actions. Traditions are almost a part of nature (C1). On the low-group side such a straightforward historical sense is impossible. B has no special selective principle from which to construct its history. A submits claims to historicity to the same competitive, sceptical criticism as it submits every other idea. Ever testing and challenging shifting perspectives on the past, low grid cosmology (A6, 7, 8) gives rise to the science of historiography. Its future is recognized as full of uncertainty (as indeed it is) but this realistic acceptance of a high-risk short-term future does not make it susceptible to millennial prophecies. Prophets of doom must make good their claims like any other people or ideas, competitively (A10).

Seen under this head, the chart suggests a way of gathering up all the work on historical perception that was developed in anthropology since 1940.[48]

The more the society is ordered by points of segmentation on a chronological scale, the more historically discriminated and the longer its perception of time past. The same applies to the sense of a well-stepped and discriminated future. The stronger the degree of insulation from the outside world and the insulation of the group's interests, the nearer may the millennium be plausibly foreseen; the stronger the consciousness of a separating boundary, the more prophetic threats are loaded with hate and vengeance.

High-grid B has no systematic criteria for judging prophecy. Drawn up in this way, certain trends in cosmological bias begin to appear across the chart linking up different boxes in more complex ways. In spite of endemic uncertainty, A can take a long view of history because of its refined critical apparatus and so it joins up with C in its potential resistance to chiliastic movements. And working the other way, B and small group D both have in common forms of insulation or withdrawal from the larger society and less historical sense: they are likely to be more syncretically open to occult practices and promises emanating from non-professional and anti-establishment sources.

2.3 Human nature

2.3.1 Sickness and health
The attitudes scatter and clump complementarily in respect of the sick role. Whether there are rewards for assuming it, and whether the role of caring for the sick is accepted and publicly valued, these are effects of the social pressures identified by grid and group. In strong group (both D and C, following the right vertical dimension), the sick role is an accepted, well-exploited means of organizing group solidarity and so of mustering support for the infirm. Failure to show sympathy and to offer help is a handy peg for blame-pinning and clarifying factional alignments. Therefore the strong group will tend to make a public show of admiration for the courage of infirm individuals, to announce bulletins on progress and to seek out causes and responsibility for ill-health as a matter of general concern. This bias will create fertile ground for the credibility of contamination theories, and for linking moral with physical causes of sickness. The difference between D and C would follow the difference of the social structure; accusations of responsibility for sickness in D would follow the covert factional lines and in C would trace the lines along which full membership is ambiguous. So in D witchcraft accusations will be challenges to existing authority (as described in *The Yao Village* by C. Mitchell[49]). In C the trend of accusations will act as a control upon persons in weakly-defined roles, such as co-wives among the south-eastern Bantu.[50] It follows from the way in which the sickness of an individual can be used to strengthen the group's sense of solidarity, that a readiness to carry responsibility for the infirm arises. Even for the heavy burden of chronic and major illnesses, there

will be well-defined roles for bed-side attendants and respect for the corporal works of mercy. The heroism of the attendant is due for praise as well as the heroism of the sufferer. However, in the small group (D) chronic illness may well be made into another stick for beating the back of the wider society of which the group sees itself the victim – in which case the double heroism of suffering and care is also a further reproach against the larger society, first for causing the menacing conditions and second for not supplying remedies and compensation.

These attitudes expected from the right side of the diagram contrast with the low-group regions on the other side. Here, ordinary people are not able to use the sick role to muster support since there is by definition no group which can harness their weakness to its purposes. At B, sickness when socially recognized can at least give a little respite from pressures to conform. But at A it is best to be brave and say nothing about personal ill-health, for the lone individualist is not going to be suddenly able to interest others in his condition, himself having spurned their judgments about everything else; and anyway it would be better not to seem off form so as to avoid adverse judgments when selective procedures are at work. A doctor's report could spoil one's chances in a competitive field. Nothing is to be gained here either by flaunting heroic wounds or by blame-pinning. Being wise to reject the sick role for himself, the individual at A will try to keep fit, and the natural bias will encourage conversation about dieting, good healthy exercise. The judgment 'He doesn't look after himself' or 'She doesn't worry about her looks' is said in a rebuking tone in square A, though it could imply admiration of a saintly dedication to others in squares D or C. There are strong implications here for medical anthropology. If people questioned about their state of health reply 'Never felt better' or 'Why should I be tired?' a grid-group rating of their social environment might help to control the medical value of the report.[51]

For low grid individualism the care of the sick is a hard problem. The basic principle of self-fulfilment for the individual absolves close relatives from sacrificing their life to an invalid, whatever the strength of the invalid's own claim to self-fulfilment. Low-grid A can solve the conflict of rights by requiring professional help to be provided (and free of charge) by the anonymous state. The self-reliance principle may go under to the welfare state for low-grid A because of the priority accorded to competitive efficiency as a condition for realizing the full scope of individual development, the latter being the continual referent for all judgments. In low grid there is a lot of sense in moving out of the individual's independent isolation when afflicted and joining up with others who carry the same burden, thus moving as a group of, say, Thalidomide Victims or Spastics Association, into square D.

2.3.2 Death

In strong groups, just as heroism in suffering is one of the ways of earning public recognition, so dying is also much discussed, and altruistic ways of dying expatiated upon. A favourite form of myth that feeds group consciousness tells of lives laid down for group survival. Funerals are an exacting public affair where tears flow unashamed. Rituals of warm support for the bereaved are consistent with their status being ruthlessly exploited for group purposes in funerary rhetoric. Everyone goes to funerals; they are judged as a major ceremonial form and how to lay on a good one is common knowledge.

By contrast, without strong group, death, having socially no place as such, is no subject to celebrate publicly. It follows that A rarely talks about death. If it has an ideal way of encountering it the best way of dying should be unexpected, painless and sudden, a heart attack at the ninth hole, a stroke in the midst of sleep. It should happen after some achievement or before some disaster so that the deceased died more content than if he had lived. Not being metaphysically inclined, being sceptical about an 'after-life' and having no group to symbolize by the death of an old person, low grid – having anyway nothing much to say about death – rarely hears of funerals until afterwards and so rarely attends them. In any case the widow is likely to get screened out of social intercourse in years to come.[52]

The lower the grid point, the more a burial gets treated as a private affair, almost of hygiene. But the memorial service is another matter (see 2.2.4 above). When we come to the right to take one's own life (suicide and voluntary euthanasia) and the right to practice abortion on one's own body, the group factor would seem to make the big difference. On the right, where group is strong, the right to take life is a matter of public concern and so attempts to abrogate the community right by the individual will tend to be disapproved. Moreover they may well contradict the typical group attitudes to heroic sickness (indicated at paragraph 2.3.1 above). But usually the strong groups are likely to disapprove of any private ways of taking life while at A neither are likely to be disapproved. They are solutions to the dilemma, outlined in the preceding paragraph, of caring for the infirm. They are the more acceptable since they fit the dominant principle of upholding the right of individuals to control their own destiny. The people at B may well adopt euthanasia and abortion as solutions to unbearable conflicts, but without any justificatory theory.

2.3.3 Personal abnormality and handicaps

In strong groups (D and C) the only unforgivable deviation is disloyalty. So physical eccentricities, including physical differences, can easily be tolerated among other in-group variations, unless of course the group is formed on a principle of racial distinction. Dwarfism, tallness and fatness, big noses, etc. are part of the group's inheritance. If the physical oddities can be recognized as part of a defining genetic strain, being seen as a 'chip off the old block' is a positive value. The physical handicap comes in for the same kindly treatment as the long-term sickness, commiserated and somewhat exploited in strong group, but not on the side where group is weak. For instance, in low-grid A where there is striving for excellence in style, for youthful appearance (2.2.2) and a general admiration of elegance and beauty, there will be an inevitable turnabout in low-grid attitudes where physical abnormality is concerned. On almost every other head, low grid is tolerant, unsqueamish, unshockable. But physical or mental defect can imply incapacity to perform in a competitive situation. The striving individual in this environment knows that pressures are on him to use techniques of exclusion where it most goes against the grain of the individualist, egalitarian ethos that guides his decisions. Physical defect is embarrassing here and this must be a reason why it is no subject for joking.[53] A physically or mentally abnormal child takes up precious time (see 2.2.1) and creates heart-rending dilemmas for its parents. Grandparents and retired or widowed aunts have been relegated to institutions (see 2.3 above); the small, stripped-for-action, socially mobile family has no redundant personnel to care for the handicapped. So these also get sent into institutions, strengthening the assumption that segregating behaviour described at 2.3.1 is both appropriate and inevitable. Then the professions specialized for helping the handicapped attract to themselves the symbols of individual self-justification in low grid and acquire some of the honour that it reaped by family bed-side attendance in strong group.

For B, where most of the social problems collect and settle, no distinctive theory of how to cope with them is expected to emerge (see 2.1.1). As to physical abnormalities which do not call for lavish expenditure of time and care, the low-grid attitude is consistently tolerant – indeed by capitalizing on personal oddities the individual can emphasize his individuality and exploit it as a personal asset for meeting the demands of the low grid pressure for specialization (A5–10). So one can make a virtue of singularity in appearance, exaggerating the interest of small size, bushy eyebrows, baldness and so on.

2.3.4 Personal relations

On the subject of friendship the attitude shifts according to grid. From A and D, where grid is low, ascribed relationships are by definition not developed; hence elective friendships are the norm, and the role of 'best friend' would need to be developed for support to the individual at the life crises of 2.3.1 and 2.3.3. At B too, especially since the individual here is bereft of group support and yet still must face sickness and death, the ideal of friend is warmly acknowledged, but too often the irrelevant gradings and insulations imposed from outside and afar prevent the friends from rendering notable help to one another. The difference between A and B would mainly be that in the former every individual knows that he cannot expect to survive socially without the sustained good offices of influential friends. The rites and language of friendship are a highly developed cultural feature, but the principle of selection encourages a readiness to take on new and better friends, while the pressure on time (A4, 6, 8) means that old friends get replaced.

The difference between C and D on friendship is governed by the way the group boundary impinges on grid insulations. At D, the elective best friend is institutionalized in the same way as for the other side of the diagram A, but the search for allies is restricted to in-group members and they are sought to promote factional advantage. Moving up-grid, where ascribed relations cover nearly every aspect of life, friendship is likely to be formally organized on universal principles such as being born in the same year or sharing a name or being at the same school, or college or regiment. There will, by definition, be a minimum of scope for choice.

Attitudes to sex should be profoundly affected by grid and group, but it is difficult (and crucial) to take into account the effects of the division of labour between males and females, and the extent to which valued property is inherited on lines laid by marriage alliances. These other things being equal, strong group is likely to control procreation and inheritance by prescribing the channels for permitted sex, and it is likely to cast its web of prescriptions over all sexual activity more and more successfully as it is found further and further up grid, with all the facilities for control outlined in C1–5. By contrast, at A, given the basic principles of tolerance and individual freedom, one might expect a 'healthy-minded', untrammelled enjoyment, easy-come, easy-go as the governing ethical principle. But in A sheer competitive exclusion by the strongest male may turn sexual disappointment into a symptom of general failure, and there will probably be as much anxiety about sex as about any other part of this anxiety-ridden cosmos: anxiety to seem adequately virile or alluring, to be seen to be open-minded about sexual abnormality, successful in holding one's own and so on.

There is another possibility that low grid itself will tip the balance of power between males and females much more decisively against the latter than in B. For if men engage in unrestrained competition, wish for alliance with those more powerful than themselves, sift and screen and drop weak allies and seek cement to bind them to strong ones, they will be tempted to break down any segregation of the political or commercial domains, and involve kinship with their other affairs. Then marriage, women and children will be used as pawns in the competitive game. It follows that there is no reason whatever to expect that a society that has settled for a long period into a low-grid style of life will have been led by the logic of its experience to accord to women equal rights with men. So we may expect some women to be sources of dishonour, ritual defilement and shame even in low grid societies, so long as marriage is such a valuable stake that they have to be kept under control. And to sustain the justification of their exclusion from equal opportunity, we will expect theories about innate sexual capabilities to explain their lowly positions.

Human nature at low grid is liable to be split between, on the one hand defilable and defiling women, and on the other, men, relatively free from impurities of sex except by contact with women. Since women have to be subjected to meet the imperious demands of group control over procreation, and are also subject where low grid is found, there is practically nowhere on the map where sexual pollution is not a part of the cosmos put to active use in threats and justifications. Once again however, the fact of withdrawal or insulation creates common cause across the diagram between B and D. So long as the division of labour and the institution of property do not separate the interests of the sexes, small groups at D can also achieve sexual freedom (but only within their ranks), while those forcibly insulated at B will take their chance when they can get it, theory or no theory, pollution or no pollution.

2.4 Society

It will be tedious to work through this programme on all the possible moral issues that may be affected by grid and group. The method is very powerful and can go on generating many more of cosmological implications. But issues of punishment and justice need to be mentioned because current psychologistic theories about personality types and attitudes to punishment could be replaced by this sociological scheme.

2.4.1 Distributive justice

D has been defined as a social environment consisting of small groups operating with over-simple organizational principles (D4–8) while C has far richer institutional resources for incorporating and classifying at different levels of status (C4–9). We would therefore expect to find at D attempts to remove inequalities, in contrast to C where attempts to justify them would be part of the cosmologizing intellectual effort. In D poverty would be treated as a burden to be shared; idealistic and stern judgments would be passed on private enjoyment of any resources and levelling distributive mechanisms such as public feasts and crippling levies for the communal chest would embody these attitudes. Paradoxically, the low-grid ethics of individual equality are daily affronted by gross inequality generated in the heat of competition.[54] Low-grid cosmology cannot understand how such inequalities come about, it questions the statistical evidence (and even the value of statistics themselves in this context, though using them confidently in others). It claims adherence to an ethic of equality (possibly only applied in voting, or to initial opportunity, or to education). It never recognizes that its own processes of screening out and selection are pushing a mass of people up-grid where they are strongly insulated, have no autonomy or scope for individual transactions. This is just one more dilemma of distributive justice, among many dilemmas in low grid social environments. Rather than dismantle the institutions which protect and promote the competition between individuals, a typical low-grid solution to the moral dilemma is to subscribe to a theory of unequally distributed native ability. 'Too bad, we can't all be clever.' 'You can't make a silk purse out of a sow's ear.' And so the pressures to exclude are justified.

2.4.2 Punishment

The basis for identifying attitudes to punishment has been laid in 2.1 on nature and especially 2.1.3 on pre-culture and 2.1.4 on cultural processes. We can already see that in C and D there would be no squeamishness about inflicting severe and physically painful punishment. As Durkheim has said,[55] the strong group has a clear vision of the need for exemplary punishment for offences against the group as such. From A to B, on the low group side, there is a very different story to relate.

Low grid A has a lot of valuable display property to protect and the concept of damage and responsibility for damage is highly developed.

All the tendencies to humanity (which sustains the egalitarian individualistic ethic at A and which is the justification cited for breaking through barriers that reduce competition), all that generalized human sympathy rejects harsh punishment. These ought to be the people that Eysenck designates as 'tender'.[56] No awkward confrontations of theory and practice arise on this point. The normal procedures of selection and screening in A make a theory of exemplary punishment unnecessary. Victims of the system drop through the meshes and become invisible. Their failure to get a following is their punishment, the most that they could dread. Moreover, no one person has the distasteful responsibility of pronouncing it. The unsuccessful deviant is left at the starting post, or squeezed out further along the race; anyway he is due to be dropped into social oblivion. From there no one who knew him before need see him again: he becomes a problem for professionals. If he should steal or kill, the kindly conscience in A sees at once that society is at fault and that he should be rehabilitated, not further victimized. Prevention is better than cure, rehabilitation is better than deterrence. So private policing and a vast number of social work professions meet the difficulties of a system which professes equality, creates inequality, and has no punitive theory for controlling deviants.

3 Examples

From Indian sociology an analysis which takes a somewhat similar approach provides a rich field of examples. The striking innovation of McKim Marriott's analysis from within Hindu traditions about their own society is that he identifies structures of behaviour from transactional analysis.[57] He has reconstituted a kind of ethno-cosmology by adding to anthropologists' field researches the traditional judgments and characterizations in Hindu culture that explain the behaviour of persons in different castes. The transactional basis is not only fixed within the traditions that establish each caste with a hereditary occupation which it offers to others, but by a spiritual scale which evaluates all kinds of exchanges. Those who give blessings, lessons, ritual or even accountancy services are providing more spiritual elements than those who reward them in grosser payments, such as money or giving services of care for the physical body. By a very ingenious chart which synthesizes the state of comparative advantage, on this scale, of all intercaste transactions and by reckoning which castes have a rational strategy of maximum or of minimum interchange with others, he proceeds to distinguish structures of behaviour which are ratified by the ethnographic and literary sources. For example, the merchant silversmiths and goldsmiths, skilled craftsmen and traders, always giving gross services according to the spiritual scale, and receiving grosser kind (money) in return, tend to be withdrawn from the full Hindu transactional system. They favour in-marrying, are more purity-minded, more diet-conscious, more observant of Sanskritic rituals than Brahmins themselves. Their strategy of self-sufficiency in the total system of exchanges, which avoids unnecessary encumbrances and closes deals quickly, encourages them to adopt something like the withdrawn sectarian behaviour of square D above. By contrast, princes and great landowners with an on-going responsibility to raise armies or to maintain a continuous supply of agricultural labour, they seek wide-ranging repetitive patterns of social relations, with diffuse obligations, no clear cut-off points. They engage in long-term intergenerational marriage exchanges, involving the widest possible network of permanent reciprocal ties. They are good company; dietary rules never get in the way of friendly social intercourse – on the contrary, they are famous for being omnivorous and not over-concerned with their place on the spiritual hierarchy. Power more than purity is their concern. They worship gods who are conspicuously violent, powerful, carnal beings, who accept bloody sacrifice. These are big entrepreneurs and could well be found in my square A. Marriott's synthesis goes entirely in the direction in which I would like to approach culture. I greatly admire a synthesis which distinguishes sets of cultic preferences, dietary behaviour and marriage rules, and places the structures of behaviour firmly on a transactional theory that identifies their relationship with the rest of society. But India is vast and remote, its ethnography highly specialized. We need some illustrative cases from our own European experience. Surely there is no need to give examples of square D since descriptions of sectarian behaviour abound. I, myself, have summarized the essentials in *Natural Symbols*, the original essay which this study glosses and elaborates. For C, the most complex group, I have already indicated some of the African ethnography that suggests suitable tribes for analysis, using Henry Sumner Maine's *Ancient Law* as a manual of instruction. Modern European examples would be any large, old established family firm which over the decades continues to build up corporately held capital, expects to maintain its weaker male members, however incapable, to expel its dissidents, to compel the women of the family to marry in alliances that will be useful to the firm or to accept undowered spinsterhood. Thomas Mann's account of such a firm and the treatment of members of the family, servants and workmen in *Buddenbrooks* gives a very excellent fictional illustration. There are really no problems in thinking about the right-hand side of the diagram.

When it comes to top left, B, high grid and weak group, several problems arise. The person found here is by definition stripped of initiative, hemmed in by rules. We have to seek illustrations of this case which explain how someone can be in such a state and yet belong to no group. The first step is to dispel the implicit assumption that all control is necessarily exercised by groups closed enough to qualify for inclusion in the right hand side of the diagram. Recall that I have given the word 'group' a limited, technical sense for the purpose of this analysis, restricting it to the kind of pressures exerted through direct face-to-face relationships. This makes it easy to recognize that some people are closely restricted by rules promulgated from distant centres of authority, so that they can find each aspect of their lives strictly defined without belonging to any group (in our technical sense) which is doing the defining. Indeed, there may be no single group responsible but a diffuse multitude of bureaucratic institutions. Plantation slavery would provide a clear illustration of how an individual can occupy that top left hand corner of the diagram and be excluded from the very group which is making the rules, but for a more modern case, consider a maidservant living in a small English middle-class family some time before the First World War. Such a residential domestic could easily have her whole day marked out by duties to be performed from before sunrise to late at night; her limited time off-duty was also subject to rules; she could be forbidden male company and expected never to marry. Not only would her speech be prescribed, so that she had to use correct forms of address, but also her manner of speaking so that no option was open to her of expressing her thoughts by a sulky or jubilant tone of voice. But even though a life-long commitment to the family she served was expected, she might very definitely know that she was not a member of it. Conversations about its affairs could cease as she entered and start up as she left the rooms. She might never be consulted on big decisions. She might never take her meals in common with the family. Even if the house was too small for a separate dining room, she might wait upon them as they ate together in the kitchen and then take her own meal alone afterwards. The cost of changing her situation was enormous, because conditions of female employment were so unfavourable.[58]

As to A, the competitive low-grid environment, the case of the turkey farmer I have quoted is one in a whole book of studies of entrepreneurs who get themselves into a competitive environment, like it there, and contribute their energies to keeping it so. A is well-documented in biography and caricatured in fiction so that it is hardly necessary to add to the discussion I gave already in *Natural Symbols* of this social context and its accompanying values. One biography that is very much to the point of this essay is J. H. Plumb's account of early eighteenth century European diplomacy. He is not describing a person and his rise to power, but a social context in which a British Prime Minister found it very hard to operate: 'The nature of foreign governments and of the men who ran them were . . . in 1722 almost a closed book' to Walpole.[59] This follows a close description of very low grid.

Questions of wealth, questions of power expressed in terms of dynastic claims and backed by highly trained professional armies gave the diplomacy of early 18th century Europe its curious flavour. There were, however, one or two other factors of exceptional importance: the character of men could influence events profoundly, and not only the character of rulers but also of diplomats. For this reason, rulers ruled usually in a detailed administrative sense – and, although they were subject continually to the pressures exerted by their ministers they were freer from restraint than rulers, royal or elected, have subsequently become, except in moment of crisis or totalitarian rule. And diplomats themselves, were less subject to detailed control. Although much improved, the means of communication were still desperately slow, and time itself became a subtle weapon of diplomacy – adding as it were a new dimension in which government could fence with government. The prevarications and delays, the decisions taken only to be disavowed, the knowledge that the whole strategy of a diplomatic campaign might be changed by the changed opinion of one prince, inflated the respect in which diplomacy was held and led also to complications almost for their own sake . . . Hence, some of the strange figures who emerged in the early 18th century . . . These were

the wild bold men brought in to take the gambles that the staid
professional diplomats would not countenance . . . Bribery became
endemic, and spies abounded, forcing diplomacy into even more
secret and personal channels, leading often to two, three or more
diplomatic exchanges being carried on simultaneously and these in
their turn, merely inflating the price that governments were ready to
pay for the treachery of another's servants . . . Dynasties, noble as well
as royal, had risen through successful treason and this tendency by
treachery was, of course, the cause of infinite anxiety to statesmen.

At this time, there was little sense of loyalty to a nation, and it is
astonishing how easy it was to buy the confidence of a highly-placed
minister of state . . . Irritating and maddening as it was to those
betrayed, yet such treachery was easily forgiven . . . within the circles
of government and diplomacy, treasonable activity was regarded with
little more distaste than the malicious and destructive envy of colleagues will arouse in tough-fibred, power-seeking men . . . The ease
. . . with which they double-crossed each other is a factor of great
import..rc? ?nd was instrumental in making Walpole depend on his
brother Horatio in diplomatic negotiations. Horatio's loyalty to his
elder brother was absolute; but Walpole's foreign policy might have
proved more successful had he depended on a cleverer man who
occasionally sold his secrets to the enemies.

In short, he was well-adapted to the social environment of England
(medium high grid, weak group) but was caught floundering in the
higher-group lower-grid environment of the European aristocracy.

At this point I can return to the examples raised by earlier scholars
interested in culture. What a weakness it was, in Ruth Benedict's
brilliant essay, to choose three cultures out of a hat and seek no
explanation for the differences between them other than the internal
consistency between propositions generated from within each culture.
For it will eventually appear that both the competitive Kwakiutl and the
sullen Dobu would be rated close together on the same square of our
diagram, if only the *ceteris paribus* rule ever allowed such distant places to
be examined simultaneously. Other things being equal, they would have
to be put into square A, though on different parts of it, if the comparison
could be fine enough. The Zuni, on her account, are in square C, strong
grid, strong group – and she has no other examples and no theory about
how culture can change. Opler supplies an example of a shift in the
history of the Chiricahua from C to weak grid, strong group, D, but he

can only introduce external social factors to operate the cultural shift; factors his theory gives no account of. Before the coming of the white man, the Chiricahua culture kept a balance between the themes of the strength of human goodness supported by benign supernatural powers and witches, ghosts and evil powers. With the beginning of Indian wars, casualties from fighting and epidemics, loss of tribal territories: 'Because of the frustrations, the uncertainties, and the pressures, factionalism flourished. In keeping with the religious pattern, Shamans sought explanations for the misfortunes and found them in the usual revelations concerning the activities of sorcerers. Charges and counter-charges increased. Murders, executions and retaliations were common, and feuds raged.[60] Instead of being *sui generis*, these cultural themes turn out to be part of universal structures of behaviour.

III Individualism

1 The hermit's choice

Earlier I gave reasons for not putting the case of the voluntary recluse on the grid-group map. I also anticipated that a certain distinctive cosmological view could be heard from that occluded quarter. Since this viewpoint becomes vocal enough to reach the ears of people fully marked up on the map and appealing enough for them to be influenced by it and to cite it in their wranglings with one another, it cannot be dismissed from this essay. All the cosmological ideas I have so far described are tied to particular sociological environments. Nothing free-floating has been allowed to appear.

Each position on the chart is here presented as an integral unit, incorporating cosmology and social experience as a single close-meshed structure. This would perhaps imply that one could equally easily unravel the relationships from any part; for instance, starting from cosmology, be led eventually to the social environment which is supposed to generate it. But no, the movement of enquiry from that direction could never have elucidated structures of behaviour (for sound reasons which do not affect the assumption of structural integrity). This was Ruth Benedict's difficulty and Opler's and many other cultural anthropologists'. It arises because several explanatory themes run crossways over the chart and appear in approximately similar guise in different structures. The only method is to assess the structure as a unit and not to let its description be dominated by any single separate elements.

For example, sexual pollution in one form or another is likely to be found everywhere. In C pollution dangers protect all the insulating lines and so sexual pollution is there as one of many; in low grid A, women are likely to be the pawns of male competitive alliances, and their subjection entrenched by pollution beliefs; in B, where group is weak, the control a man has over his womenfolk is possibly the only control he can exercise over anyone at all and he will be tempted to buttress it with theories of pollution published abroad from other parts of society.

Again, take occultism, and see that none except C have scope for synthesizing knowledge on a big scale and so all except C are prone to hope much from disconnected esoteric information. Take chiliastic prophecy, and note that the areas B and D, which are withdrawn from mainstream rewards and reponsibilities, are specially susceptible to its threats and promises. Take the belief in innate differences between kinds of humans, and it can be argued that for different purposes the competitive sector of A, and the two strong group sectors of the diagram (C and D) all are led to make it a dominant principle of explanation.

The cross-chart themes become even more entangled when the hermit's voice is added to the chorus. Therefore, though he is off the map, let us treat the isolate (whether the exile is chosen or one to which he is subjectively reconciled) to the same analytic procedures adopted for the extreme positions on the chart. We will try to identify social conditions which resemble in some ways those of the extreme bottom right (the smallest withdrawn sect) and those of extreme top left, as in the case of Thérèse of Liseux where restrictions, however senselessly imposed from without, are purposely embraced, welcomed as if they had been chosen.[61]

The experience of voluntary withdrawal rejects competition, refuses to control others and reckons not to be under control as to the essentials of human life. The following six points distinguish the social conditions of such an individual from the others we have analysed.

(1) as for (1) at A above, the social experience of the individual is not constrained by any external boundary.

(2) as for (2) at A above, nor is it constrained by substantive signs of ascribed status; the existing classifications barely concern the individual.

(3) as for (3) at A, relations between such unclassifiable individuals will be ambiguous.

(4) as for (4) at A, individuals can transact freely. But this is where the similarity ends.

(5) The individual has little incentive to transact. The rewards of competition and control at A are not for him. His transactions are sporadic, spontaneous and uncalculated.

(6) Following on (4) and (5) the individuals are isolated from the main stream energies of social life. In spite of (1) and (2) there is some insulation, partly by choice but not entirely. Too many years following this ideal will unfit the hermit for ordinary occupations. Paradoxically, the idle rich man who forbore in his youth to get trained for a professional career, has later so many careers closed to him that his life in many respects conforms to these conditions, and his case may be bracketed in this analysis with the vagrant who sleeps in the hedgerows by choice and is equally unfitted for the push and press of common society.

Let us now run through the cosmological derivatives on the same pattern as those derived from a certain point on the grid-group diagram. This is an undemanding social environment, with a minimum of abrasive challenging experiences. So here no contrast is sharply drawn between nature and culture. The more effectively withdrawn, the more the individual is prepared to find nature and the human condition at one, in a proper, pristine harmony. He selects at will only those whom he likes, so he can avoid disagreeable social intercourse. He is never trying to organize any combined undertaking (what incentives has he?) so he is relaxed. His advice to others for all their problems is to withdraw and find solace in communing with nature, thus giving scope to their own nature. This mood is inevitably anti-intellectual, and not sympathetic to high culture. It prefers bird song or children's voices to a grand concert, as we shall see as the argument develops. There are no uses for the concept of nature in moral and legal judgments, since the true hermit is little embroiled in litigious or coercive behaviour. This cosmology nourishes no particular animosity against outsiders or foreign ways. Travel is even a good way of keeping withdrawn and of admiring the wonders of nature.

As to pre-culture, the withdrawn cosmology goes for the theories of natural goodness and self-expression, and it can support them all the more happily in that it has nothing definite to teach. It tolerates mixtures happily and does not treat any boundaries as sacred. If the land is to be cultivated at all, the preference here is to keep the wild romantic look, untouched. The unit of nature and culture is honoured by preferring to eat natural, unprocessed foods and practising the simplest culinary skills of our forbears, that much nearer to nature than the intervening centuries of civilization. Where time is concerned, the hermit has plenty, he lives in the present, is not concerned with memorials to famous or private dead. As to medicine, homeopathic theories could complement other preferences for natural diagnoses and remedies. It is better for him not to think too much about sickness and death, for he has no one to help him at these crises. Perhaps he will be tolerant of euthanasia as consistent with his sturdy individualism, but he will probably rebuke abortion, babies being a sign of vulnerable nature threatened by civilization. There is a special nuance of friendship in this cosmology: animals and humans are valued almost equally. But the voluntary isolate expects no more from friends than friendly unannounced appearances, like the sparrows on the sill. In the way of reciprocal services there is really nothing much to reciprocate but crumbs and fresh water from persons who are beholden to no one. Since no great political treasure is at stake here, this life should be unencumbered by theories of sexual pollution and if anywhere at all men and women ever embrace freely, it ought to be here. But I have doubts about whether anyone ever lives here long enough to demonstrate the point. On social policy, surely great inequalities of power and wealth would be condemned as contrary to nature; but the commitment to equality would at the same time be somewhat passive and ineffectual, since the isolate by definition does not engage in political activity, he only comments upon it. His comments are always crystal clear and consistent. He has all the answers. No infliction of human punishments can be justified, nor need they be: nature is the great arbiter and will catch up with trespassers in the end.

2 The hermit's voice

If we had tried to unravel cosmology and its social setting from the side of cosmology, the pervasive influence of the hermit's views would have made the task impossible. Sweet and harmless in his life, his voice is surprisingly raucous, and it is even more surprising to note what attention it earns from people who are trying to achieve very different objectives. The withdrawn cosmology is a perennial source of metaphors of radical social change. Hence the association of prophecy, rebellion and spiritual renewal with the margins of society.[62] People who entertain no eremitical intentions for themselves exploit its theories about humanity and what social life ought to be like. We should ask why they find the exploitation of a cosmology from off the social map so easy. The answer is that its voice falls winningly on the ears of those in many different social predicaments. It speaks directly to those who have elected to withdraw from the mainstream pressures, not alone but in small sectarian groups (D). It counsels resignation to those who have been forced into lonely high-grid isolation (B). It gets more than a casual hearing from A, low-grid without group, because this social environment is specially prone to moral dilemmas, exposed to contradictions between aims and practices, and subject to frustration and tension. The attractions of a drop-out philosophy are widely appealing here. Therefore most of its metaphors are comprehensible and acceptable in other parts of the diagram and haunt the society from which the recluse has withdrawn. Only strong group strong grid would quarrel with him on most issues except the oneness of humanity with nature, and low grid low group (A) would quarrel about the pursuit of excellence, enjoyment of pomp and the value of culture with the capital C.

The more that the hermit thinks it worthwhile speaking out and seeking for his voice to be heard abroad, the more he is edging onto the social map and becoming part of the throng to which he preaches. The most silent are the most authentic representatives of this cosmology. If we can seek out the poet who never expects to be published, the pensioner growing vegetables on his allotment, the shy mumbling tramp or the isolated crofter, if we could induce them to talk, we would hear the views of the benign, withdrawn cosmology. But the more vocal, though less representative, are still extremely interesting. One thinks of Jean-Jacques Rousseau as the most famous literary exponent of these views. His ever-increasing prestige should correspond to an increasing shift of our society towards the left-hand side of the diagram. Let me take Henry Thoreau as the nearest example of a real case. Born in 1817, in the village of Concord, his father a manufacturer of pencils, he was a non-conforming individualist intellectual from early boyhood; his expected career after a Harvard education was teaching. But he soon preferred for his true profession to be a self-styled 'saunterer'. 'Sauntering meant those daily walks in the woods and fields of Concord and later cruises in a boat, made by the brothers, upon the waters of the Concord and the Assabet, in which his eyes recorded and his imagination integrated those observations which he set down in the fourteen volumes of his Journal.'[63] His editor opens the edition with the words:[64]

Henry Thoreau was the arch example in our history, perhaps in all literary history, of the man who believed in doing what he wanted . . . at the risk of over-simplification, let it be repeated that Thoreau was first and last a man determined to do what he wanted in a society which, like all societies, from Jesus Christ's Jews, to Babbitt's Americans, insisted that the individual should conform to the conventional desires of the day or be called a skulker, a heretic, a radical or a fool.

He, himself, describes how he chose his own path in some sense of having been rejected:[65]

In short, I went on thus for a long time (I may say it without boasting), faithfully minding my business, till it became more evident that my townsmen would not after all admit me into the list of town officers, nor make my place a sinecure with a moderate allowance. My accounts, which I can swear to have kept faithfully, I have, indeed, never got audited, still less accepted, still less paid and settled. However, I have not set my heart on that . . . Finding that my fellow-citizens were not likely to offer me any room in the courthouse, or any curacy or living anywhere else, but I must shift for myself, I turned my face more exclusively than ever to the woods, where I was better known.

His career was really that of a writer, supplemented by brief returns to the pencil factory when need be. His love of nature and his philosophy of life make him a very articulate representative of this quarter. Some good measure of self-conceit is probably always to be found where a person has elected to be apart from other people. Thoreau is insufferably smug. One should expect some contempt of other people caught in the toils of society, but his railing goes beyond the predictable – no mistake about his preferences.[66]

Flint's Pond! Such is the poverty of our nomenclature. What right had the unclean and stupid farmer, whose farm abutted on this sky water, whose shores he has ruthlessly laid bare, to give his name to it? Some skinflint, who loved better the reflecting surface of a dollar, or a bright cent, in which he could see his own brazen face; who regarded even the wild ducks who settled in it as trespassers; his fingers grown into crooked and horny talons from the long habit of grasping harpy-like; so it is named for me. I go not there to see him nor to hear of him; who never *saw* it, who never bathed in it, who never loved it, who never protected it, who never spoke a good word for it, nor thanked God that

He had made it. Rather let it be named from the fishes that swim in it, the wild fowl or quadrupeds which frequent it, the wild flowers that grow by its shores, or some wild man or child the thread of whose history is interwoven with its own; not from him who could show no title to it but the deed which a like-minded neighbour or legislative gave him – who thought only of its money value; whose presence perchance cursed all the shores; who exhausted the land around it, and could fair have exhausted the waters within it; . . . I respect not his labours, his farm where everything has its price, who could carry the landscape, who could carry his God, to market, if he could get anything for him . . . etc. etc.

How Thoreau harps on money. He continually compares the beauties of nature with the famous beauties of high culture and can never resist pointing out that they can be had for free.[67]

White Pond and Walden are great crystals on the surface of the earth, Lakes of Light. If they were permanently congealed, and small enough to be clutched at, they would, perchance be carried off by slaves, like precious stones, to adorn the heads of emperors; but being liquid and ample, and secured to us and to our successors for ever, we disregard them, and run after the diamond of Kohinoor. They are too pure to have a market value; they contain no muck. How much more beautiful than our lives, how much more transparent than our characters, are they! We never learned meanness of them.

Not one of my favourite writers, I confess that I have met many less preaching, less egotistical characters who are more genuine hermits than he. But if we take into account that his determination to be a writer shifted his ambitions towards the more competitive end of the scale, Thoreau can hardly be set off the social map. Indeed, he is not completely honest with himself nor fair with his neighbours.[68]

Thoreau is simply playing house at Walden Pond, yet when he encounters the Irishman, John Field, who lives in a leaky shanty with his greasy-faced, bare-breasted wife and their several children, and who ekes out a cruelly marginal existence hoeing the boggy meadows for a neighbouring farmer at the rate of ten dollars an acre he has the nerve to tell the hard-pressed immigrant how to reorder his priorities. In this appalling passage Thoreau reveals more than just a bachelor's vagueness about the sort of worries that a husband and father would have on his mind; he shows himself to be as innocent as a child:

'I tried to help him with my experience, telling him that he was one of my nearest neighbours, and that I too, who came a-fishing here, and looked like a loafer, was getting my living like himself: that I lived in a tight, light and clean house, which hardly cost more than the annual rent of such a ruin as his commonly amounts to: and how, if he chose, he might in a month or two build a palace of his own: that I did not use tea, nor coffee, nor butter, nor milk, nor fresh meat, and so did not have to work to get them: again, as I did not work hard, I did not have to eat hard, and it cost me but a trifle for my food . . . I told him, that as he worked so hard at bogging, he required thick boots and stout clothing, which were yet soon soiled and worn out, but I wore light shoes and thin clothing, which cost not half so much, though he might think that I was dressed like a gentleman (which, however, was not the case), and in an hour or two, without labour, but as recreation, I could, if I wished, catch as many fish as I should want for two days, or earn enough money to support me a week. If he and his family would live simply, they might all go a-huckleberrying in the summer for their amusement.'

What a hero for our times!

3 Low grid

Low-grid society is especially prone to contradictions. The two worst are the dehumanizing (mechanizing) of personal relations and the disparity of status, both of which result from the pressure to seek benefits of scale in all dealing, but each is compounded by troubles stemming from uncertainty. Each is a source of scandal because of its flagrant contradiction of the basic principle of individual human value. Perhaps this is the point to examine more closely that premise and see how it becomes institutionalized through the development of low-grid competitive pressures. The dismantling of classifications proceeds in the name of the unique value of the individual, so it is a constant justifying point of reference. One of the easiest inferences to make is that the principle is honoured when equality of individuals is manifest, and dishonoured by their inequality. This snugly fills the gap torn by tolerance and scepticism in the cosmological scheme. Equality is the most acceptable principle of low grid, since it is the only one that does not call for explicit re-classification. At the same time, the metaphysical vacuum turns the individual to his own interior sources for such spiritual strength as he may seek. The trend has to be away from public religion to the inner conscience, 'the still small voice'; private, even secret sympathy with the withdrawn cosmology.

When it comes to seeking remedies to the scandals of the low grid, the same culture has one favourite answer, which is to liberate the individual further. The wish to cancel the inhuman effects of screening and time-saving, so that human warmth can transform the mechanism, produces a further shift down grid. It will intensify the contradictions. This is precisely why grid is a strong enough dimension to place athwart group. Low grid, low group (A), and high grid high group (C) each have their distinctive woes. They each generate remedies which, if followed, make the later troubles worse than the first. Their own self-reinforcing energies explain why cultures built upon their premises endure. Here is the knot, the unyielding part of culture which will tend to shape the form of individual transactions. You cannot win if you try to form a strong group in a situation in which all the economic and social pressures are for open information, expansion and economies of scale. Individuals who wish to negotiate their roles, and freely to interpret the cues around them, will have to exert extraordinary force if they are to push certain doors open or close other ones. Ethnomethodologists and symbolic interactionists please note, culture is not entirely negotiable.

We have identified sources of cultural stability, but in doing so are forced to redefine it. The stability of strong group is manifest over the content of knowledge. The group remains strong so long as it filters information from outside. So new ways of doing things will not be easily introduced. But the stability of low grid has to be recognized in the very situation in which new knowledge is being continually tried. Its stability is in the spirit of experiment itself and in the hunger for widening cycles of exchange; it has a stable sense of the glory of personal genius, stable ways of organizing rivalry and ruin, a stable habit of eliciting work and defiance and of celebrating the individual; within this stable framework of low grid the scope for negotiating a new place for oneself is not necessarily more or less than in strong group. The individual negotiator within the group (at D) can manipulate tradition and by conspicuous devotion to group causes can climb the ladder of eminence. His scope is only as restricted as the world constituted by the group itself. But the negotiator of roles in low grid may be equally restricted by the strength of competition, for not everyone can be a Big Man. However, for him there exists the possibility of creating a new kind of reality and so of reconstructing the world a little in his own favour. The pressure to get benefits of scale is a pressure to differentiate. The more the individual is expected to create his own role, the more his transacting with others is entirely up to himself, then the better advised he is to corner a little resource, to specialize, or at least to offer an improved version of what everyone else can do. Hence we recognize in low-grid conditions the tendency to cultivate idiosyncracy – and this fits well with the general tolerance of deviance.

First for the rewards of specializing: better than straight returns to scale on a known product, the chance of launching a successful innovation brings rewards of esteem and following. This will result in a new field of relationships, as surely as opening new territory in frontier communities or expanding an empire. No wonder that low grid is favourable to science and the arts. The most effective way to surpass a leader, and steal away his following is to invent a new medium. This need not be a major technological change – like radio, television or supersonic transport; it need not even mean shifting interests away from one visual art to another major branch, as from painting to sculpture. If inventing a new medium were so weighty, it would be hard for individualists trying to keep ahead in low grid society. A new medium can be opened within narrow means, even between brush and canvas, as Lawrence Gowing said that Turner made paint into a new medium itself to be experienced as paint, instead of invisibly to mediate visions of objects.[69] Turner is pre-eminently a Big Man who reconstructed his own universe. He is shown to be so consciously subscribing to the very cosmology which by grid-group analysis he was likely to embrace that his case, as presented by Lawrence Gowing, belongs with other modern instances that we have cited. His conviction of the true artist's innate, unteachable powers, his competitiveness, especially with the greatest of his predecessors, his 'scorn of painters who do not aim high', the perverse-seeming defiance of criticism, his talent for paying tribute in a way that achieved a subtle victory over the recipients and his apparent alliance with and homage to the great dead artists that somehow incorporated them, swallowed them up in his own work, all this has a feel of Melanesia. There they fight with food according to rules[70] but Turner explicitly fought with paint:

> In 1832 when Constable exhibited his 'Opening of Waterloo Bridge', it was placed in the school of painting – one of the small rooms at Somerset House. A sea-piece, by Turner, was next to it – a grey picture, beautiful and true, but with no positive colour in any part of it.

Constable's 'Waterloo' seemed as if painted with liquid gold and silver, and Turner came several times into the room while he was heightening with vermilion and lake the decorations and flags of city barges. Turner stood behind him, looking from the 'Waterloo' to his own picture, and at last brought his palette from the great room where he was touching another picture, and putting a round daub of red lead, somewhat bigger than a shilling, on his grey sea, went away without saying a word. The intensity of the red lead, made more vivid by the coolness of his picture, caused even the vermilion and lake of Constable to look weak. I came into the room just as Turner left it. 'He has been here,' said Constable, 'and fired a gun'. On the opposite wall was a picture, by Jones, of Shadrach, Meshach and Abednego in the furnace. 'A coal,' said Cooper, 'has bounded across the room from Jones's picture, and set fire to Turner's sea'. The great man did not come again into the room for a day and a half; and then, in the last moments that were allowed for painting, he glazed the scarlet seal he had put on his picture, and shaped it into a buoy.

It was not by sparring on a roped-off platform that Turner dominated the scene. He had the option like every other painter 'to deploy an accepted vocabulary of representation', but he rejected that 'conventional code of configuration'. What he did amounted to introducing a new reality, one composed of painted colour. Before, the condition of painting was founded on the axiom that no traces of the means by which a work of art had been produced should appear – it was to resemble nature. But Turner's influence required painting to resemble itself more than anything else. And he got his following; in a year 'there was a host of young painters working in the new manner'. It consisted of isolating the pictorial effect, turning the painters' eyes in towards their own work as to a world in itself, a pictorial world, constituted from colour in paint. Lawrence Gowing says that even his first exhibited picture suggests that as well as light and grandeur 'one other thing was real to him, the paint itself.' 'The early critics of Turner were goaded to the point at which they almost realised that painting was uncovering, not only new means of representation, but a new substance, a different order of reality . . . Twenty years later this new kind of painting was fully formed.' Of Turner's visit to Venice, he says:

In his drawings done at daybreak the scene is made of colour, with no other substance. Shape is outlined with a marvellous economy of touch, as if discovering itself of its own accord. The colour lies intact and pearly on the paper. These drawings leave a magical impression that the specific details of a real place grew out of colour, instead of the reverse. The old hierarchy of reality was reversed. Colour assumed precedence. It existed first and provided the imaginative substance out of which the likeness of an external object could be made.

'Turner's words about Rembrandt are revealing; he imagined colour as a separate fabric, fragile and vulnerable, yet sacred and sufficient in itself to supply all the reality that is required from a picture.' And finally: 'Turner's pictures were always visibly and obviously made out of paint.'

I have said nothing here of the double structural analysis which is the other subject of this remarkable essay, the comments by Turner upon acceptable and unacceptable correspondence between painting and its subject and the further comments by Gowing tracing a deeper iso-morphism between the painter's temperament and his choice of medium, his developing emotional needs and the developing structure of his paintings. These analyses are undoubtedly relevant to the com-parison of low-grid symbolic systems with others, a comparison which must eventually be tackled. But here I am content to take the example of how an artist can not so much negotiate the categories of experience (for negotiation there was none) but can reconstrue the universe and discover there undreamed-of new resources. There is always scope for discovering a new medium. Cyril Barrett's study of Op Art has a passage that follows well on the ones on Turner. He asks 'What has Op contributed to our experience?' and answers, a new perception of space:[72]

What is important is that, by refraction, radiation and juxtaposition, these artists have been able to produce colours of intense brilliance and luminosity and great delicacy which seem to have no material base but hover in space like light: in short, disembodied colour . . . To put this another way, in place of pictures of grapes which birds can peck at you have pictures which you can bump your nose on when trying to locate them in sapce . . . Op artists . . . do not give us a substitute for our everyday space with the objects which are in it, but create an intangible perceptual space which cannot easily be reduced to ordinary space or the objects in it.

These accounts of how new media are introduced are also examples of the needed brokerage. The swift succeeding fashions in art fragment

the realm of discourse, baffle the uninitiated and call forth new professions of commentators and other intermediaries. Brokerage and insur-
ance are one way in which I would explain the vast amount of secret,
private magic in New Guinea societies. Brokers specialize in mediating
separate sellers and buyers, so low-grid times make a heyday for
promoters, historians, literary critics as they do also for scientific
research. From year to year uncertainty must increase, diversity grow
and consensus diminish more. These are costs to be borne. But there is
an advantage: the experience of continually changing media should act
upon consciousness like the discovery of new continents and new
opportunities. Low-grid conditions should cure people of thinking
restrictively in terms of zero sum games.[73]

As to personality, I have hinted at some of the effects upon it. It will be
clear from what I have said that this method invites a very flexible
approach to personality and its relation to culture, instead of the rigid,
fixed-in-infancy approach of many psychologists. Each grid-group
position suits a particular personality type. But grid-group analysis says
nothing about the weight of power. When power is weak, the personality
flowers in a very different way. Take Howard Becker's study of jazz
musicians.[74]

The musician is conceived of as an artist who possesses a mysterious
artistic gift setting him apart from all other people. Possessing this gift
he should be free from control by outsiders who lack it. The gift is
something which cannot be acquired through education . . . 'You
can't teach a guy to have a beat. Either he's got one or he hasn't. If he
hasn't got it, you can't teach it to him.' The strongest element in the
colleague's code is the prohibition against criticising or in any other
way trying to put pressure on another musician in the actual playing
situation 'on the job' . . . 'Musicians live an exotic life like in a jungle
or something. They start out, they're just ordinary kids from small
towns, but once they get into that life they change. It's like a jungle,
except that their jungle is a hot, crowded bus. You live that kind of life
long enough, you get to be completely different.' Feeling their
difference strongly, musicians believe they are under no obligation to
imitate the conventional behaviour of squares. From the idea that no
one can tell a musician how to behave it follows logically that no one
can tell a musician how to do anything. Accordingly, behaviour which
flouts conventional norms is greatly admired. Stories reveal this
admiration for highly individual, spontaneous, devil-may-care activi-

ties, many of the most notable jazz musicians are regarded as 'characters' and their exploits are widely recounted . . . This is more than idiosyncracy, it is a primary occupational value . . . 'You know, the biggest heroes in the music business are the biggest characters. The crazier a guy acts, the greater he is, the more everyone likes him.'[74]

The jungle metaphor betrays the low-grid, low-group position.

In the social world they know there are some other musicians, whose culture does not so strongly approve eccentricity. The jazz man believes that he subordinates outside pressures to his free artistic expression, while the commercial musician does it the other way round. The price that the jazz man pays for his individual freedom is uncertain pay, unsocial hours, geographical mobility, and a wrecked marriage sooner or later. So it would seem that the fullest expression of idiosyncracy appears in those low-grid systems which are weakly connected up with institutionalized power. The jazz man is not trying to exert control over others. For the musicians who do seek power, eccentricity is out; individual expression takes place within the structured media provided by others who have gone before and by others who are now in the Big Man seat of control. So education, so science, so sport, low grid provides ground rules which enable play to be compared and judged fairly. The competition has to conform to the basic premise of equality, fairness to each competitor, explicit rules to obey, rules whose object is to facilitate individual transactions. Here the competitor for the Big Man stakes cannot afford to seem crazy. But the jazz man, though down-grid, has only two of the three positive components: autonomy, competition but not control.

Since I am trying to persuade colleagues in Melanesia to try these ideas on their material, perhaps I could raise again the contrast between Dobuan and Trobriand personality, which Malinowski outlined. Reading Fortune's account of Dobu again, it appears to be an extreme type of low grid society, more advanced along that path than the Trobriands of Kiriwina. Both these island cultures extolled competition for status through exchange; both gave honour to the man who could be selected as a partner by the most prestigious foreigners, could choose cleverly among his peers, screening out the unimportant, and so build up his reputation and following with feats and famous displays. Reo Fortune, writing on Dobu, paid more attention to sorcery and marriage rules, and said less about the competitive aspects of exchange. But he gave plenty of evidence to justify the Dobuan reputation over the whole archipelago for daring merchants, brave in spite of their belief in each other's magic, utterly ruthless in their dealings, with power and status at stake. 'Gazumping' is a new word with us: to break a contract because a better offer has come along, and by breaking it, to pitch the affairs of one's colleagues into chaos and delay. The fact that we managed without that word, gazump, and that the Dobuans always had a word for it, *wabu wabu*, and that it was not specially disapproved, is significant. How did we manage before? Because we were higher on grid. Dobuans who gazumped would relish the wasted time of their rivals.[75]

> Later, when four men appear in my home . . . expecting [a famous shell] . . . only one will get it. They are furious, it is true, and their exchange is blocked for the year . . . I have become a great man by enlarging my exchanges at the expense of blocking theirs for a year. I cannot afford to block theirs for too long, or my exchanges will never be trusted by anyone again . . . I am honest in the final issue.

The complicated rules of residence by which each man lived one year in his wife's village, one in his own (with all the scope for sexual triumphs this rule gives him), these fair-play rules can be interpreted as facilitating comparison, an elaborate equalizing of opportunities of exchange throughout a society of which Fortune said simply 'there is no rank in Dobu'. Dobu had great men, but no rank, whereas in the Trobriands there were great men, but ranking classifications insulated them from the total competition of every man and boy. Rank insulates, it disqualifies some and qualifies others, regardless of talent. So the Trobriand selection for leadership was not made in an entirely open field. Higher grid, combined with the possibility of being remote from power, these social characteristics would account, I suggest, for the difference in personality between Dobu and Trobriands, as Malinowski described them.

I would propose that low marks for the power component is the crucial factor which influences the personality type in low grid. Close to power, where no holds are barred, the surface affability of the Big Man is under strain; he is tight-lipped, with plenty to worry about. The further from power, the more low grid allows individualism to indulge in a flood of eccentricity. Malinowski said the Trobrianders held the Dobuans to be

> their envied superiors in some ways, despised barbarians in others.
> The Dobuans who ate man and dog, but could produce more deadly

witchcraft than anyone else, who were mean and jealous, but could fight and raid till they held in terror the whole Koya . . . the home of cannibalism, head-hunting, or daring expeditions; the country about which there circulated fabulous tales, partly native and partly European.

And he compared their grimmer personality with light-hearted Trobrianders.[79] From Fortune's ethnography Ruth Benedict travestied them as an extreme case of cultural paranoia, ridden with fear and conspiracy. How could they have earned their great renown, collected their wealth and held their dominion, if they had really been curled up inside with fear and suspicion? They had good reason to believe that everyone was practising the black arts against them, as each indulged himself in the same. But to take the sorcery recipes out of context is to miss the other low-grid effects which make sense of the Dobu ethnography.

Many of the examples I have been using are drawn from our own culture. With us the social drive to lower grid comes because of the parallel increasing division of labour in the industrial field. But I have shown that low grid is a self-generating social condition. The contrast between the Africa of anthropologists concerned with corporation theory and the Melanesia of anthropologists working on exchange theory becomes an anthropologists' tribal model of the relation between culture and society. The more general explanation of the differences between the two models can be set out in terms of grid and group. Paradoxically, with explanation, that which was obvious becomes puzzlingly less so and that which was obscure becomes obvious. The difficult-to-explain model now is African group; the most common, world-wide model is low grid. The question now is why it has stayed so invisible (but Bernstein has answered that). As a cultural type, low grid goes with eclecticism, fashion-ridden openness to any new gimmick; then pragmatism, secularity, the privateness of access to spiritual powers; each man claiming his own secret resources, hereditary, unique and personal to himself; then the feasting which is so much less a religious communion, but more a personal political bid; then the contractual nature of the relations between individuals, and their possibility of breach; the absence of a gory criminal law – instead of fierce punishments, ridicule is the worst that can happen to a man, and rather than that, suicide as the escape. I would ask Melanesian specialists who know their field as I never can, to work out how these tribes can be placed on measurements of grid and group.

By way of conclusion, it may be helpful here to say again in general terms what the paper is trying to do. The argument throughout takes a particular kind of social environment as a starting point, and demonstrates how, given the premises involved in defining that social environment, certain distinctive values and belief systems will follow as necessary for the legitimation of actions taken within it. The dimensions of grid and group are crucial in that they provide a systematic basis for defining four main types of social environment in enough detail to allow the derivation of cosmologies to be made. Although the argument involves this directionality, it is not intended to imply that a casual relation exists between cosmology as effect and social context as cause. In any social context, it may be assumed that the chains of cause and effect between the structures of social interaction and cosmological and cultural systems which are supporting them are indefinitely interwoven and interdependent. Cosmological values, being used to provide justifications for the actions expected from a person by the constraints of his social environment, are likely to be involved in the choice of actions. Consequently a stabilizing factor is identified. However, the individual, not seen here as being passively acted upon by the forces of his social context, is himself a part of that social environment, and he will be actively maintaining and constituting it. Any individual can interact at any level and choose to accept or reject the social pressures and prevailing cosmology in which he finds himself.

The aim of this paper is therefore not to describe a causal model of cosmological values, but to propose a typology which will be reflected in the different structures of behaviour. The individual's subjective experience and conception of his social context is one part of the whole set of mapping structures. It serves as a mediating link between a more 'objective' definition of social context (which in this case would probably mean obtaining a consensus of other people's subjective perceptions) and the cosmological values to which the individual adheres. The subjective perception must, of course, also be coloured by that cosmology. The approach which is adopted here describes a structured typology, using the grid and group dimensions to trace certain patterns of behaviour through the whole system of social interactions, perceptions, values and justifications. To attempt to hold subject's perception constant while examining the relation of social context to cosmology would be fallacious. The individual's subjectivity is an important part of his way of interacting with others, and so of his system of values and his impact on them. Instead, we approach the problem by constructing a

taxonomy of social contexts and their supporting cosmologies. Ultimately this taxonomy should feed into a description of cultural processes, and provide a systematic comparative basis for cross-cultural
studies. It should also enhance our understanding of social change. The
development of typologies for understanding change has naturally
followed upon the understanding that a particular period has of itself
and its social categories. When eighteenth-century France saw itself as
constituted by three estates – a land-owning governing class, the
church, and the third estate of the powerful bourgeoisie – discussions of
social change were set in those terms. Ever since, Europe's self-
knowledge has considered social change in terms that are based upon
stratification, economic and political, and upon occupational categories.
For the anthropologist's project, the stratified hierarchical perspective
has not lent itself to saying anything very useful about the relation
between culture and ideology on the one hand or between culture and
forms of social organization on the other. The present exercise in
understanding cosmologies is intended to cut a different kind of slice
into social reality. Capable of expansion and reduction between macro
and micro scale social behaviour, it focuses on two modes of control –
processes of inclusion and processes of classification, using anthropological experience on both topics.

In sum, this is offered as an approach to culture. Define the two
dimensions, scale and mark them clearly, map the grid and group rating
of the social context and the justifying cosmology. The full programme
is to test how well the criteria have been selected to discover interlocking
structures of behaviour. Though an inter-disciplinary effort is always
fraught with danger it is good to honour Frazer by contriving to bring
together different parts of anthropology, from different regions and
times, offering a sign of peace.

Notes

I thank the Trustees of the Frazer Memorial Lecture who have given me the
occasion to present a condensed version of this argument. It is a development of
the thesis attempted in *Natural Symbols*, 1970. This means that it is one more
attempt to make a tool for anthropology from Basil Bernstein's insights into
processes of cultural transmission. I have tried to provide some precise biblio-
graphic references to this corpus, but that the debt is more general and total will
appear obvious to anyone who is familiar with it. I also thank all those critics who
have helped to sharpen the focus but who are not acknowledged in the text.

Particularly I thank the Social Science Research Council for an award in 1976–7 which enabled me to engage the help of Dr James Hampton for constructing the grid-group dimensions. I thank also David Bloor and Michael Thompson for constructive criticism. Most of my anthropology colleagues at University College London have heard me on grid-group analysis very often and I acknowledge their patience and criticisms. I also thank postgraduate students who have placed their research in this perspective, particularly Steven Rayner. I thank Bristol University for the opportunity of giving a résumé of the argument in the E. M. Wood Lecture in 1977. At the last minute Dr Stanton Wheeler's acute criticisms entailed major revisions of this text.

1   Clifford Geertz, *The Interpretation of Cultures*, Selected Essays, London, Hutchinson, 1975; Clyde Kluckholn and W. H. Kelly, 'The Concept of Culture', in *The Science of Man in the World Crisis*, ed. R. Linton, New York, 1945, pp. 78–106; Morris Edward Opler, 'Themes as Dynamic Forces in Culture', *The American Journal of Sociology*, 51, 1946, pp. 198–206; Talcott Parsons, *The Structure of Social Action*, Chicago, Ill., Free Press, 1949.

2   Margaret Mead, (a) *Sex and Temperament*, New York, 1963 (also published as pt 3 of (b); (b) *From the South Seas: studies of adolescence and sex in primitive societies*, New York, 1948; M. Mead and G. Bateson, *Balinese Character*, a photographic analysis, New York, 1942; G. Bateson, M. Mead and F. C. Macgregor, *Growth and Culture, a photographic study of Balinese Childhood*, New York, 1951; J. W. M. Whiting and I. L. Child, *Child-training and personality*, New Haven, Yale University Press, 1953; Robert A. Levine, *Culture, Behaviour and Personality*, Chicago, Aldine, 1973.

3   M. Herskovits, *Acculturation*, New York, 1938; B. Malinowski, *The Dynamics of Culture Change, an Inquiry into Race Relations in Africa*, New Haven, Yale University Press, 1961; J. Steward, *Theory of Culture Change*, Illinois University Press, 1955.

4   Ruth Benedict, *Patterns of Culture*, New York, 1934.

5   J. Steward (ed.), *Irrigation Civilisations*, Washington, 1955; L. White, *The Science of Culture*, New York, 1949; L. White, *The Evolution of Culture*, New York, 1959; E. A. Hoebel, *The Law of Primitive Man*, Cambridge, Mass., 1954.

6   S. A. Tyler (ed.), *Cognitive Anthropology*, Readings, New York, Holt, Rinehart & Winston, 1969; W. C. Sturtevant, 'Studies in Ethnoscience', *American Anthropologist*, 66, 2, 1964, pp. 99–131.

7   Mary Black and D. Metzger, 'Ethnographic description and the study of Law', *American Anthropologist*, vol. 67, no. 6, pt 2, 1965, pp. 141–65; C. O. Frake, 'The diagnosis of disease among the Subanun of Mindanao', *American Anthropologist*, 63, 1, 1961, pp. 113–82; E. Goffman, *Encounters*, New York, Bobbs Merrill, 1961; C. O. Frake, 'How to Ask for a Drink in Subanun', *American Anthropologist*, vol. 66, no. 6, 1964.

8   J. A. Barnes, 'African Models in the New Guinea Highlands', *Man*, 62,

1962, pp. 5–9; M. De Lepervanche, 'Descent, Residence and Leadership in the New Guinea Highlands', *Oceania*, 38, 1967–8, pp. 134–8, 163–89; L. L. Langness, 'Some problems in the conceptualization of Highlands Social Structures in New Guinea: The Central Highlands', *American Anthropologist*, 66, 1964, pp. 162–82.

9   M. Gluckman, 'The Kingdom of the Zulu', in *African Political Systems*, ed. M. Fortes and E. Evans-Pritchard, Oxford University Press, 1940.

10   K. A. Busia, *The Position of the Chief in the Modern Political System of Ashanti, A Study of the Influence of Contemporary Social Changes on Ashanti Political Institutions*, Oxford University Press, 1951; A. I. Richards, (a) 'Social Mechanisms for the transfer of political rights in some African tribes', *Journal of the Royal Anthropological Institute*, 90, 1960, pp. 175–90; (b) 'African Kings and their Royal Relatives', Presidential address, *Journal of the Royal Anthropological Institute*, 91, 2, 1961, pp. 139–50; M. Gluckman, *The Ideas of Barotse Jurisprudence*, New Haven, Yale University Press, 1965, pp. 39–41; Godfrey Wilson, 'The Nyakyusa of South-Western Tanganyika', in *Seven Tribes of British Central Africa*, ed. E. Colson and M. Gluckman, Oxford University Press, 1951, p. 287.

11   A. Strathern, *The Rope of Moka, Big-men and Ceremonial Exchange in Mount Hagen, New Guinea*, Cambridge University Press, 1971, ch. 9.

12   Margaret Mead (ed.), *Co-operation and Competition*, London, 1937; Paula Brown, *The Chimbu, a Study of Change in the New Guinea Highlands*, London, Routledge & Kegan Paul, 1973, p. 93.

13   Meyer Fortes, 'The Structure of Unilineal Descent Groups', *American Anthropologist*, 55, 1953, pp. 17–41; M. G. Smith, *Corporations in Society*, London, 1974.

14   Douglas Oliver, *A Solomon Island Society: Kinship and Leadership among the Sinai of Bougainville*, Cambridge, Mass., Harvard University Press, 1955; H. A. Powell, 'Competitive Leadership in Trobriand Political Organisation', *Journal of the Royal Anthropological Institute*, 90, 1960, pp. 118–45.

15   L. Pospisil, *The Kapauku Papuans of Western New Guinea*, New York, Holt, Rinehart & Winston, 1963.

16   L. Pospisil, *Kapauku Papuan Economy*, New Haven, Yale University Press, 1963.

17   P. Lawrence and M. J. Meggitt (eds), *Gods, Ghosts and Men in Melanesia: Some Religions of Australian New Guinea and the New Hebrides*, Melbourne, 1965 (especially R. M. Berndt, pp. 94–5 and P. Lawrence, pp. 218 ff); Kenneth E. Read, *The High Valley*, London, 1966, pp. 114–15; R. F. Fortune, *Manus Religion, an ethnological study of the Manus Natives of the Admiralty Islands*, Philadelphia, American Philosophical Society, 1935, pp. 5–24; Roy Wagner, *The Curse of Souw, Principles of Daribi Clan Definition and Alliance in New Guinea*, University of Chicago Press, 1967, p. 218.

18   C. Daryll Forde, 'Justice and Judgement among the Southern Ibo under

Colonial Rule', in *African Law*, ed. H. and L. Kuper, California, 1965; A. L. Epstein, 'Military Organisation and Pre-colonial Polity of the Bemba of Zambia', *Man*, vol. 10.2, 1975.

19   C. Daryll Forde, (a) 'Fission and Accretion in the Patrilineal Clans of a semi-Bantu Community in Southern Nigeria', *Journal of the Royal Anthropological Institute*, 68, 1938, pp. 311–38; (b) 'Integrative Aspects of Yakö First Fruit Rituals', Presidential address, *Journal of the Royal Anthropological Institute*, 79, 1949, pp. 1–10.

20   C. Daryll Forde, (a) 'The Context of Belief', The Frazer Lecture for 1958, Liverpool University Press, 1958; (b) 'Spirits, Witches and Sorcerers in the Supernatural Economy of the Yako', *Journal of the Royal Anthropological Institute*, 88, 2, 1958, pp. 165–78.

21   C. Daryll Forde, 'Death and Succession, an analysis of Yakö Mortuary Ceremonial', in *Essays on Rituals of Social Relations*, ed. M. Gluckman, Manchester University Press, 1962.

22   Aaron V. Cicourel, *Cognitive Sociology*, Harmondsworth, Penguin, 1973.

23   Bruce Kapferer and Don Handelman, 'Forms of Joking Acitivity: a comparative approach', *American Anthropologist*, 74, 1972, pp. 484–51; Don Handelman, 'Gossip in Encounters: the transmission of information in a bounded social setting', *Man*, 8.2, 1973, pp. 210–27.

24   E. Durkheim, (a) *The Division of Labour in Society*, New York, Free Press, 1968 (originally 1893); (b) *The Elementary Forms of the Religious Life*, New York, Collier Books, 1961 edn (originally 1912), p. 254; E. Durkheim and M. Mauss, *Primitive Classification*, trans. R. Needham, London, Routledge & Kegan Paul, 1963 (originally 1903); Robert Hertz, *Death and the Right Hand*, trans. R. and C. Needham, London, Cohen & West, 1960 (originally 1907) p. 81.

25   Harold Garfinkel, *Studies in Ethnomethodology*, Englewood Cliffs, N.J., Prentice-Hall, 1967.

26   Mary Douglas, *Natural Symbols, Explorations in Cosmology*, Harmondsworth, Penguin, 1970.

27   H. J. S. Maine, *Ancient Law*, London, Dent, 1972 (originally 1861).

28   Basil Bernstein, (a) 'On the Classification and Framing of educational Knowledge', in *Class, Codes and Control, Vol. I, Theoretical Studies towards a Sociology of Language*, London, Routledge & Kegan Paul, 1971, pp. 221–5; (b) 'Class and Pedagogies, visible and invisible', in *Class, Codes and Control, Vol. III, Towards a Theory of Educational Transmissions*, London, Routledge & Kegan Paul, 1975, ch. 6.

29   William Faulkner, *Requiem for a Nun*, Harmondsworth, Penguin, 1976, p. 10.

30   A. Forge, 'Prestige, Influence and Society, a New Guinea example', in *Witchcraft Accusations and Confessions*, ed. Mary Douglas, ASA 9, London, Tavistock, 1970, ch. 12 (q.v.).

31 Mary Douglas and B. C. Isherwood, *The World of Goods, an Anthropological Theory of Consumption*, Allen Lane, 1979.

32 David Knowles, *The Religious Orders in England*, Cambridge University Press, 1948, p. 140.

33 Richard Lynn, *The Entrepreneur: eight case studies*, London, George Allen & Unwin, 1974, pp. 118–39.

34 David F. Wilson, *Dockers: the Impact of Industrial Change*, London, Fontana, 1972.

35 Talcott Parsons, *The Social System*, Chicago, Free Press, 1952, pp. 148–9, 359–83 and ch. 9.

36 E. Durkheim, *Elementary Forms of the Religious Life*, pp. 471–3.

37 Mary Douglas, (a) 'Thirty Years after Witchcraft, Oracles and Magic', introduction to *Witchcraft Accusations and Confessions*; (b) 'Is Matriliny Doomed in Africa?', ch. in *Man in Africa*, ed. Mary Douglas and Phyllis Kaberry, London, Tavistock, 1969; (c) 'Matriliny and Pawnship in Central Africa', *Africa*, 34.4, 1964, pp. 301–12.

38 Rodney Needham, 'Polythetic Classification: convergence and consequences', *Man*, 10.3, 1975, pp. 349–69. S. Rayner alerted me.

39 Mary Douglas, *Natural Symbols*, p. 84.

40 Mary Douglas, 'The Nature of Things', ch. in *Implicit Meanings*, London, Routledge & Kegan Paul, 1975.

41 Peter Brown, 'The Rise and Function of the Holy Man in Late Antiquity', *The Journal of Roman Studies*, 1971, pp. 80–101; Louis Dumont, *Homo Hierarchicus, the Caste System and its Implications*, ch. 9 on the Renouncing Sects, English edn 1970 (originally 1966).

42 Lucy Mair, *Witchcraft*, London, World University Library, 1969; M. G. Marwick, *Sorcery in its Social Setting*, Manchester University Press, 1965; J. F. Middleton and E. Winter (eds), *Witchcraft and Sorcery in East Africa*, London, Routledge, 1963.

43 Basil Bernstein and E. Henderson, 'Social Class differences in the relevance of language and socialization', in *Class, Codes and Control, Vol. II: Applied Studies towards a Sociology of Language*, ch. 2, pp. 45–6.

44 E. R. Leach, 'Anthropological Aspects of Language: Animal Categories and Verbal Abuse', in E. H. Lenneberg (ed.), *New Directions in the Study of Language*, Cambridge, Mass., MIT Press, 1964.

45 S. Tambiah, 'Animals are good to think and good to prohibit', *Ethnology*, 8, no. 4, 1969.

46 Peter Rivière, personal communication from unpublished research on women's magazines.

47 Edward Shils, *The Intellectuals and the Powers and Other Essays*, University of Chicago Press, 1972.

48 E. Evans-Pritchard, *The Nuer*, Oxford University Press, 1940, ch. 3; I. Cunnison, *History on the Luapula: an essay on the historical notions of a Central*

African tribe, Cape, Rhodes-Livingstone Institute, 1951; J. A. Barnes, *Politics in a Changing Society, a political history of the Fort Jameson Ngoni*, Manchester University Press, 1967.

49 Clyde Mitchell, *The Yao Village*, Manchester University Press, 1956.

50 M. Gluckman, *Custom and Conflict in Africa: Section IV: The Logic of Witchcraft*, Oxford, Blackwell, 1956.

51 Gilbert Lewis, *Knowledge of Illness in a Sepik Society, a study of the Gnau, New Guinea*, London and New Jersey, 1973.

52 Colin Murray Parkes, *Bereavement, Studies of grief in adult life*, New York, International Universities Press, 1972.

53 Keith Thomas, Northcliffe Lecture, 'The Place of Laughter in Tudor and Stuart England', *Times Literary Supplement*, 21 January 1977.

54 L. Pospisil, *Kapauku Papuan Economy*, pp. 382–3.

55 E. Durkheim, *The Division of Labour*.

56 H. J. Eysenck, *The Psychology of Politics*, London, Routledge & Kegan Paul, 1954. For a critique of the scales see R. Christie, C. Hanley and M. Rockeach in dialogue with Eysenck, in *Psychological Bulletin*, vol. 53, 1956.

57 McKim Marriott, 'Hindu Transactions: Diversity without dualism', in *Transaction and Meaning, Directions in the Anthropology of Exchange and Symbolic Behaviour*, ed. B. Kapferer, Philadelphia, Institute for the Study of Human Issues, 1976.

58 Leonore Davidoff, 'Mastered for Life: Servant and Wife in Victorian and Edwardian England', Institute of Social History, Summer 1974.

59 J. H. Plumb, *Sir Robert Walpole, Vol. 2, Walpole's Europe*, London, 1960, pp. 13–17.

60 Opler, op. cit.

61 Barry Ulanov, *The Making of a Modern Saint, a biographical study of Thérèse of Lisieux*, New York, Doubleday, 1966.

62 I. M. Lewis, *Ecstatic Religion, an anthropological study of spirit possession and shamanism*, Harmondsworth, Penguin, 1971; Max Weber, *The Sociology of Religion*, London, Methuen, 1971 (originally 1922).

63 *The Works of Thoreau*, selected and ed. Henry S. Canby, Cambridge, Mass., 1937, introduction, pp. xiii–xiv.

64 Ibid., p. vi.

65 Ibid., p. 256.

66 Ibid., pp. 315–16.

67 Ibid., p. 378.

68 Kenneth Lynn, 'Adulthood in American Literature', *Daedalus*, Fall 1976, p. 52.

69 Lawrence Gowing, *Turner, Imagination and Reality*, New York, The Museum of Modern Art, 1966.

70 Michael W. Young, *Fighting with Food: Leadership, values and social control in a Massim society*, Cambridge University Press, 1971.

71   Gowing, op. cit., p. 45.
72   Cyril Barrett, *Op Art*, London, Studio Vista, 1970.
73   George Foster, (a) 'Community Development and the Image of the Static Economy', *Community Development Bulletin*, 12, 1961; (b) 'Peasant Society and the Image of the Limited Good', *American Anthropologist*, 67, 1965, pp. 293–315.
74   Howard S. Becker, *Outsiders, Studies in the Sociology of Deviance*, New York, Free Press, 1963, pp. 84–104.
75   R. F. Fortune, *Sorcerers of Dobu, the social anthropology of the Dobu Islanders of the Western Pacific*, London, Routledge, 1932, p. 150.
76   B. Malinowski, introduction to ibid., p. xxi.

10 Maurice Halbwachs, 1877–1945[*]

Maurice Halbwachs's publications are very diverse. They include statistical treatises, social criticism, reviews of the social sciences, and several major works on consciousness. Though the themes seems very various, they are not scattered or irrelevant to a central programme, the analysis of the processes of memory. This topic he acquired direct from Henri Bergson, his first master. As a pupil at the Lycée Henry IV, dazzled by Bergson's intellectual power, he was won by him to seek a vocation in philosophy. As is well known, Bergson's whole metaphysical scheme pivoted upon a particular conception of time. He would deplore his fellow philosphers' undue concentration upon space, arguing that time was neglected and misrepresented by the practice of measuring its passage only by changes in space: the spatial reference obscures the essential subjective experience. When Halbwachs's own approach was formulated it opposed nearly everything that Bergson taught, courteously but uncompromisingly.

For a pupil to have stayed with Bergsonian principles would have opened certain intellectual opportunities. For example, the phenomenologists Husserl and Schutz worked within an intuitionist theory of knowledge justified by Bergson and they counted him among their lineage ancestors. That Halbwachs did not choose this path may perhaps be explained by the counter-attraction of the other intellectual enterprises to which he eventually subscribed. Remember that Halbwachs was competent in mathematical statistics and concerned with contemporary social problems. At the turn of the century the social sciences were offering exciting prospects of new understanding. But they were aligned under the wrong banners for a loyal Bergsonian scholar.

Bergson was a very independent thinker, an innovator in European

[*] Introduction to Halbwachs's *Collective Memory*, New York, Harper & Row, 1980.

philosophy, or rather he dared to go back to an earlier philosophy of innate ideas which stood discredited in post-Kantian traditions of enquiry. Taking no notice at all of the current criticisms of intuitions, he announced his own account of knowledge comprising two kinds of thinking, one based on logical reasoning, the other based on direct intuitions which cannot be described or analysed, only intuited subjectively.[1] On this basis he put time as the central problem of philosophy; for him a direct subjective perception of inner time is the source of knowledge about the self and an assurance of free will. He contrasted the richness and self-evident truth of this intuition with the pitfalls, plodding and false analogies of logical comparison and mathematical measurement.[2] His subjectivist philosophy allowed him confidently to assert beliefs which troubled philosophers deep in epistemological criticism. In an age when many thinkers were struggling with what they called the body-mind problem,[3] he provided his own optimistic solution, in favour of mind and the autonomy of spiritual values and against deterministic, mechanistic conceptions of human behaviour.

One of the troubles with intuitionist theories is that if, after self-inspection, one is not seized by the alleged clear and immediate intuition, there is no further scope for conversation. No analysis or new reasoning can be relevant to convince you of the matter at issue: either you recognize the intuition or you do not. Presumably the young Halbwachs began to have doubts. He might well have found the necessary intellectual loyalties too constraining. Bergson was the declared enemy of materialism, empiricism and determinism. This ruled out of court any joining in new explorations in psychology and sociology or other intellectual ventures aligned however indirectly with Marxist views or the positivist methods of Auguste Comte. These so-called materialists and empiricists, because of their commitments to objectivity and therefore to measurement, were not against but rather drew inspiration from physical science, but Bergson denounced its limitations in matters of human psychology. A further attraction to a young man with a social conscience would be the implicit alliance of the nascent social sciences with critics of social injustice. Bergson was, of course, also against injustice and in favour of human freedom, but his spiritual emphasis implied that empirical inquiries, pursued with inevitably too crude measuring rods, were doomed to miss the quintessential truths about the human person. He did not go so far as to say that they are an unnecessary (if not a misguided) waste of time, but they did not figure on his agenda of urgent intellectual tasks. To share his master's loyalties, Halbwachs would have had to remain a pure metaphysician. From these beginnings he disengaged himself in two steps.

First, he went to Hanover to study the works of Leibnitz. I do not know whether Bergson blessed this journey. He might even have proposed it for his pupil. He often used to contrast his own philosophical position with that of Descartes, his greatest French predecessor. Over and over again he would criticize Descartes for leading Western thought down a mistaken path, paying undue honour to knowledge acquired from the measurable qualities of things, to mathematics as the source of truth. In particular, Descartes's focus on geometrization as a method of approaching reality resulted, so Bergson argued, in blocking our possibilities of appreciating the experience of time, since time is only measured by changes in space. Leibnitz was a near-contemporary critic of Descartes. For anyone who rejected the English empiricist line of criticism and who sought other non-Cartesian options in philosophy, to go back to Leibnitz was a reasonable strategy. That towering seventeenth-century figure had taken an attractive middle line in controversies of his time. Moreover, from Bergson's point of view he was doctrinally sound on spiritual autonomy, freedom and the immortality of the soul. Halbwachs's new master, for such Leibnitz was to become, was a brilliant mathematician, who had challenged the great Newton with his claim to be the first to invent differential calculus. Halbwachs worked on Leibnitz's unpublished papers and helped to catalogue them. He was nominated to be one of the editors of an international edition of Leibnitz's works, a scheme put off by the outbreak of the First World War. Leibnitz is frequently quoted by Halbwachs in many unexpectedly apt places. His little textbook on the philosopher describes in admirably simple style what he himself, Halbwachs, found important in Leibnitz.

First he emphasized Leibnitz's attack on intuition. Next, he quoted his recommendations on behalf of logic and mathematics as the superior forms of knowledge. Third, he followed the model of differential calculus for developing a little-by-little, gradualist approach to philosophical controversies. According to Leibnitz, most discontinuities in thought are artificial and misleading; tracing minute changes over many strands is a way of dismantling the formidable old boundaries of philosophical dispute; even the intractable problem of mind versus matter takes on a milder aspect when the hard dichotomies are gradually dissolved.

Between clear and obscure, there are little transitions.[4] An intuition is
a calculation without signs. It does not belong to our nature, which is
able to proceed by continuous movement from cruder to finer
symbolising.[5] The mind is not a *tabula rasa*, empty of experience,
nor does it start with innate ideas awakened by experience.
The Cartesians and the empiricists both fail to take gradual changes
into account. Innate ideas are neither all ready made, nor pure
potential . . .[6]

Two more of Halbwachs's quotes from Leibnitz show how relevant
he found this philosophy of over two centuries ago. According to
Bergson, forgetting is due to obstacles, remembering is a removal of
obstacles. Later Halbwachs would argue that forgetting is due to vague
and piecemeal impressions and remembering a process of fitting them
together under suitable stimulus. Bergson's view supposed that the
whole of past experience is always present to us, like the printed pages of
a book, complete and entire in subterranean galleries of the mind.
Leibnitz, according to Halbwachs, held a very similar view:[7]

Our present thought is not only heavy with thoughts to come – all
thoughts and all impressions leave their trace in us in the form of
conscious memories and indistinct recollections . . . our perceptions
lose their clarity; but they remain active and thanks to them we have
the notion of our own identity. Nothing is forgotten; once attention is
renewed these little perceptions become clear once more, and so we
remember.

Halbwachs's own formula played up the indistinctness and incomplete-
ness of past recollections and attributed the ability to remember to
partial renewal of the old experiences, seeing a friend, revisiting a scene
or other external stimulus. We remember when some new reminder
helps us to piece together small, scattered and indistinct bits of the past.[8]

Bergson needed his concept of the unity and completeness of past
experience stored up in the unconscious: it was part of his theory of the
intuition of personal identity. So Halbwachs's insistence on indistinct
and partial memories undermines his first teacher's theories more
critically than would appear out of context.

One can recognize a charter for Halbwachs's future un-Bergsonian
work from the following attributed by him to Leibnitz: 'Individual
consciousness is not the only way in which personal identity is constituted: contacts with other people and with other things can supplement

it.[9] After this, Halbwachs could relegate the body-mind problem to a lower status than Bergson claimed for it. He probably expected to have no more worries about differences of degree and differences of kind, differences of quantity and differences of quality, intuition and intelligence, inner-time and outer-time. By immersing himself deeply in the dead metaphysician's thought, he emancipated himself from the living one, and absolved himself from having to do metaphysics on his own account.

After the sojourn in Hanover, Halbwachs called upon Emile Durkheim in Paris. He claimed to have finished with philosophy and asked to be trained as a sociologist. One might suppose from the sequel that he then stopped concerning himself with philosophical problems such as the experience of time. But Durkheim himself was a proponent of an alternative view on the subject. In choosing Durkheim rather than another sociologist, Halbwachs was decidedly going over to the enemy. He was not leaving Bergson's territory in any neutral sense, but rather moving into a good position from which to prepare an attack upon it. For Durkheim and Mauss had consistently developed conceptions of time which did not in any way rest upon the discoveries of individual psychology; they presented time not as an intuition, but a social construct. However, it was going to be long before Halbwachs addressed the subject. He turned first to contemporary social problems.

In 1908 an article criticizes municipal authorities for not providing public parks for the enjoyment of workers. The argument is couched in terms of surplus value created by the workers but not accruing to them, it is avowedly socialist, quotes Fourier, and relays to French policy-makers the news of experiments in town planning legislation and progressive taxation in Germany and Great Britain. A 1909 dissertation describes the urban dislocation caused by private enterprise in the development of Paris over 100 years. The account is supported by statistical analysis of changes in the value of land, the unequal rates of compensation allowed for dispossessing the rich as contrasted with the poor landowners. If he had continued in this field of direct economic and political analysis, which was becoming more and more professional and effective in his lifetime, he would surely have made his mark. However, the influence of Durkheim drew him towards abstract philosophical issues. In 1913 and 1924 two long essays appeared on social statistics; criticizing utilitarian philosophy, in particular its starting point of individual psychology. In 1913 a major study on working-class living standards; in 1924 L'Origine des sentiments religieux: these are both extensions to modern life of Durkheim's philosophy. Not until all this was accomplished did he return, at the age of 48, to memory and time: *Les Cadres sociaux de la Mémoire* (1925). Before discussing this, which is our central topic too, it is helpful to say a little more about his third teacher, Durkheim, with whom he was associated as a student and collaborator in *L'Année sociologique* until Durkheim's death in 1917.

Here was another stern founder of a school of thought, who, like Bergson, brooked no disagreement among his followers. One might say that Durkheim was a sociologist first and foremost. He became, as it were, a philosopher by necessity since his central concern was to uncover the sources of social solidarity, through a theory of collective consciousness. In Halbwachs's work, Bergson and Durkheim are confronted, the former individualistic, psychologistic, subjectivist, the latter collectivist, sociological (indeed rather outspoken against psychology doing duty for sociological explanation) and seeking objectivity in the tradition of Comte's positivism. In spite of these contrasts, there is a curious parallelism between them in their choice of fundamental theoretical issues. In post-Kantian philosophy the major initiatives had been taken by Hegel and Marx. To engage in dialogue across the Franco-German border after 1870 was perhaps less congenial than before, and certainly the flow of international communications in psychology and philosophy that was still quite strong at the turn of the century gradually diminished until 1914, when it almost stopped. One senses an increasing need to prove the value of French culture, its uniqueness and independence. Both Bergson and Durkheim wrote as if what had happened since Kant need not count. Neither was interested in empiricist criticism in the theory of knowledge. Both tried to improve upon Kant's work. They took him up at the fundamental level of his criticism of innate ideas and his theory that there are two necessary categories of understanding, time and space; that these categories are definitely not intuitions, not ideas nor modes of reasoning, but conditions of thought. Both offered large, system-building alternatives. Bergson started by separating the experience of time from that of space, insisting that the former had never been studied apart from its spatial measurements. He identified inner-time (not the external time which is susceptible of objective measurement) as a direct and immediate intuition of the mind. This approach explained and justified the sense of personal identity and asserted the dominance of pure thought over physiological processes in the brain. Durkheim, for his part, proposed not two but three necessary conditions for human understanding, adding the social condition to the categories of time and space. It is as if they had both looked at Kant's achievement and both decided that the best place to enter the argument would be to say something more about those fundamental Kantian categories of the understanding.

For Durkheim the prospect of individual thought is impossible to contemplate, almost an absurdity, since language and categorization arise together in social intercourse. The source of morality and religion is the individual's experience of society as a moral force greater than himself, requiring his allegiance. From time to time moral sentiments are fanned into strong emotions by ceremonies of intense social inter-action, times of religious effervescence when the moral authority of society is easily assimilated to the idea of God. To understand the social factors sustaining individual consciousness was his central programme of research.

Two questions in this programme were to be taken up by Halbwachs, the totally convinced disciple. One was how moral and religious fervour remain alive between the moments of effervescence. In the quest for an answer, Durkheim emphasized the physical props and spatial mappings that sustain cognition. But this kind of answer only forced the question about religion to be formulated more sharply: if most categories of thought can be held in the mind because of the possibility of pointing to the physical object of reference, do not religious categories have special difficulty in remaining stable since they have no physical reference, but only refer to society itself, an abstract idea in the minds of those who live together? To answer this, Durkheim had developed his theory of totemism and other religious beliefs which require physical representa-tions of abstract ideas. He also argued, following Comte, that spatial categories have a natural stability that makes them capable of sustaining the evanescent moods of social consciousness.

Of the second generation of Durkheim's colleagues, Halbwachs was the only one interested in modern industrial society and capable of drawing his examples from it; his early training in metaphysics made him subtle, his interest in social criticism and his statistical bent gave him a specific role to play.

Here I should mention briefly the studies which are specifically sociological, less concerned with philosophy, before introducing his other works on memory and this volume on *The Collective Memory*.

To start with *La Classe Ouvrière et les niveaux de vie* (1913), Halbwachs used two important sets of German statistics, collected in 1909, to analyse workers' expenditures and to propose a sociological theory of needs. A characteristic expenditure pattern among workers was already established and known as Engels's law, according to which the lower paid spend a larger proportion of their income on food than other income groups, an expenditure pattern which is typically not responsive to small changes in income. The kind of easy theorizing that has accompanied the observation then and since tends to explain it by reference to the bed-rock necessities of survival which supposedly control the lower paid worker's expenditures. We still find economists subscribing to physiological theories of needs. Halbwachs counter-proposed that perception of needs is determined by social class. He used Durkheim's theory of collective representations to give a sociological definition of class and a sociological approach to consumption. Goods are used for establishing social relations. Hence the worker, by reason of his isolated and powerless position in society, has no call for unlimited expenditures on housing, travel or other things: he can relate only to two social groupings, his family and the public life of the streets, the first with food, the second with clothing; hence their nearly constant value as proportions of expenditure over the time series Halbwachs examined. One regrets that his idea about the social structuring of pressures to consume was not pursued with more energy, for it is still a necessary corrective for the individualistic thinking in the theory of demand. Likewise, the sociological definition of class, based upon shared values, is good, but reading this book one is impressed with what it does not say. It is fair enough that in 1913 he should have found the individualist assumptions of utility theory inadequate. It is only a pity, given his mathematical training, that he did not recognize that utility theory is not really a philosophy to be disproved by philosophical arguments: it is the philosophical support of an operational device which works well enough not to be discarded until a correspondingly powerful mathematical apparatus can be offered to do the same analytic tasks equally well. Consequently, Halbwachs missed out on the real dialogue about tools of analysis which preoccupied the most brilliant thinkers in economics in his lifetime. More worrying in this book is the shadow play with Marxist concepts. Josep Llobera has concluded, after much research, that the sociologists of *L'Année sociologique*, like their British counterparts before and later, never took Marx's conceptual and theoretical contributions to their own subject seriously enough to warrant a sympathetic reading of his texts.[10] But this meticulous reinventing of alienation, false consciousness and lumpen proletariat in Durkheimian terms suggests appropriation rather than ignorance. *Les causes de suicide*, is introduced by Mauss

as precisely an up-dating of Durkheim's famous work of 1897. Halbwachs improves the statistical analyses, enlarges the data base and
generally confirms the value of the original insights. Like the other
books, it is a disciple's tribute.

In 1930 Halbwachs visited the University of Chicago. *L'évolution des
besoins dans les classes ouvrières* came out in 1933 with analyses of a large
number of budget surveys covering American as well as European
households. The challenge to his earlier study was to find that among
American workers the proportion of expenditure on food had shown a
marked downward trend. This should have led him to develop his
earlier sociological theory of demand by calling for empirical data on
possible changes in the social environment of American working-class
families. Presumably, the changed pattern of expenditure should lead
him to seek signs of less isolation, less fragmentation, less frustration in
the American workers' households. He could have developed his theory
of thirty years earlier by connecting a relative absence of the restrictive
social effects in American life and class structure which in Europe were
causing the workers' search for esteem to stop at the immediate family
and the street life society. Instead, he weakly argued from his initial
assumptions that the isolation, fragmentation, etc. of the American
worker had kept him ignorant and consequently vulnerable to the wiles
of advertisers in the new technology, so that he bought vacuum cleaners
and improved his own house when his income rose. Likewise, in *Analyse
des mobiles dominantes* (1938), and *Morphologie sociale* (1938), Halbwachs
remained uncritically faithful to an inflexible model of working-class
collective representations. In 1940 his comprehensive survey of international work on sociology, economics and demography (for *Actualités
scientifiques et industriels*) is an extraordinary revelation of how isolated
from other thinkers the *Année sociologique* group had become in the
inter-war period. The review covers all that was important and contemporary in those growing fields. In economics, Halbwachs concludes his
competent summary of Keynesian theory with a competent account of
Joan Robinson's criticism. He seems to be perfectly in touch with
colleagues overseas. Such reviews are intended to facilitate transmission
of ideas across continents and seas. But when such an able scholar with
that particular trained bias summarizes a foreign corpus of work, the
effect is to break the circuit. No one reading that review in France would
feel any need to take the Keynesian argument too seriously, for the
reviewer ends by dismissing it on the authority of François Simiand's
vague disparagements. In 1935 Halbwachs had become a member of the

International Institute of Statistics. Clearly he was interested and capable in sociological analysis, but he never made his best contribution in this direction. His regular reviews of economics and demography for *L'Annèe sociologique* were laconic and dull. The sharply critical, idealistic tone of his two early essays on Paris was so different that one presumes that his voice in this area was muffled by editorial policy.

To turn from this to the work on memory is refreshing. *Les Cadres sociaux de la mémoire* (1925) was the starting point. In the first part he distinguishes dreams from memory. Discussing Bergson and Freud, he defines dreams as individual fragments of experience; the defining character of memories, as distinct from dreams is that memories are supported by those of others, they are public and shareable. He emphasizes the importance of spatial memory for locating memories of past experiences. The body of the book examines how different social segments each with a different historical past, will have different memories attached to their respective landmarks. The book was attacked because of his brushing aside individual psychology and his insistence that even our most personal feelings and thoughts arise in social situations. His critics felt the threat of sociological determinism. He answers these criticisms much later in *La Mémoire collective* (see p. 15 *et seq.* of the French edition). To his claim that there are no individual intuitions or memories his challenger declared: even if you claim that 99 per cent of memory is reconstructed and only 1 per cent is real individual recall, this one per cent gives enough basis for questioning the importance you assign to the social processes in remembering. But Halbwachs is steadfast, as his answers (pp. 23–33) show. Even the child's world is never empty of human beings, benign or malevolent, still less the adult's world. Even a solitary perception of being alone is itself a recognition of the state of being in society. In reply to these criticis, he confirms one of their suspicions, as he comes out emphatically in favour of social determinism. Referring to Bergson's theory that we have an intuition of a unified consciousness, Halbwachs retorts: we think our consciousness is unified, this is an illusion just as we think our actions are undetermined: they are not (pp. 33–4).

Les Cadres sociaux de la mémoire is programmatic, somewhat of a manifesto. One could call the two works which follow it applied exercises demonstrating the value of the programme. The first of these is the short essay on the collective memory of musicians (1939). The second is the book on the Christian memory of its holy places: *La Topographie légendaire des evangiles en terre sainte* (1941). The first considers remembering processes which essentially do not have spatial orientations, the second considers how the spatial framework of memory is continually deformed and remade according to the changing concerns of the living people who do the remembering.

Since the essay on musical memory is reprinted at the end of this volume, there would be no need to say much about it here. But of all Halbwachs's works it is most widely known today in the form of a summary by Alfred Schutz in his much reproduced essay on 'Making Music Together' (1951). Unfortunately for Halbwachs's modern reputation, Schutz's account is grotesquely inaccurate. A close reading of both essays reveals strong sympathy between them. Their only serious disagreement is on the question of innate ideas brought into prominence by Schutz's loyalty to Bergson. Natural allies are often separated by sectarian disdain. In this case Schutz's curt 'So much for Halbwachs' is the harsher because in the forty years since 'La mémoire collective chez les musiciens' first appeared, phenomenology and cognate disciplines for exploring consciousness followed the directions where Halbwachs led. Where else could they go by inspired combinations of observation and introspection?

Let me use David Sudnow's remarkable book on learning to play jazz as an illustration of the points that Halbwachs makes. *Ways of the Hand: The Organization of Improvised Conduct*[11] is a study that fits just as well in the positivist tradition developed by Halbwachs as in the ethnomethodological tradition of Garfinkel, the acknowledged teacher, and of Harvey Sacks to whom it is dedicated.

First, Halbwachs wants to convince the reader that remembering music is a difficult feat. He insists that the isolated individual could not do it, a claim that Schutz finds absurd. It is particularly difficult because musical notes are not connected with anything but each other. They do not signify solid objects or events which can act as triggers to the memory. As Suzanne Langer said: Music has all the earmarks of a true symbolism except one: the existence of an assigned connotation.[12] Music unfolds in its own musical medium. The puzzle of remembering music is an acute form of Durkheim's problem about how religious cults persist in the minds of their worshippers without a physical, visible point of reference. Halbwachs remarks that all students of music make private schemata for remembering tunes, recognizing patterns in the timing, intervals and rhythms. Without such schemata nothing would be recalled at all. This private symbolizing, the first effort to remember music, does not achieve very much. It becomes easier if the hearing can be accompanied by reproduction, for example singing, so that movements in the brain are supplemented by movements in the larynx, which register further movements in the brain to carry the pattern in memory; easier still if there are words and rhymes and associated ideas which support the faltering musical memory by non-musical props. Best of all is the written score, which gives a spatialized summary of the music, a visible support. If music were not a social activity, it could not be remembered and so could not exist: the more the community is intensively specialized for music the stronger the attention and the richer the range of their remembering. Musicians, lay or professional, can only achieve their appropriate level of musical experience by making music together.

Schutz would disagree on the difficulty for an isolated individual of remembering music. But Sudnow says:[13]

> I got a first taste for the magnitude of the problems I was in for when I tried to listen to a piece of jazz melody on a record and then go to the piano to play it. . . . Even when taking a portion of a melody from a record where I thought I knew the improvised section well (and it is worth noting that the existence of the recording gives improvised melodies a status they would otherwise not have that they can be heard and learned as 'fixed melodies'), a symptomatic vagueness in my grasp of these familiar improvisations was discovered. I knew these melodies only in certain broad outlines. . . . I had been glossing the particularities of the notes in many of my hummings, grasping their essential shape perhaps, but not singing them with refined pitch sensitivity.

When it comes to trying to remember a tune, Halbwachs says that we represent tunes in symbols '*a notre manière*'.[14] Sudnow draws elegant trajectories of his own to remind himself of different rhythmic styles.[15] All through the apprenticeship he is describing, his teacher is in the background giving his weekly lessons, and Jimmy Rowles in the foreground, the model jazz pianist, and the other players, even when he was practising alone:[16]

> Every once in a while the time would get into the fingers as I sat and tried to move like Jimmy Rowles, setting a beat first by getting my shoulders going around a little, while I tapped my foot and snapped my fingers before play; counting off the time with a care I had never taken before, a care for the jazz to be played, a care for the others with

whom I could have been coordinating my moves, for that bass player and drummer who were never around, that we might stride into the song together . . .

Like Halbwachs, Sudnow assumes that music is a language to be laboriously learned by social processes:[17]

> I learned this language through five years of overhearing it spoken. I had come to learn, overhearing and overseeing this jazz as my instructable hands' ways – in a terrain nexus of hands and keyboard whose respective surfaces had become known as the respective surfaces of my tongue and teeth and palate are known to each other – that this jazz music *is* ways of moving from place to place as singings with my fingers. To define jazz (as to define any phenomenon of human action) is to *describe* the body's ways.

Such lyricism is beyond Halbwachs's style, but the hard and lucid analysis conveys exactly his message about the physical, spatial and social elements in learning.

Shortly after this, Halbwachs turned his attention to the spatial aspects of memory. The phenomenologist, disagreeing with his declared determinism, would have done well to challenge Halbwachs here, because his analysis never allows him to suggest that spatial orderings of memory fix it for good and all; quite the contrary, they are elements used by human intentions one way in one decade and quite differently when social concerns have changed, in another decade. The holy places revered by Christians in Palestine shift according to historically significant doctrinal and political changes. This is a very careful empirical study following in the steps of Renan, striving to identify the original spots revered in Christian tradition, finding some lost, some duplicated many times over and some clearly wrong. Halbwachs adds his own surmises to make sense of the pattern on the ground as remembered, after the rebuilding of Jerusalem, after the discovery of the true cross by Constantine's mother and other shifts of cultic enthusiasm.

These two studies represent a big effort towards empirical demonstration of the positivist sociologist's main work. What is amazing is that he never thought of more exact methods of testing and never seems to have had any relation with his renowned contemporary, Frederick Bartlett, who spent his life contriving clever laboratory tests for memory. Halbwachs had far richer ideas than Bartlett, though the latter actually claimed to be looking for a sociological approach to memory.[18] It is not difficult to imagine experiments with musical memory and spatial memory that these pioneers could have worked out together. But in this case Halbwachs was not the circuit breaker. The author of a famous book on *Remembering* could hardly omit any reference to his contemporary colleague's work, but his account of the assumptions and conclusions of the *L'Année sociologique* group is almost as disdainful and quite as misleading as that by Schutz.

In Bartlett's travestied account, Halbwachs is dismissed for accepting from Durkheim a unitary conception of society and for reifying collective memory into a quasi-mystic soul with its own existence. According to Bartlett, Durkheim 'believes that the social group constitutes a genuine psychical unit, and is possessed of nearly all the characteristics of the human individual'. He struggles to distinguish memory in the group, which he regards as a legitimate concept, from an illegitimate idea of the 'memory of the group' which he wrongly foists upon Halbwachs.[19] This is particularly unfair, as readers of *La Mémoire collective* will realize.

Halbwachs's gift to Durkheim was to unpack and separate clearly the elements of social life that contribute to the collective memory. His concept was of a flexible, articulated set of social segments consisting of live individuals who sustain their common interests by their own selective and highly partial view of history. This is not only in accord with modern analyses of ideological forgetting, structural amnesia and theoretical blindspots in science but it is an achievement which has been largely responsible for contemporary sophistication on the subject. To have worked this out within the strong constraints evidently imposed by Durkheim upon his colleagues was a signal service to Durkheim himself and a contribution to Durkheim studies.

No wonder that Halbwachs wanted to write, in his late sixties, one more book on the collective memory, a synthesis and final justification. Friends close to him expected an important contribution and deplored his untimely end, as much for the interruption of this work as for the crime and sorrow of his deportation and death in Buchenwald. Indeed, it is an important synthesis and it shows extraordinary advances on the preceding work.

Much of the book contains criticisms of Bergsonism with support from Leibnitz. All the discussion of private experience of pain[20] and of whether time can be conceived as passing more quickly for some people than for others,[21] of the concept of a universal, empty time frame encompassing all existences,[22] of solipsist problems arising from a concept of subjective inner time experience – these are all aimed against Bergson's subjectivist theory of knowledge. They are good arguments; phenomenologists have the opportunity here of deciding whether they need to carry that particular philosophical burden of innate ideas in order to follow the important new programmes of research which propose themselves as soon as human intentions are taken as the initial point of departure.

When it comes to the concept of time as used by mathematicians, Halbwachs used Bergson's own account with approval. Mathematical time is an attempt to enlarge and universalize time, it is a uniform perception like the geometrization of space. Historians' use of time is again very different from the ordinary experience of individuals. Historians create historical periods which have meaning for their professional concern with tracing synchronies and sequences, but have no correspondence with any historical experience anyone ever lived through, no anchorage in any collective memory. No one arrives at the dawn of a great historical period exclaiming 'Today we begin the Hundred Years War!' The argument expresses a deep debt to Bergson; it is not always critical. The most significant Bergsonian idea is the conflation of the future and the past in the present. Interspersed with the dialogue with Bergson are the rich insights into the social reconstruction of history, the elliptical collapse of long periods of time when nothing significant is observed to happen, the social structuring of time and other important insights. The memory of a society, he said, goes back only as far as it can; that is, it goes back as far as the memory of its constituent groups. Vast quantities of information are forgotten, not from spite or intention, but merely because the groups which used to remember them have disappeared.[23] The divisions of time in the collective memory correspond to the divisions of society. Whereas this message has been received and accepted by sociologists and historians, the use made of it has been partial and *ad hoc*. It has fallen to anthropologists to develop the simultaneous analysis of the structures of a society and the structure of its experience of time and to consider their respective time frameworks as bases for comparing historical societies.[24]

Jean Duvignaud in his preface to the first edition, wrote that time recollected was a specially important cultural theme in the first quarter of this century. He cited Proust, Joyce, and Henry James as novelists experimenting with new uses of memory's perspectives; he also cited Freud in psychology and Einstein in physics. He introduced Halbwachs as one having taken up that contemporary theme and having so well adapted sociological thinking in this respect to an Einsteinian relativism that nothing can be said on the subject of memory now that does not owe him a debt. Let this be my conclusion too and let the book speak for itself.

Notes

1 *Essai sur les données immédiates de la conscience*, Paris, 1889.
2 See his criticism of Einstein's theory of relativity, *Durée et simultanéite (à propos de la théorie d'Einstein)*, Paris, 1922.
3 *Matière et mémoire, essai sur la relation du corps à l'esprit*, Paris, 1896; 'L'Ame et le Corps', lecture published in *Le Materialisme actuel*, Paris, 1916.
4 *Leibnitz*, p. 72.
5 Ibid., p. 79.
6 Ibid., p. 68.
7 Ibid., p. 71.
8 *La Mémoire collective* (hereafter *LMC*), pp. 64–5.
9 Ibid., p. 80.
10 Josep R. Llobera, 'Techno-Economic Determinism and the Work of Marx on Pre-Capitalist Societies', *Man*, June 1979, vol. 14, no. 2, pp. 249–70.
11 Sudnow, London, Routledge & Kegan Paul, 1978.
12 Suzanne Langer, *Philosophy in a New Key*, Harvard University Press, 1942.
13 Sudnow, op. cit., pp. 20–1.
14 'La Mémoire collective chez les musiciens', p. 171.
15 Sudnow, op. cit., pp. 130–2, 137, 138.
16 Ibid., p. 141.
17 Ibid., p. 179.
18 *Remembering, A Study in Experimental and Social Psychology*, Cambridge University Press, 1932.
19 Ibid., ch. 18, paragraph 2.
20 *LMC*, p. 91.
21 Ibid., p. 114, 116.
22 Ibid., p. 87.
23 Ibid., p. 73.
24 For an exemplary case study, see E. Evans-Pritchard, *The Nuer*, Oxford, Clarendon Press, 1940; and for a summary of references to subsequent work, *Evans-Pritchard*, by Mary Douglas, Modern Masters Series, Fontana Viking, London, 1980.

Maurice Halbwachs's principal publications

1907   *Leibniz*, Les Philosophes.
1908   'La Politique foncière des municipalités', *Les Cahiers Socialiste*, no. 3, pp. 3–32.
1909   'Les Expropriations et le prix des terrains à Paris, 1860–1900'. Revised version published 1928 as 'La Population et les tracés des voies à Paris depuis cent ans.'
1913   *La Classe ouvrière et les niveaux de vie: recherches sur la hierarchie des besoins dans les sociétés industrielles contemporaines* (primary doctoral dissertation).
1913   *La Théorie de l'homme moyen: essai sur Quetelet et la statistique morale* (secondary doctoral dissertation).
1924   *Le Calcul des probabilités à la portée de tous*. Co-author with M. Frechet.
1924   *Les Origines du sentiment religieux d'après Durkheim*, Paris, F. Alcan. English translation published 1962 as *Sources of Religious Sentiment*, Free Press, New York.
1925   *Les Cadres sociaux de la mémoire*, Les Travaux de L'Année Sociologique, Paris, F. Alcan. Republished 1952 by Presses Universitaires de France.
1928   'La Population et les tracés de voies à Paris depuis cents ans' (revised version of 1909 article).
1930   *Les Causes de suicide*, Les Travaux de L'Année Sociologique. Foreword by Marcel Mauss, Paris, F. Alcan. English translation published 1978 as *The Causes of Suicide*, Free Press, New York.
1933   *L'Evolution des besoins dans les classes ouvrières*, Paris, F. Alcan.
1938   *Analyse des mobiles qui orientent l'activité des individus dans la vie sociale*. Republished 1952 as *Esquisse d'une psychologie des classes sociales*, introduction by George Friedmann, Presses Universitaires de France. English translation published 1958 as *Psychology of Social Classes*, Free Press, New York.
1938   *La Morphologie sociale*, Presses Universitaires de France. English translation published as *Population and Society: Introduction to Social Morphology*, Free Press, New York.
1939   'La Mémoire collective chez les musiciens', *Revue philosophique*, pp. 136–65.
1940   'Sociologie économique et demographie', *Philosophie: 9, Actualités Scientifiques et Industrielles*.
1941   *La Topographie légendaire des évangiles en terre sainte: étude de mémoire collective*, Presses Universitaires de France.
1950   *La Mémoire collective*, preface by Jean Duvignaud, introduction by Michel Alexandre, Presses Universitaires de France. English translation published 1980 as *The Collective Memory*, introduction by Mary Douglas, Harper & Row.

11 Judgments on James Frazer*

'Times have changed and so have our ears.' This line from Tacitus is the
first reference in Roman antiquity that E. H. Gombrich finds to the
psychology of perception and its relation to styles. His extraordinarily
rich discussion of this whole subject, *Art and Illusion*, treats the history of
art as a continuing tension between the stability of a style and the
struggle against it, the struggle of an artist 'to win freshness of vision'.[1]
He gives many examples of the artist's ambivalence towards tradition,[2]
cites the many exercises in copying the masters, and the common fear of
becoming a slave to tradition.[3] Like other great art historians, his powers
are taxed to account for innovation, but this is not the principal task of
his book. Rather the other way, he deploys the psychology of perception
to explain why innovation is so difficult. A current style imposes a
closure on the possibilities of perception. A style is a contemporary
organization of experience: 'A style, like a culture or climate of opinion,
sets up a horizon of expectation, a mental set which registers deviations
and modifications with exaggerated sensitivity.'[4] Constable succeeded
in establishing a new way of transposing our awareness of brightness
into painting, but beside Corot's work the brightness of Constable's
painting is eclipsed. 'It recedes behind the ridge which separates, for us,
the contemporary vision from that of the past.'[5]

This essay explicitly seeks to use Gombrich's ideas about style as a
framework within which to discuss the changes in the reputation of
James Frazer as one generation has succeeded another. One hundred
years ago Frazer took finals in classics and then prepared to compete for
the fellowship in Trinity College, Cambridge. He won it, aged twenty-
four, with a dissertation entitled 'The Growth of Plato's Ideal Theory'.[6]
In that hundred years his reputation grew so that he completely

* From *Daedalus*, Fall (Generations) 1978, pp. 151–64.

dominated a large area of European thought. He dominated classics –
no small feat – and he dominated archeology. Above all, he dominated
the whole horizon of thoughts about man and his nature, his origins, his
capabilities and destiny, within which the widest literary efforts were
engaged. No one reputation in the subject rivals his until we reach
Lévi-Strauss. In his inaugural lecture to the Collège de France, Lévi-
Strauss remarks that fifty years had elapsed between the founding of his
Chair of Social Anthropology in 1958 and Frazer's inaugural lecture[7] in
Liverpool on taking the first university post in the world ever to be thus
entitled. Fifty years earlier still, Lévi-Strauss also remarked, were born
Franz Boas and Emile Durkheim, the founders of modern anthropology, the one American, the other French. This pretty trilogy of dates is
enclosed in a century, and frames a Franco-Anglo-Saxon dialogue on
Frazer's chosen subject. But note that the contemporary vision held
within this horizon does not count Frazer as a founder. It would be
difficult for Lévi-Strauss to salute him as such. Nothing matches the
greatness of Frazer's fame so well as the completeness of its eclipse
among anthropologists today. Malinowski recognized him as a powerful
influence in his own work. But there will be few now to say that standing
on the shoulders of this particular giant they were able to get a longer
view.

Frazer is now attacked as a theorist. He is attacked as a serious
thinker. He is even attacked as a stylist, the one reproach that would
really have surprised him and hurt his feelings. On the first count we
shall see that the theoretical field which he was confronting was a very
different one from that in which we work now. On the score of the
profundity and scope of his thought, his ghost might expostulate that he
is taken out of context and sadly misunderstood. For settling the
question of style there is the lack of any general theory of style. Without
understanding the problems of style that Gombrich has discussed, it is
difficult even to judge the seriousness of a thinker. All in all, it is
obviously difficult to set a writer in the perspective in which he perceived
himself to be. When we follow Gombrich's discussion of how the
prevailing culture or style closes the possibilities of perception, we can
be sure that the painters who carefully copied admired past masters were
not fully understanding or faithfully copying what they saw. 'All thinking
is sorting, classifying. All perceiving relates to expectations and therefore to comparisons. . . . We have to speak of expectations, guesses,
hypotheses, which can become so strong that our experience runs ahead
of the stimulus situation.'[8] This being so, the following account given by

Gombrich of the transmission between generations has something missing: 'If Constable saw the English landscape in terms of Gainsborough's paintings, what about Gainsborough himself? We can answer this. Gainsborough saw the lowland scenery of East Anglia in terms of Dutch paintings which he studied and copied . . . and where did the Dutch get their vocabulary?'₉ What is left out is the whole history of art and the series of misunderstandings each generation takes for its starting place. According to Gombrich, it is only the vocabulary and probably only a part of it that stays, while at each historical stage there cannot be a real seeing in terms of another viewpoint. Lawrence Gowing has called attention to the creative aspect of that misunderstanding:[10]

> One might write the history of that order of originality which this century identifies as the essence of art – and eventually it must be written – as a history of inveterate misunderstanding. We cannot claim that the view of Delacroix that inspired Cézanne represented a true evaluation of him. The guiding star that Cézanne followed shone far more steadily than the flawed jewel of Romanticism ever did. And Delacroix himself, how shallow his interpretation of Rubens! Then Rubens – was not his merely sensuous appreciation of physical rhythms as the basis of style a gross misconstruction of the philosophical meaning that the human body held for Michelangelo? And so on. . . . Yet this succession of creative misunderstandings was nothing by comparison with the way that the 20th century used Cézanne.

Within each new dimension of understanding the project of passing judgment on another generation's work seems necessary. The judgments partake initially in what Lawrence Gowing calls the 'apparent arbitrariness of a continued and unending process of redefinition, on the basis of a past which is itself in a perpetual state of rediscovery and revaluation'.[11] But if later judgments upon one-time achievement are not themselves to be devalued and arbitrarily dismissed, we should seek laboriously the means for reconstructing the old dimension of understanding.

In 1910, when Frazer remarked, 'My sun is westering',[12] he was more likely referring to his expected life-span (he was then fifty-four years old) than to his reputation, which was nowhere near its zenith. He did not listen to his critics. If he had wished to answer them, he might have said: First, mythology is my subject matter, I have rescued it from the toils of philologists; second, my insight has opened a unitary vision of human history, and supported a noble view of human progress. Above all else, I am writing literature, my work is largely an imaginative effort, my greatest achievement is in the development of a style in which to present my insight. The things he took seriously were literature and human destiny, the one in the service of appreciating the other.

I shall try to establish these three points, starting with his subject matter, the strange state of mythology as he found it. In 1878, the Ninth Edition of the *Encyclopaedia Britannica* was launched. Its editorial announced a new policy of expansion for 'the modern sciences of anthropology and sociology'. It guaranteed that henceforth 'Mental Philosophy and the important topics concerned with Biblical Criticism, Theology and the Science of Religion' would be treated 'from the critical and historical rather than the dogmatic point of view'.[13] Indeed, when the volume for S was reached in 1886, there was Robertson Smith's famous article on sacrifice, which subverted many pious presumptions. In due course, Frazer himself wrote the article on taboo in 1888. This was his first major step towards transforming the study of mythology, and closely modelled on Robertson Smith's ideas.

We can hardly imagine now the high excitement that focused on the origins and fate of human culture. A modern audience misses the emotional violence of Ibsen's play when Hedda Gabler stuffs into the stove her lover's manuscript on the future of civilization. In 1890 the horror of the deed was that she had deprived humanity of profound insights into its very self. Not a mere petty act of caprice or jealousy, it must have ranked as an irreparable crime, a public tragedy for all posterity.

To recapture that mood of intense interest we should realize what a great race was on. In France, Germany, America, and in England the researchers were competing on work deemed of the utmost importance. In the apparent nonsense of beliefs in ghosts, female deities, instant transformations and transportations, there had to be some systematic sense that would show us how we humans here and now are constituted. Whoever solved the riddle would be sure of fame. So completely had the literary public taken the project to heart that writers could use it to enhance their dramatic moments. How else could George Eliot have convinced anyone in 1872 that the ardent clever heroine of Middlemarch should have ever consented to marry the dreary Mr Casaubon? Only by showing the girl dazzled by his noble enterprise: 'with something of the archangelic manner he told her how he had undertaken to show that all the mythical systems or erratic mythical fragments in the world were corruptions of a tradition originally revealed. Having once mastered the true position and taken a firm footing there, the vast field of mythical constructions became intelligible, made luminous with the reflected light of correspondences.' Later, when the plot has to discover Mr Casaubon's egotism and plain unworthiness, the trick is done by showing that he is not seriously working on the 'Key to All Mythologies', distracted from his high mission by envy of other scholars. But long before that denouement, the worst blow had fallen: Mr Casaubon did not even read German.[14]

> The Germans have taken the lead in historical enquiries, and they laugh at results which are got by groping about the woods with a pocket compass when they have made good roads . . . the subject Mr. Casaubon has chosen is as changing as chemistry: new discoveries are constantly making new points of view. Who wants a system based on the four elements, or a book to refute Paracelsis? Do you not see that it is no use now to be crawling a little way after men of the last century . . . and correcting their mistakes? – living in a lumber room and furnishing up broken-legged theories about Chus and Misraim?

So the man is first built up as a hero and then demolished as a fraud – all on the strength of his dealings with mythology.

In the history of ideas, before some major figure has arrived on the scene, the old perspectives often seem littered with a crazy jumble of broken bits and loose ends. Just such a state is summed up in a critical article on mythology by Andrew Lang in the same edition of the *Encyclopaedia Britannica*. He singled out the central puzzle of mythology as follows. The myths of civilized peoples, for example those of the Greeks and Aryans, contain two elements, rational and irrational. The first are completely intelligible, but the second constitute the puzzles:

> The rational myths are those that represent the gods as beautiful and wise beings . . . there is nothing not explicable and natural in the conception of the Olympian Zeus . . . or in the Homeric conception of Zeus as a god who 'turns everywhere his shining eyes' and beholds all things. But Zeus . . . who played Demeter an obscene trick, by the aid of a ram, or the Zeus who, in the shape of a swan, became the father of Castor and Pollux, or the Zeus who deceived Hera by means of feigned marriage with an inanimate object . . . is a being whose myth is felt to be unnatural and in great need of explanation.

Max Müller called this irrational, unnatural element 'the silly, senseless and savage element in mythology'.

That great philologist proposed to solve the puzzle by tracking the names of deities back to the original meanings of words common to all the Indo-European languages. Traced to its Sanskritic form, *Athene* is revealed as the word for dawn and *Zeus* as the word for sky. Now, according to Müller, at the beginning of human life and language, in a premythopoeic period, those words could have been chosen to mean powerful spiritual beings. But it is in the nature of abstract ideas that they are difficult to hold on to, and it seemed likely that the religious meaning would have been lost in the course of time and only the particular material reference of words be left. So the word *Zeus*, from a sky god with male gender, would have degenerated in the mythopoeic period to something like 'the shining one' (male) and the word for *Athene* to something like 'the burning one' (female). Müller thought that the rough-hewn language of our forebears would only be able to say 'the sun follows the dawn' in a way that might also be interpreted as 'the brightly shining man pursues the ardent woman'. And so to explain the odd result, the myth of the sun god pursuing a female would be invented. The argument almost anticipates jokes about translation machines that turn 'the spirit is willing but the flesh is weak' into 'the wine is good but the meat is bad'. But quite certainly Andrew Lang was being very unfair on Max Müller. His general idea that false theories circulate as a result of a concretization of abstract ideas has many resonances today. But his actual theory had technical difficulties.

Lang, in his article, went on to compare Müller's theories with those of Spencer, who had a similar speculation about the inadequacies of first human speech. As Lang said of them both: 'The chief objection to these processes is that they require as a necessary condition a singular amount of memory on the one hand, and forgetfulness on the other.' But he was in real sympathy with the questions expressed by Müller: 'was there a period of temporary madness which the human mind had to pass and was it a madness identically the same in the south of India and north of Ireland?' Lang answered affirmatively to both.

Against these protagonists with their convoluted schemes, bristling with technical difficulties, Frazer entered one simple theory adapted from Robertson Smith. Partly because he far surpassed his colleagues with sheer narrative skill, he succeeded in absolving mankind from the charge of an ancient temporary madness. The savages were philosophers, poets, not simpletons. Incidentally, he also absolved his contemporaries from any dilemma posed by their attitude to dogmatic religion. Frazer's theory was that all religions tend to deify kings and to make their gods die as sacrificial victims; all teach that by the ritual act of king-killing the world will be renewed. The central doctrine of Christianity was that god incarnate was put to death under the label of king; the same god is treated doctrinally as sacrificial victim: the rite of the sacrifice is credited with powers of renewal. The analogy with Christianity is there, very complete and compelling. But Frazer had too much respect for the poetic aspect of religion to press it home offensively. He never explicitly made the parallel between Christianity and the ancient beliefs he reclassified.

If anyone now seeks to convict Frazer's enterprise of superficiality, surely anyone in his time would have been astonished. What else could be more profound? It would surely always be thought serious to explore this unitary experience of the human race and to find all humanity, even in its dimmest, remotest past, meditating upon the relation of man and nature and developing an understanding of that relation which culminates in emotional power and beauty in the great religions. Anatole France declared: 'Il nous fait entrer dans la pensée des barbares d'aujourd'hui et des temps lointains, il a éclairé d'une lumière nouvelle cette antiquité grecque et latine que nous pensions connaitre; il a substitué aux fables que l'homme imagine pour expliquer sa propre origine, les premières données d'une science rigoureuse qui n'existait pas avant lui.'[15] Called upon to address the Société Ernest Renan in 1920, Frazer declared his loyalty to the same project at which Renan had laboured: a rediscovery of true religion, divested of archaic trappings.[16] The contrast he drew between Renan and Voltaire is revealing of his own methodological preferences: Voltaire was more prosaic, more analytic; Renan, the Breton, more poetic. He insisted that Renan was deeply religious, destroying images which he loved, to put better ones forward. He took to heart Renan's judgment that the Christian historic effort represents 'half the poetry of mankind'. There is no question that he was dealing with matters judged profound by his contemporaries, whether they disagreed with his conclusions or not. There is a question whether he would have liked Anatole France's description of his contribution to a rigorous science – for he frankly preferred the path of poetry.

It was from Renan, he said, that he got the idea of ending the *Golden Bough* with the tolling of bells from Rome.

In the 1890 edition he describes his journey at an end; he climbs the Appian Way to the Alban hills and sees the sunset behind St Peter's; then he pursues his way, darkling, along the mountain side to Nemi, to look once more at the lake of Nemi. Finally, 'There comes to us, borne on the swell of the wind, the sound of the church bells of Rome, ringing the Angelus. Ave Maria! Sweet and solemn they chime out from the distant city and die lingeringly away across the wide Campagnan marshes. *Le roi est mort, vive le roi! Ave Maria!*' But in the foreword to the 1900 edition he notes:

> To a passage in my book, it has been objected by a distinguished scholar that the church bells in Rome cannot be heard, even in the stillest weather, on the shores of the lake of Nemi. In acknowledging my blunder and leaving it uncorrected, may I plead in extenuation of my obduracy the example of an illustrious writer? In *Old Mortality* we read how a hunted Covenanter, fleeing before Claverhouse's dragoons, hears the sullen boom of the kettledrums of the pursuing cavalry borne to him on the night wind. When Scott was taken to task for this description, because the drums are not beaten at night, he replied in effect that he liked to hear the drums sounding there, and that he would let them sound on as long as his book might last. In the same spirit I make bold to say that by the lake of Nemi I love to hear, even if it be only in imagination, the distant chiming bells of Rome.

However, in the last edition, strict geographical scholarship prevailed over imagination. He confided to the Société Ernest Renan that a friend made him change the bells to the church of Aricia from which they could really be heard at the lake.[17]

Having dealt with the theory of mythology as Frazer found it and touched upon the greater philosophic seriousness of his view compared with the other mythologists, I will return to the question of seriousness when I have said something more about his interest in the literary imagination, on which the tribute to Renan gives a hint.

Frazer's early essay 'The Growth of Plato's Ideal Theory' used stylistic criticism for attributing chronology to the different parts of the corpus. From this beginning his later prejudices on style are already clearly formulated: 'in the later Dialogues. . . . The vivacious manner of a great dramatist, enthralling his hearers by the alternate play of high tragedy and light comedy, is exchanged for the dry as dust manner of a professor lecturing to his pupils . . . it is a transformation like that of a Shakespeare into a Kant.' Later in the essay, he suggests that Plato lost by being 'guided by the pale cold light of Reason, instead of by the purple glow of the Imagination'. In the many volumes of the *Golden Bough*, meticulously footnoted on obscure places and peoples, he never gave up his own light touch and dramatic contrasts. He also managed to write on purely literary themes: an essay entitled 'London Life in the Time of Addison, 1672 to 1719', a 'Biographical Sketch of William Cowper', a series of imaginative reconstructions on Sir Roger de Coverly give some idea of his stylistic preferences.[18] In the same volume an essay on Condorcet is a good example of his mixing tragedy with farce. He greatly admired the philosopher, and saluted his calm survey of human progress and his firm trust in the essential goodness of mankind and the glorious future awaiting it. Revolutionary Paris was at the height of the terror then. Frazer describes the paradox of the philosopher politician who had actually prepared a new constitution in the legislative assembly, but was now condemned to death himself because he had criticized Robespierre. He describes his hiding for several days:

> On the third day, driven by the pangs of hunger he entered a humble tavern and called for an omelet. They asked him how many eggs he would have in it. As a philosopher and secretary for many years for the Academy of Science, Condorcet knew much but unluckily he did not know how many eggs go into the making of an omelet. He answered at random, 12. The reply excited surprise and suspicion. He was asked for his papers, but he had none, nothing but a copy of the Epistles of Horace.

And so Condorcet was hustled off. However much he admired his hero and felt the heroism and tragedy of his life, he could not resist recounting the famous, farcical ending. With Addison and Steele for his models, why should he?

Now we can begin a more serious consideration of the style and of the seriousness of the writer. The passage cited from Lawrence Gowing describes a happily creative misunderstanding between generations. But the theory of Gombrich implies that there must at the same time be unhappily destructive misunderstandings. Could it be pleaded for Frazer that he exposed himself to this misunderstanding when he chose his version of the light amusing style of eighteenth-century essayists for a life-work which required no less than twelve ponderous volumes? Or in the period from the 1880s to 1910, when he was most creative, was that read by his contemporaries as exactly the appropriate style for his great themes?

Gombrich says of painting that it is never a copy, always a transposition of nature. The success of the transposition depends on the artist's and the viewers' learning a notation. Our response is not to colour as such, but to relationships, to gradients in light intervals. The proper business of mind is 'assessing gradients and relationships'.[19] He uses the metaphor of being attuned. Our expectations of style are as receivers already attuned: 'When we step in front of a bust we understand what we are expected to look for. We do not, as a rule, take it to be a representation of a cut-off head.'[20] This becomes a problem in the case of copying, because a change in scale changes all the relationships.[21]

> We can speak of a real facsimile only when the copy is of the same size as the original. For size affects tone . . . since the same color will look different when the size of the area changes, a facsimile reduced in scale will look false when all colors are identical with the original.

To illustrate the difficulty our generation has in assessing Frazer's work, we can use the adverse judgment of a philosopher who always wrote in a highly condensed, elliptical style and can ask whether his complaints against Frazer arise out of the constraints of a different cultural horizon. Wittgenstein exclaimed: 'What narrowness of spiritual life we find in Frazer. And as a result: how impossible for him to understand a different way of life from the English one of his time.' And then, pettishly, he adds, 'Frazer cannot imagine a priest who is not basically an English parson of our times with all his stupidity and feebleness.'[22] He was pondering on the *Golden Bough* and using it as an illustration of the difference between explanation and a way of life.

> Every explanation is an hypothesis.
>
> But for someone broken up by love an explanatory hypothesis won't help much. It will not bring peace.
>
> Frazer's account of the magical and religious notions of men is unsatisfactory: it makes these notions appear as *mistakes*.
>
> Was Augustine mistaken, then, when he called on God on every page of the *Confessions*?
>
> Well – one might say – if he was not mistaken, then the Buddhist holy-man, or some other, whose religion expresses quite different notions, surely was. But *none* of them was making a mistake except where he was putting forward a theory.
>
> Even the idea of trying to explain the practice – say the killing of the priest-king – seems to me wrong-headed. All that Frazer does is to make this practice plausible to people who think as he does. It is very queer that all these practices are finally presented, so to speak, as stupid actions.

But it never does become plausible that people do all this out of sheer stupidity.

When he explains to us, for example, that the king must be killed in his prime because, according to the notions of the savages, his soul would not be kept fresh otherwise, we can only say: where that practice and these views go together, the practice does not spring from the view, but both of them are there.

Frazer says it is very difficult to discover the error in magic and this is why it persists for so long – because, for example, a ceremony which is supposed to bring rain is sure to appear effective sooner or later. But then it is queer that people do not notice sooner that it does rain sooner or later anyway.

I think one reason why the attempt to find an explanation is wrong is that we have only to put together in the right way what we *know* without adding anything, and the satisfaction we are trying to get from the explanation comes of itself.

And here the explanation is not what satisfies us anyway. When Frazer begins by telling the story of the King of the Wood at Nemi, he does this in a tone which shows that something strange and terrible is happening here. And that is the answer to the question 'why is this happening?': Because it is terrible. In other words, what strikes us in this course of events as terrible, impressive, horrible, tragic, etc., anything but trivial and insignificant, *that* is what gave birth to them.

We can only *describe* and say, human life is like that.

Frazer is much more savage than most of his savages, for these savages will not be so far from any understanding of spiritual matters as an Englishman of the twentieth century. His explanations of the primitive observances are much cruder than the sense of the observances themselves.

These comments on Frazer amount to a grave charge of superficiality, of failure to match interpretative powers to the depth and height of human experience to be interpreted. Wittgenstein strives to seize the true nature of the human predicament: 'the crush of thoughts that do not get out because they all try to push forward and are wedged in the door'.[23] His criticism of Frazer parallels the oft-told story of John Constable's argument with Sir George Beaumont. The older man is saying that the greenness of grass has to be shown within the mellow tonalities of the whole picture; Constable is saying that nature is not like that, but is much lusher, much greener, more alive. He seizes an old

violin whose soft hues are like those used then to transpose natural
greenery to the picture's painted range. Laying it on the lawn he
triumphantly demonstrates that the green in nature is nothing like the
brown violin. No doubt about it; but Gombrich points out that
Beaumont never said it was. The problem of transposition between the
natural and the painted set of gradients still remained. What Constable
had to do was to work out 'how to reconcile what we call "local colors"
with the range of tonal gradations which the landscape painter needs to
suggest depth'.[24] This he succeeded in doing.

The very success which Frazer enjoyed argues that he was working in
a well-understood style and that his transposition from life to book form,
with its self-imposed constraints, successfully picked up the great
themes and related them to lesser ones, so that he seemed to his
generation to be talking very seriously about religion and half the poetry
of the world. Wittgenstein's complaints are background to his own
attempt to break through the prison of style, and to come to a fuller
awareness of nature. Wittgenstein was one in a movement of many
thinkers who won and to whose eyes Frazer has a fusty, narrow view.

To stop here would be to espouse the negative relativity which some
of Wittgenstein's followers adopt. We can go a little further by exploring
the nature of the change in perspective. Wittgenstein himself used his
reflections on the *Golden Bough* to illustrate his idea about a special kind
of explanation, the concept of perspicuous presentation: 'a way of setting
out the whole field together by making easy the passages from one part of
it to another . . . the way in which we see things. . . . This perspicuous
presentation makes possible that understanding which consists in just
the fact that we "see the connexions".'[25] The translator notes that
Wittgenstein constantly used '*übersichtlich*' in writing of logical notation
and mathematical proof: 'It is clear what he means. So we ought to have
an English word. We have put "perspicuous" here, but no one uses this
in English either.' Others have used 'transparent proof'. But in the
context of the remarks on anthropology, it seems to a modern ear that
Wittgenstein was thinking of a form of presenting a proof by showing the
fit between all the steps. He was groping for structural analysis before it
had become available in anthropology. His words recall Bartlett's
remark:[26]

Perhaps the mathematician or thinker in any form of closed system,
who quickly stops doing something that he has begun in error, has
something of a pre-perception of the 'fitness' of the structure he is

building to that of the complete structure within which he is working. Exactly how or through what mechanism such pre-perception can be achieved is still exceedingly hard to understand; but the process is, in function, precisely that of 'matching'.

A philosopher has recently placed Wittgenstein's thought on Frazer in the larger context of his philosophy and shown the direct influence of the latter on Clifford Geertz.[27] The process of matching and searching for intermediate links is the process of finding metaphorical structures. Wittgenstein would obviously have encouraged structural anthropologists to seek the cultural pattern of metaphors with the deepest, widest scope for human meaning. This need to enlarge the canvas presents, no doubt, the problems of facsimile that we have noted already. Clifford Geertz responds wholeheartedly by deepening his tonal range, enriching his hues and by using a very powerful literary style. His discussion of the moral imagination uses the case of Balinese practice of burning the widows of a great man.[28] The whole colourful emotive style escapes the reproach which Wittgenstein levelled against Frazer's account of the burning of a man in Fire Festivals. It is not frivolous; it is not superficial; it does try to grasp the intervening links which make sense of the events for the people who organize them. By comparison Frazer's style alone makes him seem to be trivializing. This has nothing to do with his attempt at explanation. He could always find a minor superstition among frolicking harvesters or New Year celebrants to match any more grandiose theme. The switches of scale give us a sense of flippancy.

If we ask why this scale-switching was acceptable to his contemporaries, we recall that at that time his readers had as much ambivalence as he did about the value of religion. Frazer firmly believed that the *Golden Bough* recorded a long history of human folly – the trail of religious institutions and wars prosecuted and crimes committed in their name. To treat these horrors delicately and to show their universal origin in man's prehistory was the stylistic challenge which he met by switching from lofty to the humble scale, from tragedy to humour.

I would conclude this question by suggesting that the glass he held to nature was the glass in which his contemporaries were prepared to see, that he was not more superficial in moral imagination than they, and not mistaken as to the style in which to present his version.

Though our present generation reacts against this perspective, there is a part of Frazer's work which they accept quite happily. I can explain the paradoxical influence of Frazer's distinction between two kinds of magic on present-day thought by comparing Frazer with Lévi-Strauss. The two scholars, their theme, their method, and their achievement are interesting to compare. 'The deeper philosophy of the relation of the life of man to the life of nature' was Frazer's main concern. Lévi-Strauss seeks to reveal the functioning of the human mind, especially its age-long meditation on the difference between nature and culture.

The pair run in double harness on other points as well. Each generated in his turn an industry of imitators who collected materials according to the master's scheme and who found it made sense that way. Both are rebuked for taking their material out of context and for imposing the pattern of their own thought upon it. Each is accused of lacking sociological insight and political sensitivity. Both are especially liable to be misunderstood unless they are recognized to be speculating on the origins of thought.

When it comes to comparing their methods, the modern toolkit does not seem all that superior to Frazer's method of analysing magical thinking. Leach has remarked that Lévi-Strauss uses much the same analytical methods as Frazer, emphasizing resemblance and contiguity, though he calls them metaphor and metonym, while Frazer calls them similarity and contagion.[29] Of course, there are important differences. Frazer focused on resemblance. He thought that the likeness between two stories jumped to the eye of the reader, just as readily as likeness between two colours or two parts of the body struck the mind of the primitive. He did not think that resemblance needed analysis, and there he was naïve. The method of modern structuralism focuses on difference, particularly upon close contrasts, for example between relatively up or down, hot or cold, wet or dry, dark or light. Tracing the pattern of such binary distinctions, the method traces how a whole system of symbols is constructed of similarities and juxtapositions. It is extraordinary to see Frazer's two favourite tools sharpened up and put to new use by his severest critics. But the modern mythologists did not get their idea of the structure of a symbolic system from Frazer, nor is it a coincidence that they should rely so heavily on similarity and contiguity for their work. With the aid of linguists,[30] they have raided the same old attic storeroom of ideas, the long traditions of European philosophy, but without really knowing where the furniture came from.

When Frazer taught that there are two ways of looking at the world, one modern, scientific, and the other primitive, and that the latter divides again into two, religious and magical, and that magical principles are also just two, similarity and contagion, he was making a series of binary distinctions. Binary distinctions are an analytic procedure, but their usefulness does not guarantee that existence divides like that. We should look with suspicion on anyone who declared that there are two kinds of people, or two kinds of reality or process. The self-same European tradition which we all draw upon makes an old favourite division of mental faculties, one slow, logical step-by-step reasoning, the other quick, pattern-perceiving, intuitive. Often the second is called feminine and the first masculine. Pattern-perception is contrasted with linear reasoning. Two kinds of computer thinking are often compared, analog with digital. Among the structural analysts you will find echoes of this in their use of the two axes of analysis, whose names are switched over and over again. For Frazer's principle of similarity you will read metaphor, paradigm, resemblance, substitutability, equivalence, classes, system, and for his principle of contiguity you will find continuity, juxtaposition, syntagma, syntax, structural proximity, sequencing rules, metonymy. Just like Frazer, the practitioners admit it is often difficult to tell which one applies, and then some of them sink into a morass of metonymic metaphors contrasted with metaphoric metonyms, paradigmatic syntagmas, and syntagmatic paradigms. Never mind; when it comes to practising the analysis (instead of saying how it is done), they forget the clumsy apparatus and invent delicate ways of tracing cross-references back and forth and nesting layers of meaning, from smallest to greatest. This bears out the justness of William James's view that there is no elementary principle of mental association other than contiguity.[31] How can you tell whether two patterns are similar except by tracing the internal positioning of parts? How can you compare except by prior sorting of like properties? According to James there is only one elementary principle of association, and to follow it means tracing and numbering all the connections that can be identified:[31]

> The manner in which trains of imagery and consideration follow each other through our thinking, the restless flight of one idea before the next, the transitions our minds make between things wide as the poles asunder, transitions which at first sight startle us by their abruptness, but which, when scrutinized closely, often reveal intermediating links of perfect naturalness and propriety – all this magical, imponderable dreaming has from time immemorial excited the admiration of all whose attention happened to be caught by its omnipresent mystery. And it has furthermore challenged the race of philosophers to banish something of the mystery by formulating the process in simpler terms.

The problem which the philosophers have set themselves is that of ascertaining *principles of connection* between the thoughts which thus appear to sprout one out of the other, whereby their peculiar succession or coexistence may be explained.

For James the important explanatory principle about how ideas sprout up or saunter carelessly into our minds is habit, association by being frequently connected in our experience.[33]

Seen things and heard things cohere with each other, and with odors and tastes, in representations, in the same order in which they cohered as impressions of the outer world. Feelings of contact reproduce similarly the sights, sounds, and tastes with which experience has associated them. In fact, the 'objects' of our perception, as trees, men, houses, microscopes, of which the real world seems composed, are nothing but clusters of qualities which simultaneous stimulations have so coalesced that the moment one is excited actually it serves as a sign or cue for the idea of the others to arise. Let a person enter his room in the dark and grope among the objects there. The touch of the matches will instantaneously recall their appearance . . . the feeling of the garments or draperies which may hang about the room is not *understood* till the look correlative to the feeling has in each case been resuscitated.

William James sums up the law of mental association by contiguity by saying that 'objects once experienced together tend to become associated in the imagination, so that when any one of them is thought of, the others are likely to be thought of also, in the same order of sequence or coexistence as before'.[34] He sticks to the traditional word 'contiguity', though recognizing that perhaps 'association by continuity' or 'external association' might be better. James places everything in this process upon habit, and this he traces to laws of habit in the nervous system. He refers to able writers on the subject who rely on two principles of association, one contiguity, the other similarity, but he dismisses the claims for similarity to be treated as an elementary law[35] for interesting reasons which I shall need to refer to again. So there it is, a long European and American tradition of analysing the association of ideas, and of classing them by laws of contiguity and similarity. According to James, Frazer was wrong in distinguishing similarity from contagion as principles of thought. But if so, he erred in good and modern company. Frazer and Lévi-Strauss, both using a tone of voice that suggests the awe and splendour of their subject, diminish the meaning it holds. Frazer belittles the faculties of the primitive mind. Lévi-Strauss uses heavy equipment for dredging up nearly vacuous thoughts. He claims to reveal how the human mind has been reflecting on the differences between nature and culture. Ask bluntly, well, what *does* it say about the difference? Usually all that structural analysis reveals is that the myths are saying over and over again that there is a difference. All we have is the possibility of a structure on which possible meanings could be hung. However much Frazer is castigated by a succeeding generation of anthropologists, they do not see that where they uncritically use his ideas they get their most disappointing result. Gombrich enables us to locate a blind spot.

Among all the other bric-à-brac we were lumbered long ago with a division between the passive and the active faculties of the mind. The first, the association of ideas, merely fed into the mental machinery the stuff for logic to work upon. It was hardly Frazer's fault that he took up this theory, for it was widely accepted in his formative period. So it is understandable that he should use the accepted division between two mental processes, and credit the active one with the achievement of gradually overcoming the delusions which the association of ideas is likely to introduce when left uncontrolled. But more recent writers have a better chance. The separation of passive and active faculties is now realized to be a much more dubious line to draw. The whole process of recognizing, comparing, classing, and performing other logical operations is seen much more as a unitary process, an active organizing effort by the perceiving subject, a pressure towards transparency and match. Any myth analyst who just sets up the framework of contrasts and similarities and stops there, claiming to have discovered something that is happening in the mind without the knower being actively involved, is espousing a passive theory. He is applying his craftsmanship to an old store of broken-legged materials, rather passive himself in his attitude to what means are available. Meanwhile the lumber room is being cleared and sorted and daylight shows up the dust. Gombrich shows that there cannot be making without matching, innovation without copying. First there has to be a model, then the critical dissatisfaction and the struggle to improve upon it. He also shows that there is no way of making all experience available at once. Any awareness depends on areas of invisibility and insensitivity. Blind spots there must be. If they surface on the periphery of vision, it can only be because some new synthesis is ready.

To return to the matter of judgment between generations: I clearly have profited greatly from Gombrich's applying the theory of perception to style in painting. But I have only found a few not especially illuminating things to say about the misunderstanding of Frazer by his successors. It might not have been necessary to refer to Gombrich in order to say that the theoretical field had changed, that Frazer thought of himself as a stylist and literary scholar, and that his style is a clue to his mood and thought. The importance of Gombrich's contribution is more precisely his demonstration of how the theory of perception, established in its main outlines at the beginning of this century, itself has led to a new horizon of expectations.

In writing so lucidly about the constancies between gradients and relationships, and about judgment and perception as the attuning of the mind to a particular key, Gombrich reintroduces a theory of rationality to a twentieth century that has always had access to it, but still has not been able to adjust to its depths. Reintroducing is the word. Admittedly it was only anticipated by Newman's account of the illative sense. But it has been here, as Gombrich shows, for a long time. Perspicuous presentation or transparent proof in Wittgenstein, preperceptual matching in Bartlett, structuralism in Jakobson and Lévi-Strauss – there is a convergence of meanings in our generation which is gradually setting up a cultural ridge, as it were, which will separate the contemporary vision from that of the past.

This should enable us to take the next step. So far we are limited to a very general statement about swings of the pendulum, creative and uncreative misunderstandings, stabilizing and constraining pressures, and the individual thrust towards innovation. At this stage we seem to be limited to agnosticism. No judgment can be passed, either on the past generation, or on the rejecting or admiring judgments of the present. But if this approach to style and culture is hanging over us as the new style, with all its closures and constraints, but fully available, a priority immediately appears among projects for this generation. Nothing else will prosper more than an examination of our own style, pushing its possibilities of comparison to their limits. When such a project is developed, it may be possible to say convincingly that Frazer was a flawed jewel of neo-classicism, or a perfect gem for all time, or a stumbling block.

Notes

1   E. H. Gombrich, *Art and Illusion: A Study in the Psychology of Pictorial Representation*, the A. W. Mellon Lectures in the Fine Arts, 1956, Bollingen Series/Princeton, Princeton University Press, 1960, p. 33.

2   Ibid., p. 174.

3   Ibid., p. 175.

4   Ibid., p. 60.

5   Ibid., p. 58.

6   J. G. Frazer, 'The Growth of Plato's Ideal Theory', an essay, New York, 1930.

7   Claude Lévi-Strauss, *Anthropologie Structurale Deux*, Paris, Plon, 1973, p. 12.

8   Gombrich, op. cit. pp. 301, 303.

9   Ibid., p. 316.

10   Lawrence Gowing, 'The Logic of Organized Sensations', chapter in *Cézanne, The Late Work*, ed. William Rubin, New York, Museum of Modern Art, 1977, p. 66.

11   Ibid., p. 70.

12   James G. Frazer, *Totemism and Exogamy, a Treatise on Certain Early Forms of Superstition and Society*, 4 vols, London, 1910, p. ix.

13   Thomas Baynes, Editorial for Ninth Edition of *Encyclopaedia Britannica*, Scotland, 1878.

14   George Eliot, *Middlemarch*, London, 1872.

15   Anatole France, Preface to J. G. Frazer's *The Gorgon's Head and Other Literary Pieces*, London, Macmillan, 1927.

16   James G. Frazer, 'Sur Ernest Renan', Paris, 1923.

17   Ibid., p. 66.

18   James G. Frazer, *The Gorgon's Head and Other Literary Pieces*.

19   Gombrich, op. cit., p. 57.

20   Ibid., p. 50.

21   Ibid., p. 326.

22   Ludwig Wittgenstein, 'Remarks on Frazer's *Golden Bough*', trans. A. C. Miles and Rush Rhees, originally published in *Synthese*, 17, 1967, quoted from *The Human World*, no. 3, May 1971, pp. 28–41.

23   Ibid., p. 30.

24   Gombrich, op. cit., p. 44.

25   Wittgenstein, op. cit., p.35, note.

26   Frederick C. Bartlett, *Thinking: An Experimental and Social Study*, New York, Allen and Unwin, 1958, p. 151.

27   Richard H. Bell, 'Understanding the Fire-Festivals: Wittgenstein and Theories in Religion', *Religious Studies*, 14, 1978, pp. 113–24.

28   Clifford Geertz, 'Found in Translation: On the Social History of the Moral Imagination', *Georgia Review*, 13, 1977, pp. 787–810.

29   Edmund Leach, *Lévi-Strauss*, London, Fontana Modern Masters, 1970, p. 49.
30   Roman Jakobson and Morris Halle, *Fundamentals of Language*, The Hague, Mouton, 1956.
31   William James, 'Principles of Psychology', chapter on *Association of Ideas*, first published 1880.
32   Ibid., pp. 551–2.
33   Ibid., pp. 555–6.
34   Ibid., p. 561.
35   Ibid., pp. 581–2.

12 The debate on the Holy: review of *The Making of Late Antiquity* by Peter Brown*

The history of the second to the fourth centuries of late antiquity can be seen as a debate on the nature of the Holy. The debate itself is a part of a political movement that reaches its peak in the sixth century. As the political action unfolds, men accept or reject the options before them. They press for advancement, they either displace their rivals or are themselves routed. The outcomes change the character of social life in villages and towns. With each new phase in the political history, people make different appeals to the supernatural powers around them, so that the face of supernatural changes, decade by decade.

This is the outline of an anthropologist's reading of *The Making of Late Antiquity*. The assumptions are familiar and well-established. No anthropologist can go into fieldwork with one ear listening for a debate about political power and the other ear cocked to catch a separate debate about spirituality. If anthropology has anything to say to history, it is to suggest that the spiritual beings in which people believe are not interesting to the believers in an academic or theoretical sense. They are interesting at a particular time because they can credibly intervene in particular ways. They can back a threat, punish impiety, see into the future, and warn of dangers. If the believers stop wishing to threaten, punish, or warn each other in these ways, the spiritual beings become otiose and their cult languishes. This sounds so obvious that one would hardly think it worth repeating. However, among the many kinds of historians some are not convinced that this point of view, faithfully followed, will yield good insight into a complex period. All right for simple spear-and-arrow cultures in Africa that beliefs should be such an intimate part of social life, but for interpreting a civilization as advanced as ancient Rome or Byzantium, one must take the local theories about

* Review published in *Religious Studies Review*, April 1980, vol. 6, no. 2, pp. 96–9; Peter Brown, *The Making of Late Antiquity*, Carl Newell Jackson Lectures, Cambridge, Mass., Harvard University Press, 1978.

spirituality on their own terms. To the minds of a particular age, their philosophy had a strictly intellectual fascination, and that is that. In these terms a reviewer dismissed the core argument of *Religion and Society in the Age of Saint Augustine* (1972). He felt that something more should be done to appreciate 'the great clash, on a philosophical and theological level, of pagan and christian conceptions of evil', the stark philosophical appeal of Manicheeism and the compulsion of a nexus of ideas from which the philosophical elements in an average classical training of the fourth century, and earlier, were hardly able to effect a release' (Anonymous, 1972).

Apart from the fact that in Rome and Byzantium effective political power did depend on spears and arrows, disdain of civilizations that do not head our own genealogy should not distract us here. Nor should ignorance of other interpretive disciplines protect a Manicheean-like assumption that pure minds, though inhabiting vile bodies, produce visions of the universe that are too ethereal to be subjected to the earthy analysis of political and economic motives. If we have to appreciate the intellectual attraction of bygone philosophers, we need some resource other than undisciplined empathy.

Elsewhere, Peter Brown has described himself as the kind of historian who grabs any theories that seem to help, indiscriminately and unprejudicedly picking ideas from psychology, literature, sociology, anthropology or whatever comes to hand. This book is the latest and probably the most coherent product of his anti-methodological method. In reviewing it I do not arrogate to myself any scholarly status for commenting upon the historical sweep or the sound use of texts or the plausibility of the interpretations, as they would be seen from the point of view of historians who have spent their lives working on this period. All that I can do is summarize an anthropological theme that runs through it.

It seems that historians concerned to understand the period A.D. 200–600 have tended to treat Late Antiquity as an amorphous passage of time without its own distinctive claims to periodization. It appears as a confused jumble of pressures leading through the collapse of the Roman Empire to the foundation of medieval Christendom. Focusing on prejudged politically or culturally unified blocks allows an easy explanation of whatever seems to be happening where the focus is blurred. The periods or places defined as interstitial are thought to be undergoing crisis and the events of the third century are explained as effects of crisis: the pains of social change, the loneliness of urban life, the rootlessness of migrants into great cities, the shock of public disaster, the collapse of old religious cults unable to compete with new ideas. This litany of what it feels like to live in the vortex of wars and upheavals can hardly stand as an explanation; it is a list of social changes coloured by the evaluations of modern sociology. When interpretation has no rule but sympathy, inevitably those things which seem peripheral and bizarre in contemporary life are interpreted as such. One of our dearest beliefs, that the life of the spirit floats free from physical constraint, is also uncritically imported into the story. Consequently, the central dialogue about recourse to supernatural powers and the use of sorcery and magic are brushed aside by historians, treated as a blot upon the otherwise brilliant intellectual achievements of the age.

The Making of Late Antiquity deals with the two hundred years from the mid-second to the mid-fourth centuries. It opens by putting a close focus on the record to see if it fits the current scholarly assumptions. The pagan world is thought to be rigid and because rigid, vulnerable to new ideas, so much so that the arrival of Christianity is a source of threat. But the record shows the pagan world around the Mediterranean in the second century was pliant, syncretist, and so long used to confronting new ideas that it could be said to be immunized. It is thought by some to display a highly emotional temperature, continually scared of interference from supernatural beings or full of holy dread. But, as anthropologists have often found, what would be signs of nervous jitters among ourselves can be part of a perfectly calm and practical relation with ghosts and demons. Urbanization is another question: to explain forsaken temples and attrition of old beliefs by a secular trend naturally accompanying the growth of cities and a rootless proletariat is plausible to us; but according to Peter Brown the only city was Rome, the others were scarcely more than villages which scrutinized their members with such relentless demands for conformity and reciprocal exchanges that people suffered more from claustrophobia and the tensions of over-control than from the lost loneliness of an atomized urban population. As for the shock of great military defeats, this did not greatly affect the general populace, only the political leaders. Instead of treating religious beliefs as another and separate problem, they can be followed as a thread for disentangling the skein.

At the beginning of this period the human and the supernatural communicate across an open frontier. Divine power is very much in evidence, but access to it is unspecialized. Anyone can have a dream visitation, anyone can consult the oracles. The gods are accessible, impersonal, and available to uphold community morals. Their power stands in opposition to human forms of political power. Their effect is to control competitiveness. They cut the exceptional individual down to human size, rein his ambitions, and recall him to his public obligations. Such a religion works locally. It reduces uncertainty and supports the stabilizing, levelling intentions of its worshippers. Through the period A.D. 200–400 the nature of the holy becomes a matter of debate as the locus of the supernatural shifts.

First, the local communities break up as leaders of great stature arise, whose influence stretches across large regions. Men were driven by great ambition in the second century, but somehow in the age of the Antonines it was kept under control. The traditional oracular institutions spoke with a collective voice to restrain competition, not to serve it. But in the third century the controls gave way. It is common to read that the life of the upper classes of the Roman world collapsed under pressures from outside. But on Peter Brown's analysis the people themselves were no passive objects responding helplessly to external causes. They themselves and their ambitions caused an explosion. City against city, great landowner against great landowner, army leaders against emperors, the third century saw a general release of competitive drives for larger prizes than ever before. In the third century human power is fluid, ambiguous, and incoherent. By the fourth century coherence is restored to institutions and power runs in large clear channels which extend far beyond the local community. Inevitably through the two new phases, the old conception of divine power is successively adapted to the new intentions. Instead of acting spontaneously at close quarters as brakes upon overmighty individuals, the supernatural seems to retreat. It is no longer accessible to the average person, only to great leaders. Cults which traditionally had a levelling role wane before the rise of the individual. Supernatural power now works on the side of social mobility and grandiose ambition. Individuals claim divine support, their claims, like all others, are competitively contested. The debate on the Holy shifts to tests for identifying fraudulent claims to supernatural strength and revealing imposters. The new cults are cults of holy men who have to prove their friendship with God by conspicuous powers and by stripping themselves of private interest. In the second phase the shakeup is over, new political boundaries much larger than the old local communities are established. The sensationalist feats of individualistic holy men now have to compete with the steady talents of great administrators. Prophets give way to bishops,

who develop new communities and eventually re-establish local community life at the grass-roots level.

The argument about the rise of Christianity, under this close focus, is
that the temples and the sacrificial rites of pagan worship were not
abandoned because of unsuccessful competition with foreign religion,
but because of secular trends well-established in pagan society itself,
trends to individual glorification and a channelling of wealth away from
civic institutions into private competitive display. The parallel change
took place in pagan religion from impersonal cults of holy places and
holy objects to the cult of conspicuously holy persons. The Christian
church also took part in and benefited from these secular trends. Rising
on the new tide of individualism, the Christians contributed to the
debate about the Holy the concept of martyrdom. First, the deaths of
martyrs were idealized as the heroism of special friends of God. Then
came the bishops' claims to earthly power on the grounds that they too
had access to specialized spiritual backing. So far from being born of the
relative deprivation suffered by an urban proletariat, the attraction of the
Christian church is here presented as its absolving of individuals from
the restrictive demands of kinship and neighbourhood and its allowing
them to elect communities of new friends. It is the flight of individuals in
an age of individualism from the oppressive life of small towns that
explains the success of the Christian bishops, the escape of ascetics into
the Egyptian desert, the continual dialogue of challenge and testing of
claims to holiness.

The Making of Late Antiquity does not make easy reading. The style is
difficult. One is aware of seeing only the tip of a massive submerged
iceberg of scholarship, clued by careful footnotes. Peter Brown tries to
carry the reader swiftly through the dense scholarship by lively allusion.
The result is an elliptical style, laden with names of persons and places,
names of men of late antiquity and names of scholars commenting upon
them, and citations from all. The result is a text overdecorated with
energetic metaphors and references in many languages, always apt and
very enlightening, but the pace is too fast for covering such rough
ground. The copy editor has made the pages unsightly by using
quotation marks as a visual form of emphasis. Why should 'crisis',
'heavenly', 'earthly' sometimes but not always be in quotation marks?
One gets a vision of the Carl Newell Jackson Lecturer gesticulating and
speaking with strenuous changes of emphasis in voice every few
minutes, his fingers perked up to his ears to indicate 'quote-unquote', as
he says that he is 'dissatisfied with the idea of a general "crisis" of the

third century as a *passe-partout* explanation for the emergence of the distinctive features of Late Antique Religion.'

The author had clearly been reading widely in anthropology before his first published essay on sorcery and demons (Brown, 1970) using the insights of Evans-Pritchard (1937). There he argued that the great legacy of written magical prescriptions and accounts of sorcery attacks in late Roman society need not be taken by historians as evidence for a general resurgence of superstition. Assuming that such accusations do not fall randomly, a closer focus allowed him to locate their incidence in times of maximum uncertainty and in social institutions undergoing specially strong conflicts. The growth of a new bureaucracy, recruited from the traditional aristocracies and equipped with new learning, put the old imperial cadres under strain. Men tried to settle scores with ambiguously defined rivals by accusing them of sorcery. Through the fourth century such accusations mark the pressure to clearer definition in the secular governing class. A twilight world of talent presses upward, held back by accusations of illegitimate uncontrolled supernatural power. Christianity had to divorce the belief in dangerous occult powers from the political uses of accusations. In its rise it dissociated the spiritual powers of evil from human enemies, checked blame-pinning, and gathered its recruits into a fold where they would be safe from demons.

The present book presents a more mature and less mechanical use of anthropology than that earlier essay. The insights have been absorbed without strain and used flexibly to trace out the complex pattern. The value of a certain approach to religious history has been triumphantly demonstrated. Surely now that the way has been shown, there will be a decisive change in the assumptions historians bring to the study of philosophical ideas.

References

Anonymous (1972), 'Late Roman Realities', *The Times Literary Supplement*, 26 May, p. 608.

Brown, Peter (1970), 'Sorcery, Demons and the Rise of Christianity from Late Antiquity into the Middle Ages,' in Mary Douglas (ed.), *Witchcraft, Confessions and Accusations*, ASA Monographs, 9, London, Tavistock Publications, pp. 17–37.

Brown, Peter (1972), *Religion and Society in the Age of Saint Augustine*, London, Faber & Faber.

Evans-Pritchard, E. (1937), *Witchcraft, Oracles and Magic among the Azande*, Oxford, Clarendon Press.

Name index

Subject index